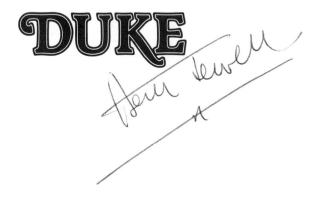

DUKE

DUKE

A Portrait
of Duke Ellington

Derek Jewell

W · W · Norton & Company · Inc ·

· New York ·

Copyright © 1977 by Derek Jewell

Published simultaneously in Canada by George J. McLeod
Limited, Toronto. Printed in the United States of America.

All Rights Reserved

Library of Congress Cataloging in Publication Data

Jewell, Derek.
Duke: a portrait of Duke Ellington.

Discography and bibliography: p.
Includes index.
1. Ellington, Duke, 1899–1974.   2. Jazz musicians—
United States—Biography.
ML410.E44J5   785.4'2'0924 [B]   77–2271
ISBN 0–393–07512–5

1 2 3 4 5 6 7 8 9 0

Dedicated to the memory of
EDWARD KENNEDY ELLINGTON
and to all those who loved him and his music,
especially
RENEE AND LESLIE DIAMOND
and
EDMUND ANDERSON

Contents

Illustrations

Following page 166

Acknowledgments

There will never be a definitive biography of Duke, who was the least definitive of geniuses. This does not pretend to be one; simply his story written with affection and an attempt at understanding. I am deeply indebted to many people: to his musicians and family and friends with whom I have talked down the years; to all those who have chronicled his achievements in the past, and whose writings have consciously or unconsciously made an impression upon me, notably his most loyal observer, Stanley Dance. For my editor, Colin Webb, his picture researcher, Phillipa Lewis, and for all those others who have so greatly helped me—they especially include Steve Allen, Robert Ducas, John Gensel, Carole Haynes, Herb Hendler, Louis Herchenroder, Max Jones, Colin and Patricia Kyte, Dan Morgenstern, Roger Earl Okin, Anita Porter, Sinclair Traill, and Lauri Zimmerman—I am grateful. Above all, there is the Duke himself who, whilst he lived, was more tolerant of my company and questions than I had the right to expect.

1

Caravan to Everywhere

Cigarette smoke hung on the air; another bottle of champagne stood flatly half empty. Someone had just left the suite at the Dorchester, where he always stayed when he was in London. Someone was always just leaving or arriving, since few men at the summit gave so generously of their time to the curious as did Duke Ellington. He was sprawled in a chair, in working gear of blue slacks and dark blue woollen shirt, and he spread his hands when I said I was very happy to see him and I was sorry to disturb him, but my newspaper was set on an interview, and so . . . "You know me," he interrupted, "I'm a great talker. I'm always duly flattered by being asked."

Nothing, as I learned often in meetings with him during the last decade or so of his life, was more calculated to throw an interviewer than an opening Ellington wisecrack. He salted his talk with gently sardonic self-mockeries and soft-spoken irony. The face, crisscrossed with the lines of endless years of early mornings around the globe, would turn itself toward you, eyes very lively above the huge pouches beneath them. "Don't look at my bags that way," he'd say. "They're an accumulation of virtue."

You could never quite be sure how to take Edward Kennedy Ellington. People who had known him far longer and better than I have said he remained an enigma to them until the day he died. "Duke," as Miles Davis once observed, "puts *everybody* on." Ralph Gleason, the critic, christened him "The Artful Dodger." Yet he could be remarkably consistent, too. Of all the words he spoke at that meeting in the early days of 1964, a few sentences stayed in the mind most vividly. Knowing, as everyone did, that most of the musicians in his orchestra at that time had been with him for years and years, I'd asked about the band book—how much of the music was simply in the heads of his sidemen, how much they needed to look at the sheets, since his scores were often not published complete.

"We hardly ever keep scores. We have nothing to go back to. Out of the thousands of numbers we've done, only about ten percent of the scores remain. They disappear. People wrap their lunch in them. Strays knows, don't you Strays?" And he inclined his head toward Billy Strayhorn, short, dapper, and, at the time, barefoot, his collaborator and musical *alter ego* during an intensely productive quarter century of Ellington's career.

Later, when Duke had disappeared to take some vitamin pills, Strayhorn pushed his black hornrims firmly on his nose and spoke with engaging seriousness, his voice even softer than his partner's. "He really doesn't care about this sort of thing, you know—collecting his stuff. To him it doesn't matter at all. Not too long ago, for his birthday, we thought it would be a good idea to collect all Duke's work together and present it to him. John Sanders, he used to play trombone with the band, did the work. There was no time to find more than a small part of it even in a year. It ran to several leather-bound volumes. Now it's in a warehouse."

Arthur Logan, Ellington's doctor and close friend for more than forty years, also described how he and Strayhorn had made the presentation. "Duke was impressed. He made polite noises and kissed us all, but you know, the son of a bitch didn't even bother to take it home."

Duke's words at the Dorchester, his behavior at the presentation, can be construed as a majestic disdain for self-aggrandizement, and doubtless that was true of him in one respect. Equally important, however, is the fact that he wasn't much interested in yesterdays. The most fascinating piece of music for him was always the one he was writing at any given moment, the one he would hear played the next day by the orchestra he kept together for almost fifty years in a fashion totally unparalleled by any other artist in the whole history of music. He had so much music within him, he appeared to find it as easy to discard as to keep. The trumpeter, Rex Stewart, who spent a decade with the band, once told of his fascination when he first saw Ellington deliberately tear into tiny pieces some music upon which several hours of writing had been spent. "Then he flushed it down a toilet drain. I couldn't contain my curiosity, so I asked him why he had destroyed it. His reply stunned me. He answered with a smile: 'Well, I'll tell you, Fat Stuff. If it's good, I'll remember it. If it's bad, well, I want to forget it, and I'd prefer that no one catches on to how lousy I can write.' " Too many stories of that kind have been told down the years for anyone to believe that Ellington's customary indifference to his earlier work was entirely a pose.

Until the last few months before his death at the age of seventy-five, Ellington was doing exactly what he had been doing for approaching half a century: being a professional bandleader, playing in every conceivable context from boozy clubs to cathedrals for virtually fifty-two weeks a year on the non-stop grind of one-night stands and world tours. He and his remarkable caravan probably travelled ten million miles or more across the years; and Ellington seemed to accept this as the condition for which nature intended him. "What is there to retire to?" he said when he was asked about quitting the road. "Stagnation wouldn't look good on me. My band and I travel all over the world, see the sights and see the people. You can't beat that. The road is my home, and I'm only comfortable when I'm on the move. New York is just where I keep my mailbox." Incredibly, except in his teens, he never owned a house he called a home in his life.

It was while he was indulging in this frenetic, non-stop, creative madness that, between 1923 and 1973, he composed the thousands of minor and major compositions (not counting the ones he flushed down the drain) which stand in his name, or partly in his name. Add the performing and the composing together, and in quantitative terms there can indeed never have been another musician of any description to approach him in any century.

Men from what are customarily conceived as different worlds of music from Ellington's—Percy Grainger, Constant Lambert, Igor Stravinsky, Leopold Stokowski—all said at different times and in different fashions that he was one of the greatest living composers. Stravinsky, indeed, compared Ellington with Stravinsky, and when he arrived in New York for a visit in the 1930s told the reception committee (on being asked what he wanted to see) that his top priority was to hear Ellington play at the Cotton Club in Harlem, a venue quite unknown to the committee. Kenneth Tynan included Duke with Chaplin, Hemingway, Orson Welles, Cocteau, and Picasso as among those sharing "a fixed international reputation that can never be tarnished."

Such tributes can be duplicated a hundredfold, and are scarcely subject to dispute; and, fortunately, because Thomas Edison invented the record machine, much of Ellington's genius has been captured forever. Yet how little even the music and what has been said about it explain the enigma of Ellington as artist and human being. He was, in truth, as easy a man to misunderstand as to comprehend. Set down just some of the paradoxes and contradictions his life contained, and his elusiveness becomes clear.

He was both showman and serious artist. He was a stunning innovator, yet extremely conservative, never deflected from his chosen path by the treacherous tides of popular music fashions like bebop or rock 'n' roll. At the same time, his ear was always sensitively cocked to what was happening around him, and he was never unwilling to praise the work of others who succeeded in making music of whatever kind that *sounded* good. "Take rock 'n' roll," he once said to me. "Perhaps Ella, she says, I'm gonna make a rock record, and you'll wind up with a real jam. Is it jazz, is it rock, is it music? Now you take a symphony, something by Britten, and put it in the hands of some old cat with no finesse, and you get the worst noise you ever heard." Such slang-laden phrases, incidentally, were in stark contrast to the formal elegance, frequently verging on the poetic, with which he could turn sentences when he set words down on paper.

Ellington was without doubt the most remarkable jazz musician of all; indeed, his life, from 1899 to 1974, spanned virtually the entire history of jazz. Yet to speak of him simply in terms of the elusive, syncopated, Afro-American music we call jazz seems absurdly to underestimate him. "I don't write jazz, I write

Negro folk music," he once observed, gently chiding me for an unwise question during a television interview. He used to say that the music he played had outgrown the word "jazz," which was increasingly true. "We've all worked and fought under the banner of jazz for many years, but the word itself has no meaning," he said on radio in 1968. "There's a form of condescension in it," by which he doubtless implied the black-ghetto connotations of jazz in the public mind.

More paradoxes. He was a romantic, as his music and his words, both written and spoken, dazzlingly show; at the same time he was intensely practical, a trait most demonstrably proved by the fact that he kept together his orchestra of unpredictable, individualistic virtuosi with consummate skill—and large sums of money—for so long. "I won't let those goddam musicians upset me. Why should I knock myself out in an argument about fifteen dollars when in the same time I can probably write a fifteen-hundred-dollar song?" He nearly always chose great instrumentalists, but hired some indifferent singers. Rarely has an artist been so available, yet so secret; so ready to talk, yet so inscrutable; so utterly public, yet so private. Edward Kennedy Ellington was a miraculous jigsaw, and seldom did anyone pick up more than a few pieces at a time.

I remember one December flying into Las Vegas and discovering, to my intense joy, that he was playing at one of the hotels in what the management were pleased to term, Vegas-style, the lounge. That lounge turned out to be a huge light-spangled kandy-kolored room in which 3,000 people were sitting around and drinking madly and talking about how much they'd lost and other grievances, including the dollar, the state of their marriages, offspring, grandmothers, livers, obesity, and suntans. A friend and I sat at a bar along the wall where the sound of ice being hurled into glasses provided the biggest percussion section ever heard with the band, and the barman looked up at us and said: "Jesus, don't doze guys play *loud*," before starting to whistle "Satin Doll" in agonizingly near-unison with Duke's reed section.

And yet, after fifteen minutes Duke had got most of that hallful of hustlers hooked. He charmed them, yet musically made no concessions. He played some crowd-pleasing ballads, true, but he also put on a large hunk of his latest composition, "Afro-Eurasian Eclipse," and insisted on telling them about its relevance to the then fashionable Canadian oracle, Mr. Marshall McLuhan. They shut up, more or less. Most of them listened. And they didn't throw things when he told them that "Mister Jewell of London, England, and M'sieur Rob-air Dook-ah of Normandy, France" (my friend, Robert Ducas, having this polyglot name, but being as English as Eton could make him) "are honoring us with their presence." And when he packed up till the next show (three a night: at 10 P.M., midnight, and 2 A.M.) to go back to his dressing room and resume his attempts to find winning numbers at Keino—a sort of electrified and high-kitty Bingo—they gave him applause as warm and as long as any I've ever heard. How did he feel about that kind of show? "Well," he said wryly, "I'm sure glad I learned social significance in the poolroom."

That was Ellington in one context: the loud, rough, smoky atmosphere of hard-nosed professional entertainment which, as an American Negro born at the turn of the century, had to be the road (almost the only road) along which he and other lucky ones ground out their way to the top. In total contrast was the man who, in the last decade of his life, performed scores of what he termed Sacred Concerts at churches of every denomination around the world—music which was *his* music, in the modern idiom. To him it was an immensely serious business. His simple faith ("There's one God, and that's all," he once told me) was powerful. He always used to say he'd enjoyed three educations—"the street corner, going to school, and the Bible. The Bible is the most important. It taught me to look at a man's insides instead of the outside of his suit."

The complexities, apparent contradictions, and endless fascination of Duke Ellington were further inflated by the many words of the unpredictable artist himself. Mostly he would be warm and gracious in conversation. At times he would be preoccupied, his words monosyllabic; at others he would spin endless stories about his early life or about how he came to compose particular pieces. To a questioner whose pretensions he disliked, he might say: "Such talk stinks up the place." Once he sighed and said: "You've got to be older to realize that many of the people you meet are mediocrities. You have to let them run off you like water off a duck's back. Otherwise they drag you down." He must have completely confounded one interviewer who, baffled by the power and subtleties of Ellington's music, requested him to state his artistic philosophy.

"I like great big ole tears," said Duke in one of his most celebrated replies. "That's why I like Whetsol" (one of his trumpeters in the early days). "When he played the Funeral March in 'Black and Tan Fantasy' I used to see great big ole tears running down people's faces." Then Ellington remembered another of his early trumpet players. "Bubber Miley! Well, Bubber used to say, 'If it ain't got swing, it ain't worth playin'; if it ain't got gutbucket, it ain't worth doin'!' "

Revealing and imaginative obliqueness of that kind was not Ellington's only way with those who sought in vain to discover his nature. He would withdraw from conversations as readily as he started them, ignore questions he had no wish to answer. He fulfilled his passion for privacy—since this is what it was—by acting as if he were public property; he secured the isolation he esteemed, since to be a composer demanded it, by never taking a holiday, by working in one way or another every waking hour, wherever he happened to be. His continual movement around the world helped to keep him secure as a private person, for no one could ever get too close. His word for his behavior was "skilapooping"; he explained it as "the art of making what you're doing look better than what you're supposed to be doing." He fended off would-be biographers all his life. "I'm not old enough to be historical, and I'm too young to be biographical," he once said memorably. "Biographies are like tombstones. Who wants one?" Even his autobiography, published just before his death, turned out to be a potpourri of biographical sketches, poems, and statements rather than a straight or particularly gripping story.

The truth is that Ellington had a host of incipient artistic gifts—in writing, painting, theatrical production—as well as one of the most idiosyncratic characters imaginable. But nothing mattered to him except his music. *Music*, as his book declared, *Is My Mistress*. And in music his greatness is founded.

He worked, despite his dislike of musical categories, in one of the few new art forms of our century: jazz. He wrote and conceived most of it for the unique orchestra he ran, building the tones and harmonies around the personal style of each of his players and their collective sounds. He used just a plain old dance band format—saxophones, brass, and rhythm—and yet managed to be an outstanding innovator, in form and in the tones he squeezed from these instruments. It was his *use* of the orchestra, as much as the notes he wrote for it, which led to the often drawn comparisons between Ellington and conservatoire composers like Delius, Debussy, Mozart, and Bach—the latter most appropriately in one sense, remembering how important improvisation was both to Bach's art and to jazz. Duke did once observe, "Bach and myself both write with the individual performer in mind," but mostly, all he ever said in response to that kind of statement was typically laconic. "If I didn't like the way the band played, I wouldn't pay so damn much for the pleasure of listening to it and writing for it."

So true. He never became rich on the scale to which other superstars of his own jazz-and-crooner generation, still less of the rock generation, have accustomed us. Despite his reputation, he often played to half-empty halls. In the late 1960s, with the costs of his band, himself, his entourage, his girl friends, and his family, he needed to make at least a million dollars a year to break even. He could probably have become richer just being a composer or studio star, for what he wrote was astonishing. Who has not heard his (or his and Strayhorn's) heritage in the past century? Pop songs and mood pieces like "Satin Doll," "Solitude," or "Sophisticated Lady"; swingers like "Caravan" and "Cotton Tail"; major suites and tone poems from "Black, Brown, and Beige" to "Afro-Eurasian Eclipse"; movie scores, TV scores, theatre mood music, ballet settings, and, pre-eminently for him, the sounds of his Sacred Concerts.

Yet, oddly, few of these works in their day became really monstrous commercial hits, because however delicious and tuneful they were, half their essence seemed to vanish when Ellington's men weren't playing them. Since his musicians often gave *him* ideas too, sparking off phrases to fill in scores he hadn't completed, this was even less surprising. Often Duke himself didn't want to play his best-known numbers, preferring to move on to new material. At a concert in 1965 when he was presenting parts of his "Far East Suite," he faced cries for his old repertoire from some loudmouths in the audience. "We arranged the wrong program for you. I'm so sorry," Ellington finally said with heavy irony, and deliberately led the band into the corniest medley of his hits they'd ever heard. No wonder

Duke later observed: "What I have written and what I have performed is something else."

All these things he wrote, this torrential flow of sustained composition, in circumstances which most people would consider ludicrous. There were no quietly contemplative country cottages for him, no seashore retreats, no guarded apartments. He worked and travelled so much, he had no time or taste for that. If ever he achieved Wordworth's emotion recollected in tranquillity, then he did so under monumental difficulties. His musical drawing board was the overnight railroad coach, the glass walls of recording studios, seats in dim-lit darkened buses and airliners, the backs of hotel menus, or the telephone.

Only a man with an iron constitution could have survived the work pattern and the habits of sleep which Ellington imposed upon himself. He usually went to bed at dawn and breakfasted at some time in the afternoon. He was a big man: six foot one, weighing somewhere around 185 pounds at his mean, although the poundage varied wildly between his later years, when he dieted rigorously, and the early days when he was plump and shiny, and consumed food in so gargantuan a fashion that his trombone player. "Tricky Sam" Nanton, declared: "He may be a genius, but Jesus, can he eat!" Duke had a very low pulse rate, which perhaps explained his continual equanimity. Rarely was he angry; seldom did he appear to be ill, until the last few months before his death. He was, however, a health fanatic. For most of his adult life Dr. Arthur Logan was at his beck and call. When you inquired how he was, he'd say, "How can *I* tell you? I haven't called my doctor yet to find out how I'm feeling today." The joke was almost true. Ellington carried countless medications with him, dispensing them to the band if necessary. His life and music defied almost every myth about "typical jazzmen." He had some musicians who were more like ministers of God, others who destroyed themselves with drugs. He himself smoked untipped cigarettes and once observed, "I never in my whole life smoked anything which hadn't got printing on it."

Beauty in all things delighted him, particularly in women, and he was beautifully correct in addressing them. Not that beauty was the point; Ellington's golden rule seemed to be to make *everyone* happy, and he could make any woman feel like a million dollars. "You make that dress look so beautiful," he would say; or to an airline stewardess during his South American tour of

1968: "Does your contract stipulate that you must be this pretty?"

His life as a composer was so inextricably interwoven with his life as a performer that he presents a unique artistic image. Undoubtedly he was a genius. He was to many a god, but he was far from a saint: rather, just a human being of a kind with which the world is blessed too rarely. When he died, a light went out for millions of people who had loved him and his art as madly as he always, onstage, declared he loved them. The caravan rests; but the music, his heritage, plays on. Its roots, like the foundation of his faith in God, were planted early, in Washington, D.C.

2

1899-1926
Roaming around the Jungle

Few childhoods can have been as idyllic as Edward Kennedy Ellington always made his sound. He worshipped his mother and his father (as well as his sister, Ruth) and every portrait of them justifies his claim that they were respectively very beautiful and very handsome.

From the moment of his birth on April 29, 1899, he was, in his own words, spoiled rotten by a multitude of relatives, mostly female. He was no child of the ghetto. His father, James Edward, called Ed by his mother and J. E. by his closest friends, was at first a butler who was occasionally employed at the White House, and later a blueprint maker for the U.S. Navy. Ellington said his father always acted as if he had plenty of money, and the family was modestly well-to-do. As a youngster, Ellington ate well and lived a pampered civilized existence. When he travelled to Europe for the first time on the S.S. *Olympic* in 1933 he had no trouble choosing the right silverware at table (as he liked to recall), because his father had taught him all about that. And it was from his father—together with a high-school principal who impressed upon all her charges the importance of good speech and manners to winning respect in the world for the Negro race—that he picked up his grandiloquent habits of speech and, perhaps, much of his wit. His father, Ellington said, could sweet-talk anyone.

The bond with his mother was even more remarkable. Her death in 1935 stunned him; but the artistic result of his grief was one of his first great extended compositions, "Reminiscing in Tempo." Even toward the end of his life he was continually mentioning her, sometimes in surprising circumstances. When he made his reply at a fabulous party given in honor of his seventieth birthday by President Nixon at the White House in 1969, the sophistication of his words finally collapsed. "There is no place I would rather be tonight," he concluded, "except in my mother's arms." From her, more than anyone else, sprang his deep and abiding religious faith. She took him every Sunday to at least two services, usually at her own Baptist church and his father's Methodist church. She sent him also to Sunday school. The God she described to her child had no racial color, nor had his creations. She told her son he had nothing to worry about because he was blessed—and many times he spoke convincingly of his belief in her words because, he said, of the inexplicable good fortune he always encountered throughout his life.

Before he was out of his twenties, Ellington claimed, he had completely read the Bible four times, and he went through it thrice after the death of his mother. So, although it was scarcely surprising that the world outside did not suspect the beliefs of the emergent hip entertainer, those who were close to him were always aware of Duke's faith. Otto Hardwick, one of Ellington's earliest friends in Washington, recalled how Duke would come home at night and read the Bible in his bath till the water turned cold. Ellington was meticulous about saying grace before meals, and he wore a gold cross on a chain around his neck from his middle thirties, which was odd, since he had an aversion to other jewelry, and refused to wear watches or rings.

At times the borderline between his religious beliefs and his various superstitions, most of them connected with his refusal to contemplate death, was uncertain. Once, going to interview him early in 1966, the photographer with me, Ian Yeomans, was coincidentally constructing a magazine feature on what men carried in their pockets. So he asked Duke, unforewarned, to turn out his. There wasn't much in them, in fact, but in his hip pocket was a wad of crumpled dollar bills, each one wrapped around a St. Christopher medal and other religious emblems. "People send them to me," he said. "This is their way of showing that they know my feelings. I never like to be without them." Yet he was just as decisive over things as simple as colors. Blue was his favorite, his lucky one. Green he loathed and would never wear. Once I asked why. He shrugged off the question. He was a city boy: green was like grass, and grass reminded him of graves. In this, as in so many ways, Ellington was a mixture of the naïve and the sophisticated. But the religion, as well as the superstition, was a powerful strand from the start. The Sacred Concerts, a surprising development to so many people in his later life, were really no surprise at all.

Any black American with a religious family would have gained a good grounding in music from churchgoing in those days, and Ellington's home was a place for music too. His mother played pretty piano; his father played operatic music, learnt by ear; and soon their son was being taught the piano with a teacher called Mrs. Clinkscales, and if the name sounds apocryphal, well, that's what Ellington always insisted it was. Not that he got too far with Mrs. Clinkscales in this stab at the only formal musical education he had in the whole of his life. He'd only begun learning because his mother decided it was something to take his mind off baseball, at which she'd seen him get a violent crack on the back of the head from a bat with which a schoolmate was demonstrating his free-swinging skill. He needed other incentives to awaken his urge to practice, because his main interests at the time were similar to those of most other teen-agers or sub-teen-agers: baseball (he worked part time selling popcorn at the Senators' stadium); pulp magazines—he read the Sherlock Holmes stories too; acting grown up; and girls.

The last two were to prove most useful. When he was twelve he was sneaking in, under age, at the local burlesque theatre, where the girls did their bumps and grinds and genteel titillation, and had begun to get a taste for show business. At fourteen, also under age, he was a regular visitor to poolrooms, especially one on T Street close to the Howard Theatre in Washington, where musicians as well as students, doctors, lawyers, and hustlers of every description congregated. These poolrooms were the social clubs of the neighborhood, a piano was available, and here Ellington met several of the people who were to help him in evolving his keyboard technique and who were also to form the nucleus of his earliest bands.

A summer vacation trip to Atlantic City and Philadelphia helped. In the latter he heard a pianist called Harvey Brooks who, he always claimed, was the first musician in his life he really wanted to emulate. He was in his middle teens—some have claimed it was much earlier—when a school friend (Edgar McEntree), snappy dresser and "socially uphill," as Ellington put it, first nicknamed him Duke, for no apparent reason except that those deemed fit for Mr. McEntree's company had to have *something* special about them. It was that same McEntree, pushing Duke forward at a high-school party as a piano player, who first taught him that music had charms other than the notes. Ellington had continued to fool around on the piano after his formal lessons had ended, and he'd come up with two compositions—"Soda Fountain Rag" (written when he was rising sixteen and had a part-time job as a soda jerk in a Washington rendezvous called the Poodle Dog Café) and "What You Gonna Do When the Bed Breaks Down?" He played the second at a party, and the next day there were three pretty girls calling for him. He was invited to many parties after that; and there was usually a girl leaning on the piano when he played.

The names of the pianists mean little now: Sticky Mack, Doc Perry, Louis Brown, Blind Johnny, Shrimp Bronner. But whenever he was asked about the early days, Ellington recited them as if they were geniuses, these poolroom Paderewskis who befriended him. To Oliver "Doc" Perry he paid special tribute in his autobiography: "my piano parent," Duke called him, the man who taught Ellington about reading a melody line and recognizing chords—and for nothing.

The atmosphere of the times, attested to by Duke and a thousand others, really did seem to be a musical free-for-all. You hung around, you listened, you asked questions, and advice was freely given by the local ruling deities in New York, Washington, Chicago, New Orleans, St. Louis, wherever jazz was being made in those days, when the world (including, in 1917, America) was at war. Duke, as his long-time associate Tom Whaley was to observe of his later years in New York, didn't waste the opportunity. "His great asset," Whaley said, "was listening"—and that, too, was to be the way he grew as a composer and orchestrator. He fed on the sounds around him, picking up bits of tunes and styles, molding them to his purpose.

A teacher at his high school, Henry Grant, heard about him and gave him harmony lessons. Soon Ellington was making a reputation as a relief player for Doc Perry and other local musicians at local dances and parties, already demonstrating his flair for showmanship. Copying a trick he'd seen used by Luckey Roberts at the Howard Theatre, he took to throwing his hands in the air off the keyboard. Sometimes, however, he was too weary for that. One of his earliest professional engagements in his teens was at a private party, where he played four hours without stopping. His fingers actually bled, he said later. The pay was seventy-five cents. "It was the most money I had ever seen," he recalled. "I rushed all the way home to my mother with it. But I could not touch a piano key for weeks after—not till my raw fingers had healed again."

That incident was scarcely typical of his apprenticeship. At this early stage of his career, everything he did seemed to make friends for him, even an encounter with the pianist James P. Johnson, who was already a legend. Duke learned, note for note, Johnson's "Carolina Shout" from a piano roll. When the great pianist played in Washington at Convention Hall and performed the tune, Duke's gang screamed for him to get up on the stand too. James P. smiled, went along with it, let Duke play "Carolina Shout," applauded, and later invited the upstart to be his guide around the town. The friendship that began was to be helpful when Duke went to New York City.

The emergent Ellington also proved a sharp businessman. Sent out one night on a $10 wage to play as a soloist at a country club, he collected $100 and had to pay $90 of it to the booker who'd fixed the job. So Duke put an advertisement in the classified telephone directory and soon became a booker himself. When he was rung up, he was such a sweet-talker he ended up sometimes sending out several bands a night and making $150 a week before he was twenty. He had shown a great talent for painting at school, but when he left he never made use of an art scholarship at the Pratt Institute of Applied Art, awarded to him in 1917 after he won a poster competition sponsored by the National Association for the Advancement of Colored People. At the same time, his strong feeling for color was evident throughout the music he composed. His portraits were painted in sound and often called "Portraits"; scores of his titles were expressed in colorful terms: "Black and Tan Fantasy," "Blue Bubbles," "Mood Indigo" (there was also the lesser-known "Flame Indigo"), "Sepia Panorama," "Azure," "Magenta Haze," "On a Turquoise Cloud," "Golden Cress," "Silver Cobweb," "Red Garter." In 1917 and 1918, however, he could make more money running bands, for which there was a big demand in wartime Washington. Trying to get the best of all possible worlds, he ran a sign-painting business in tandem with the band booking. He painted backdrops for the Howard Theatre and for a time he also had office jobs in the Navy Department and the State Department. He built a ten-room house and bought a Cadillac; he was into the music business for good.

Although Ellington, the private man, never mentioned the fact, and grew very angry if anyone asked questions about it, there was another reason why around this time, with the war drawing to a close, he was working flat out. He needed the money to meet his extra responsibilities. On July 2, 1918, he married Edna Thompson, who had been born across the street from his house, had played with him and had been a classmate for years. Duke's only son, Mercer Kennedy Ellington, was born in 1919 before either parent was twenty-one; a second son died in infancy. "It was too close to the first," Edna Ellington later told a magazine. "We were very young then. Kids, really. I think we both thought Mercer was a toy."

The marriage was not happy and, although he never divorced her, Ellington stayed with his wife for only a few years before they permanently separated. He continued to support her generously, however, and she lived in a spacious Washington apartment which contained a baby grand piano. She claimed to have taught both Duke and Mercer how to read music. Early in 1959, long after he had formed a close relationship with Beatrice (Evie) Ellis, a former dancer who made homes for him in New York City—particularly at his final (and only) permanent address on the city's West Side—and was always introduced by him as Mrs. Ellington, the magazine *Ebony* printed an article, with pictures, about Edna Ellington.

Duke was furious. He had never talked about his wife, and in thousands of interviews no one who wanted to avoid his drying up at once had ever dared question him on the subject—if, indeed, the interviewer knew of Edna Ellington's existence. He continued to maintain a total silence on both Edna and Evie for the rest of his life. Yet—another Ellington paradox—he gave a copy of the *Ebony* issue in question to a close friend in London, presumably to ensure that some record of the piece on Edna survived and might be noted. And to that same close friend he once explained the facial scar which many people did not notice on his left cheek in later life, although it ran from his left ear almost to his lips, and reputedly slightly affected his hearing and the sight of one eye. Edna Ellington, according to Duke, had attacked him after she suspected him of going out with another woman, crying bitterly that she would "spoil those pretty looks." Many stories, indeed, circulated about that scar. The trumpeter, Rex Stewart, told the British jazz authority, Sinclair Traill, that a letter opener wielded by Ivie Anderson, the singer who performed with the band during the 1930s, had caused it. According to Stewart, there was a romantic attachment for a time between singer and bandleader; she discovered another woman in his room, and slashed at him. Whatever the truth, it's undeniable that Duke's eye for a pretty woman never dimmed—and often caused him problems. Yet women were placed in a definitively relative category with him; something else was far more important.

Edna was in part, as Evie was later to be, a sacrifice to his art, for already back in those early Washington days, music was his passion. Nothing, including marriage, was allowed to stand in the way. He chose his own directions, demanded freedom, and was already acting like a fully fledged musical leader. Those who have experienced his personal magnetism can easily understand what William "Sonny" Greer, one of the first musicians with whom Ellington worked in Washington, meant when he said that he loved Duke from the start. "There was some sort of magnetism to him you wouldn't understand. In my whole life, I've never seen another man like him. When he walks into a strange room, the whole place lights up."

Greer wasn't quite the first to fall under the Ellington spell. Otto Hardwick, who picked up the nickname Toby, lived a block away from Duke. He was five years younger, and as their schoolroom friendship, founded on music and baseball, grew, Duke took it on himself to look after Toby. He persuaded his junior to switch from double bass (which Hardwick's father had to carry, so small was he) to C melody saxophone. He got the boy jobs, and by the age of sixteen Hardwick was an essential part of the group of musicians who were revolving around Ellington in the city. The others included a trumpeter, Arthur Whetsol, and a banjo player, Elmer Snowden, but none were so close as Hardwick and Ellington. When Sonny Greer arrived on the Washington scene in 1919, brandishing like a torch his reputation as a flashy drummer, a fly fellow, and a knowledgeable fixer—he had, after all, been playing in a trio in Asbury Park, New Jersey, with a young pianist called Thomas "Fats" Waller— the essence of Ellington's first important band was formed. Ellington recalled standing on the corner, acting big-time, and accosting Greer. "I'm sure I look a killer in my new shepherd plaid suit. I take the lead in conversation. Sonny comes back with a line of jive that lays us low."

Ellington, Hardwick, and Greer quickly became inseparable. After playing at the Howard Theatre for a time—a job he picked up in the poolroom, of course—Greer joined the Ellington band. He knew how to organize cheering sections to win band contests for his new friends. He filled their ears with tales of the glamorous clubs and personalities up in New York. They acted, entering their twenties, as if they were already there, swilling down pints of whisky or gin, toting fat cigars, buying big cars (Hardwick had one fondly named the Dupadilly, in which they raced against other musicians), and generally living it up on the considerable funds they were now making out of music. "He was the nearest thing I ever had to a brother," Ellington said of Greer. He was, even more importantly, the nearest thing they had to contacts in Harlem, the crowded and flamboyant black section of New York.

The call came in 1922. A bandleader in New York, Wilbur Sweatman, whose gimmick was to play three clarinets simultaneously, offered Greer a job in his band, and he agreed to come provided there were berths for his two friends. Going on ahead of Ellington, who was reluctant to give up his going concerns, Hardwick and Greer found that the jobs were almost on the point of evaporating. When Duke finally arrived, they had run out of money. So they had to go the rounds of the clubs, looking for chances to perform. Sometimes they got tips, which they split three ways. They didn't eat much, mainly hot dogs. Greer and Ellington played as much pool as they could afford for small side bets, hustling to turn twenty-five cents ɔ a couple of dollars, at which point they might eat. A good ʋ ᴸ of the small-time pickings they made went to buy their eɕ ation, for al-though they weren't making jazz history, theʸ never wasted their time. This was the New York of rent partie. held in black apartments to raise funds when rent money was ɕ e, and of the piano virtuosi who played at them. James P. Johnson was there; so was Willie "the Lion" Smith; and Greer's old partner, Fats Waller, was also around, learning just like Duke, but soon to become a master himself. The classroom for Duke and Fats—or university, in Ellington's phrase—was the endless circuit of par-ties and barroom explosions where the piano professors, with pounding cross rhythms and striding right hands, could always be found.

Both Johnson and the Lion thought Duke was a nice boy. He bought them as much liquor as his tips from clubs would permit, but the traffic wasn't one way. The Lion gave Duke fifty cents one day when he thought his protégé needed a haircut. "I can't," Ellington wrote in a foreword to Willie's autobiography, "think of anything good enough to say about the Lion, Willie the Lion, Willie the Lion Smith." He proved his feelings in ways more substantial than words, helping the Lion financially in later years, ensuring that his teacher was beside him on his seven-tieth birthday. Ellington learned well, absorbing rather than copying, for he changed the "stride" styles of his teachers out of all recognition, despite the traits (especially of Waller, who was five years his junior) which he retained.

It's important, though, not to oversimplify the development of Ellington, and turn it into a picture of him as a graduate of the gin-mill pianists. Never a *poseur* about his music intellectually, he was completely frank about his influences in the early New York days. He wasn't worried about the *kind* of music he heard, only its quality. Of his early piano professors—from Doc Perry to the Lion—he confessed to *Newsweek* in 1969:

> I never could play anything I heard them play, although they all
> tried to teach me. So I had to sit down and create something to fit
> under my fingers. I used to hear Paul Whiteman records, taking
> the snobbishness out of the music and opening the doors for musi-
> cians like the Beiderbeckes and Dorseys, who had great talent and
> impeccable taste. When we started to build a band, Fletcher

Henderson was what we tried to sound like. Another great source of inspiration in those days was the Broadway movie houses. They all had symphony orchestras in the pit playing classical selections before the performance. If there was a good Western on you'd probably sit through three performances of a symphony.

Listening and absorbing, however, was not enough. The three Washingtonians had no jobs and no money. When Duke found fifteen dollars on the street they bought rail tickets back to the capital to sort themselves out, make some money, and bide their time. They hadn't long to wait, and next time it was Fats Waller who sent them running. He came to play in Washington in the spring of 1923, told them there was a job for them in New York, and encouraged them to believe there'd be work for Snowden and Whetsol as well as the three who had already tried their luck in Harlem.

Again Ellington's friends departed in advance of him; again, the old old story. Waller wasn't around, there was no job. Greer said they felt lost without Duke, so with optimistic blandishments they sent for him. Typically, he set out with a billfold, but one luxury seat in the parlor car, one expensive dinner in the diner, and one large cab fare later, he arrived at 129th Street to meet his friends with empty pockets. They shrugged, started the round of auditions, and despite tempting individual offers refused to split up. The spirit of the Ellington band was already brewing. Finally, they were lucky. A night-club singer, Ada Smith—who as "Bricktop" was to become a major name in the clubs and, later, the darling of Paris—had known Ellington's crew back in Washington, where they worked a spot called the Oriental Gardens together. She persuaded Barron Wilkins, who ran a popular night club, Barron's, at 134th Street and Seventh Avenue, to hire them. The Washingtonians, all five of them, were on the way.

Duke's view of those early days was essentially romantic. He forgot the drugs, the booze, the harshness, the violence. Soft lights and sweet music disguised the rough edges. For him, night life was glamorous and fun. No one hustled anybody. In an era when the stereotype was the gambler or hoodlum lighting cigars with fifty-dollar bills, Barron's was the place where the top entertainers and gamblers and sports stars would come in, get a handful of coins as change for a $100 note, and scatter the lot all over the dance floor between numbers for the singers and the musicians to share. The pay for Ellington's men was $50 a week; but five men plus four singers would split up to a thousand dollars a night in such tips.

There were other ways to earn money besides playing "sort of conversation music, soft yet gutbucket," as Hardwick put it, at Barron's. With a lyricist called Jo Trent, Duke began to compose songs for the Broadway music publishers at $50 a time, all rights sold. "The first time I was offered money for a song, the man asked for a lead sheet. I'd never written a lead sheet. But it was four-thirty in the afternoon, and I knew the check-book closed at five, so I learned to write a lead sheet real quick." "Blind Man's Buff," "Choo Choo" ("I Gotta Hurry Home"), and "Pretty Soft for You" were among these early songs. Duke also wrote his first complete score for a show, *Chocolate Kiddies*, with Jo Trent. They completed it in one evening. "I didn't know composers had to take to the hills or the beach and talk with the muses for a few months to get out a show," Ellington later observed ironically. His life's pattern was being set. This time the composers split $500 between them after the producer, Jack Robbins, pawned his wife's engagement ring to raise the wind, but with no later regrets, since the show, featuring Adelaide Hall and Josephine Baker, ran for two years in Berlin and made him a rich man.

All this time, Ellington was gently asserting his leadership of the band. Whetsol was the disciplinarian. Snowden looked after the business side, but the others insisted that Duke should take this over and Freddie Guy came in on guitar to take the place of the banjoist. "Even then," according to Hardwick, "we were already pulling for Duke. He had everyone on his side, he was that kind of guy."

In the autumn of 1923, the band switched clubs, to the Kentucky (at first, it was called the Hollywood) in a classier part of midtown New York—Broadway and Forty-ninth Street—and the four years they spent there, mixed with tours up to New England, was the final stage before the major breakthrough, both commercially and musically. This was the start of Ellington's "jungle" music, for musicians joined him who could, with the aid of mutes and embouchure effects, "growl" and wah-wah in a way scarcely heard before. The "growl" sound, usually produced by drawing a rubber plunger in and out of the trumpet or trombone bell, was described by an early witness as "like a demented soul in hell." Who invented the technique no one quite knows. The ancient New Orleans trumpet master, Joe "King" Oliver, was an early exponent; Sidney Bechet, the great soprano saxist, also of New Orleans, would growl on his instrument, too. No matter. Three virtuosi with mutes and "growls" came to Ellington. The first was Charlie "Plug" Irvis on trombone, who used varied implements to modify his tone—an old tomato can, smashed in at the bottom like a cone (according to Sonny Greer), and also, in Ellington's description, one of the bits that were left after he dropped and smashed a special mute made in the 1920s to fit a trombone and turn its sound into a saxophone imitation.

After Irvis came James "Bubber" Miley, a trumpeter who replaced Whetsol (he took time off to study medicine at Howard University, but returned to the band later), and, finally, a replacement for Irvis called Joe "Tricky Sam" Nanton, who formed a brilliant and complementary partnership with Miley. Duke listened to these men before he plunged. He wasn't writing much of his own music in the years 1925 and 1926; rather he was twisting the pop hits of the day to the band's developing colorings and capacities. But Nanton and Miley, and what they were capable of, were to be the biggest influence on *how* Ellington wrote music when he had lived with their sounds for a couple of years. This, again, was consistent with Ellington's methods down the years. His musicians gave to him, as he did to them; tonally as well as with musical phrases, they helped to build many of his greatest compositions. It was a perfect example of two-way musical empathy.

The club life was hard, from 11 P.M. till around eight in the morning, and already Ellington's way of life was putting a strain on his marriage. Edna Ellington, in 1959, said of those early days:

> We left Mercer in Washington and went to New York. I was one of Ellington's show girls, though really all I had to do was walk around and lend atmosphere. Those were the days when we lived in one room and beans were only five cents a can. Some days we didn't have the five cents.
>
> Like all things, times began to get better. But I was young and jealous and didn't want to share him with the public. I couldn't stand around waiting until the public had their fill of him before

he could give me some of his time. If there was something important I wanted to say to him, I wanted to rush up and tell him then.
But I had to wait. Then came the big break-up. Ellington thought
I should have been more understanding of him. I guess I should
have been.

As his marriage crumbled, with Edna ultimately returning to
Washington, Ellington prospered at the Kentucky. For entertainers, it was a rewarding scene. Greer, sharp as ever, would
scan the people as they came downstairs into the club. This was
the period of Prohibition in America, the "noble experiment"
which failed, and Greer was the one who okayed that it was safe
to continue serving illegal booze as each new party entered (they
never had a raid or a pinch, he boasted) and who also singled
out the big spenders when Duke and he worked the floor as a
piano/drums/vocal duo when the band wasn't on. The pair of
them could count on $200 in tips between them on most nights.
The band began to make radio broadcasts, and became so popular that the club capacity of around 130 was usually strained.
    Paul Whiteman, already the "King of Jazz," and his musi-
cians—Bix Beiderbecke, Tommy Dorsey, Joe Venuti—and
scores of other big-name players were regular visitors after other
clubs around town had closed for the night. Later, Whiteman
and his arranger Ferde Grofé (composer of the "Grand Canyon
Suite") spent many hours listening to Ellington performances
until finally (so the story goes) they gave up their attempts to no-
tate what Duke's men were playing. Later still (in 1938)
Whiteman commissioned Duke to write a longish concert
piece, "Blue Belles of Harlem," for his orchestra.
    Inevitably, the visiting musicians at the Kentucky Club would
sit in for a jam session. Sidney Bechet, the classic soprano saxophone king from New Orleans, came in one night, jammed
with Irvis and Miley, and later he joined Duke's band for a
spell, making it into a seven-piece. He used to join in the battles
of the bands which were already becoming a feature of New
York and other cities with a vigor belying the sometimes wistful
tones produced by some players from the soprano saxophone.
One night, visiting a ballroom where the house band had gold-
painted instruments and a big reputation, Bechet held a table
napkin (as well as his reed) in his mouth so that it hung down
and covered his fingers whilst he was playing. He outplayed the

house band—"cut" them, in the jazz vernacular—so completely that the manager told the men with the golden horns to play waltzes for the rest of the evening, and not to risk any jazz.

Other men were important to Duke in this period. He met Irving Mills, a manager and impresario whose stock-in-trade was to pick up the complete rights to "original" blues from needy musicians at twenty dollars a time. Whenever he didn't like a number, or was short of a few dollars, he'd tell the hopeful "composer": "No thanks. I've got that one." Mills offered them their first recording sessions—four numbers at a time—and under a handful of different names (the Jungle Band, the Whoo-pee Makers, the Harlem Footwarmers, as well as Duke Elling-ton, depending on the label) the band was in the studios once or twice most weeks. Then Mills became their manager, and this was the beginning of an association that lasted a decade or more and was crucial in making Ellington's orchestra an international attraction. Sonny Greer believed Ellington wouldn't have made it so far or fast without Mills's guidance, and Duke paid similar warm tributes to Mills, though rarely without a spice of irony, which suggested that the relationship wasn't always happy and that the manager made plenty of money out of the band.

Harry Carney was another piece of the mosaic. He was from Boston, Massachusetts, a clarinet player who'd taken up the in-strument for one of the reasons that Duke persevered with piano: it pulled in the girls. Carney changed to the alto sax-ophone because he heard it was easier to play, and with a near neighbor, a boy called Johnny Hodges, they started listening to all the fashionable records, especially those of Sidney Bechet. He and Hodges ended up playing in New York, Hodges with a band led by Chick Webb, the drummer who first employed and nurtured Ella Fitzgerald, and Carney at a spot called the Bam-boo Inn, which was where Duke first heard him in April 1927 on his night off. That summer he invited Carney to join him playing one-nighters up in New England for the local impresarios, Char-lie and Sy Shribman. Carney jumped at the chance to see his home town again, and when summer was over, Ellington sweet-talked the boy's mother into letting him stay with the band in-stead of going back to school. As Carney was only seventeen, Duke became a kind of guardian to him, and he stayed until Ellington's death. Carney also introduced Hodges to the band—another lifelong member, virtually—and became Duke's closest friend and confidant on the road. "A great fellow," Carney once observed of Duke. "It's not only been an education being with him, but also a great pleasure. At times I've been ashamed to take the money." To which Carney, one of the nicest men who ever lived, would add a characteristic postscript. "I guess I'll stay with him as long as he can afford me."

Duke's tours were as important to him as his sessions at the Kentucky Club. He learned how to cope with the dancers on the jumping ballroom circuits of Massachusetts and Pennsylvania. He learned how to look after himself in the band battles in which it was quite common for a local group to put down a Paul Whiteman and his thirty pieces. Any musician, as Ellington said later, had to keep with it, get out on the battlefield, not stay at home. "You may read where so-and-so lost this particular battle and so many men were washed away, and it's all a little terrifying. If you come out from home cold—bang!—and all the other cats have been roaming around the jungle, fighting the different animals who're growling with their plungers, honking with their tenors, screeching with their flutes and clarinets, then these animals can sound pretty wild after the comforts of home."

Out in the touring jungle, Duke saw the sights, heard the sounds, and pictures began to form in his mind. His great collaborator of later years, Billy Strayhorn, used to say that musical inspiration came from very simple things, like watching a bird fly. For Ellington, driving from job to job around New England, the source of inspiration was sometimes more prosaic, even the names on signs. One sign they kept seeing on the highways was LEWANDO CLEANERS; and every time the band would start singing "Oh, Lee——wan—*do!*" Out of that lick, according to Ellington, came "East St. Louis Toodle-oo," which became the Ellington signature for years until "Take the A Train" was written by Strayhorn. Hundreds of other compositions, phrases, titles were to be suggested from the scenes and people Ellington surveyed on the road. By 1927 his early education was over.

3

1927-1939
Gangsters, Girls, and Princes

New York City in 1927 was made for an entertainer as energetic, innovative, and expansively optimistic as Duke Ellington. The roaring 1920s were aptly named, for America, casting memories of world war behind her, was in ferment. Piety with profit was the motto. People worked hard, and played hard. There was money to be made, by grabbing opportunities in business, by gambling on Wall Street—few foresaw the crash which was coming—by flirting on the fringes of the law or, in the case of the hoodlum gangs which were now an established feature of the major cities, by plunging mercilessly into the unlawful. The money made, legally or illegally, was lavishly spent. People demanded entertainment, and the clubs which sprang up by the hundreds extracted millions of dollars from uninhibited customers.

They were paying, of course, for something special. Theoretically America had been "dry" since the Prohibition laws of 1919, but this didn't stop the clubs serving booze, both good and bad, brought in by warring gangs. Prohibition provided another racket to add to prostitution, protection, and gambling. So prices were steep, the atmosphere was hectic, hollering, and nervous, and the music was jazz. Its catchy rhythms, its easy appeal to the emotions, its effervescent excitement seem now to have been exactly right for the times; yet in retrospect it is astonishing how quickly it conquered America, for as the 1920s dawned it was identified in the minds of solid-thinking white citizens with the supposedly inferior and certainly poorer black culture of the United States.

Paul Whiteman—employing Bix Beiderbecke, the Dorsey brothers, Joe Venuti, and other stars—began to break down the barriers with his soft-jazz approach and his flirtations with symphonic compositions like Gershwin's "Rhapsody in Blue." Singers like Al Jolson and Bing Crosby were hearing the music and amending it for their own uses, while, on so-called "race" records for the black market, Bessie Smith and the blues singers provided other ingredients of the recipe. Middle-aged white America, pushed forward by the young, took to jazz and the embryonic crooners slowly. As in a later generation when the under-twenty-fives ensured that rock 'n' roll changed the face of popular music, so in the 1920s America's young people—with far less economic power than their peers enjoyed three decades later—provided the zest which swept away the standard popular fare of straitlaced ballads and waltzes. This younger generation, again like the teen-agers of the late 1950s, was in a state of rebellion. Theirs, however, was a comparatively lighthearted revolt, very unlike the sullen heavy-toned dissent of the rock age. These rebels wanted not to demolish society, but to enliven it and amend the restraining conventions of the pre-1914 social order. Their weapons weren't demos, politics, pot, jeans, and doomful Bob Dylan battle hymns, but slang, dancing cheek to cheek, the hip flask, raccoon coats, and jazz. They embraced the music which Whiteman had made whiter and which Ellington was to make his own. Music which was unique, often sophisticated, but always with its roots somewhere in the black America of blues, gospel songs, and half-remembered African tribal rhythms and calls. Soon, the radio and the microphone were to ensure that jazz and its more commercial derivatives, from crooning to novelty numbers, filled the ears of all America as, in 1929, the prosperity bubble of the 1920s burst and the nation slid toward the Depression and the New Deal of Franklin D. Roosevelt.

In the autumn of 1927, however, there was nothing to be depressed about, if you were fortunate enough to be scrambling up the ladder in a career or making money on the stock market. There was still plenty of poverty in the country, to be glaringly revealed in the 1930s; and the black population was still largely poor and underprivileged. But to be a successful black entertainer was desirable, and the mood of the nation remained entrepreneurially exuberant. Ellington matched that optimistic mood. Egged on by Irving Mills, who already realized he had a hot property on his hands, Duke looked for the next step up from the Kentucky Club, the ballroom circuit, and occasional forays into vaudeville. He found it in Harlem, upstairs at 142nd Street and Lenox Avenue, in one of New York's most prestigious night spots, the Cotton Club.

Ellington, however, needed some luck. The job wouldn't have been available at all had not Joe "King" Oliver, the classic New Orleans trumpeter, turned it down because it didn't meet his cash requirements. Duke heard about the vacancy very late, and the six-piece which was his bedrock group wouldn't do for the Cotton Club. Rushing around for players to make the number up to eleven, Duke arrived more than two hours late for his audition. So, fortunately, did the club's owner. Ellington's was the only band out of the six in contention that he heard, and he hired them immediately. Even then, a final arrangement had to be made before Duke could work, for he was contracted to appear at a theatre in Philadelphia. So some associates of the Cotton Club operators in Philadelphia called on the theatre manager and put a proposition to him: "Be big about this, or you'll be dead." The manager was as big as he could be.

When Duke opened at the Cotton Club on December 4, 1927, he felt he had everything going for him. It was a biggish place, with room for up to five hundred people. It had twenty beautiful girls in its floor shows, for which songwriters as distinguished as Jimmy McHugh and Dorothy Fields (and, later, Harold Arlen and Ted Koehler) composed the material. On the big night of the week, Sunday, most of the stars playing Broadway would turn up; Sophie Tucker, Duke recalled, was a regular, sliding toward the spotlight to take a bow while the band played her hit, "Some of These Days." Customers had to behave. If anyone talked loudly during the show, he was cautioned and, if he didn't quiet down, was thrown out. Every evening between six and seven the club band had a coast-to-coast broadcast, which was good for the Cotton Club and even better for

Duke Ellington. Into his expanded band came, over the next few years, several more of the men who were to become great Ellingtonians. Johnny Hodges was hired to sit by his fellow Bostonian, Harry Carney, in the reed section. Barney Bigard, a clarinet player from New Orleans whose "woody" tone Duke adored, joined another player from the same city, the bassist Wellman Braud, who had been recruited in 1926. In 1929, the great trumpeter, Cootie Williams, took over from Bubber Miley, while Juan Tizol, one of Duke's many co-composers (and sole composer of one of the band's greatest hits, "Perdido"), brought his valve trombone into the band and a certain Latin-American feeling too, for he had been born in Puerto Rico.

Not all of the original Ellingtonians liked the change from small to medium-sized band. Greer said it broke his heart because as a quintet their music had been quiet and tasteful and they hadn't needed written arrangements. But the high salaries at the Cotton Club—as the management could easily afford, with whisky at around $14 a bottle—soon took the edge off his heartbreak, as did the fame which broadcasts brought the band, and the presentational flair which went with its new stature. For a spell, Duke employed a sousaphone player who had blinker lights in the bell of his instrument and played five-chorus solos with the colored lights twinkling over his head. Greer himself soon had a drum kit which was fabulous for the time—snare and bass drums, tom-toms, cymbals, chimes, vibraphone, timpani, and much more, all worth around $3,000. He claimed to be the first in the world to put his leader's name and his own monogram on the bass drum.

There were other compensations for the musicians. When the Cotton Club closed its doors at around four in the morning, they didn't go home. Nearby clubs stayed open much later, with floor shows including singing waiters and twirling trays, starting at perhaps 6 A.M. There would be jam sessions with twenty or thirty visiting musicians from other bands joining in, and at breakfast time the crowd of merrymakers would spill into the streets, the men in their tuxedos and the girls in their long dresses, still looking for a jam session to blow at or a card game to join. If all this sounds today like a romantic version of the truth, then a fearsome number of musicians must have fevered imaginations, for the descriptions reside in volume after volume of jazzmen's memoirs from the period. "The average musician hated to go home in those days," Sonny Greer remembered. "He was always seeking some place where someone was playing something he ought to hear." They were dangerous as well as exciting times. Ellington recalled that he was frequently asked by the police if he'd seen a particular person at a particular time, if he knew named people, if he'd ever been asked to perform favors for acquaintances. Like others who wanted to stay healthy, he saw, heard, and spoke no evil.

Nevertheless he was sometimes asked to do favors. A dangerous gangster, just out of prison, came into the Cotton Club one night and requested "Singin' in the Rain." Duke overlooked the request until the manager urgently reminded him; the band scarcely stopped playing the tune for almost an hour. On another occasion, according to Barney Bigard, the club management telephoned Al Capone in Chicago when the grapevine said some gangsters intended to kidnap Ellington and the famous dancer, Bill "Bojangles" Robinson. Three of Capone's men came down from Chicago and warned off the kidnap party inside the club with drawn guns.

Certainly this was not Ellington's only brush with gangsterdom or Capone. He must, sometimes, have been in real danger, but whenever one asked him in later years about the tribulations of his early existence—the insults because of his color, the dives, and the gangsters—he would usually turn the question away, find a funny side to the story, never drawing the curtain on his privacy too far aside. This was another side of his pragmatism; he usually sought ways round obstacles rather than confrontations. Even as early as the Cotton Club years, he had no real interest other than his music and his band, and he could be ruthless—with people, with time, with himself—in protecting that interest. His every action reflected his obsessiveness, from paying his musicians lavishly to sidestepping the gang of hoodlums who pushed for protection when Duke's name went up in lights outside an establishment on the West Side of Chicago, ineptly called The Paradise, during a visit in 1931.

Duke heard about their demand for $500, or else, from his road manager, who had intimated to the visitors, brazenly but ludicrously, that since all the boys in the band carried guns, they'd give as good as they got if the hoods wanted a shoot-out. Ellington at first considered moving his gunless men out of town fast, but when he was asked for money again at his hotel ($200 this time), he rang up some connections. Duke claimed later that, as a result, Al Capone warned everyone to lay off Ellington. The hoods rang him finally asking for twenty dollars because they had to leave town in a hurry; Chicago had become too hot for them.

An environment like this must have helped the spirit of any band. You stuck together to survive, as well as to make music. The Ellington band's sense of togetherness was developing well. Bigard pushed Duke, as hard as Harry Carney did, to bring Johnny Hodges into the band because, he said, he was afraid that Ellington might otherwise recruit the most prestigious clarinettist of the period, Buster Bailey. Later, it was Hodges who talked the leader into employing Cootie Williams. "In the beginning," Cootie said, "you didn't think about money. It was exciting, and we were very young. Everybody made suggestions. It was a family thing." It wasn't exactly a cooperative, but Duke did not behave magisterially toward his men in the fashion of a Glenn Miller or Benny Goodman. He used his musicians, listening to their improvised solos and sometimes picking up phrases to form the basis of his tunes, as much as they used his steadily growing innovations.

At first, Bigard thought Duke was getting the arrangements down wrongly on paper "because he wrote so weird." He'd put down the chords unusually, giving to another instrument the part which seemed natural for the clarinet as, later, he was sometimes to score as a lead instrument the baritone saxophone which Harry Carney took up at the Cotton Club to provide more variety in the band's sound. It was tricks like this which, with the mute-and-growl playing of his brass section, swiftly made Ellington's sound so distinctive. Otto Hardwick was another who said that all Ellington's early musicians believed his numbers sounded weird. "We found out, before the fans did, that you've got to give Duke's compositions a chance to grow on you. That's how original they are."

Ellington's originality now began to show in a spate of compositions mostly featuring the "jungle" sound, but already containing catchy lyrical passages and touches of novelty. Among these early titles were "Black and Tan Fantasy," "Black Beauty," "The Mooch," "Mood Indigo," "Rockin' in Rhythm," and "Creole Love Call," the last-named modelled on a solo by the clarinettist, Johnny Dodds, but still a major innovation because of the exquisite fashion in which the wordless vocal of Adelaide Hall was blended with clarinet. The ingenious and delicate "Mood Indigo," which ultimately became a vehicle featuring a trio of muted trombone, clarinet, and bass clarinet, grew into an alternative signature tune for Ellington and drew from him this idiosyncratic description: "Just a story about a little girl and a little boy. They are about eight and the girl loves the boy. They never speak of it of course, but she just likes the way he wears his hat. Every day he comes to her house at a certain time and she sits in her window and waits. Then one day he doesn't come. 'Mood Indigo' just tells how she feels."

"Black Beauty" was one of the earliest of his musical portraits of black artists, written especially for Florence Mills, the singer, and "Creole Love Call" was similarly intended as a vignette of Bessie Smith. The singer who helped him create it, Adelaide Hall, was, incidentally, never a regular vocalist with the band. She was one of those guests—Joe Turner, Ella Fitzgerald, Mahalia Jackson, and Alice Babs were others in later years—whose styles were needed for particular effects which Ellington's tone-palette demanded. During his history he employed no fewer than thirty-one regular band singers. Some of the best were Ivie Anderson, Joya Sherrill, Al Hibbler, Herb Jeffries, Trish Turner, and Kay Davis. But generally Ellington wasn't the greatest selector of singers.

At this time, however, he relied chiefly on Sonny Greer for vocals, and it was his instrumental sounds and his compositions which were beginning to persuade the white college kids and more elderly playboys who had at first gone to the Cotton Club for kicks and a tourist's look at the blacker side of life to return time and again for a musical experience which they sensed was the start of something exciting and radical. Looking back on this period, nearly fifteen years later, Duke spoke very revealingly and with considerable candor. "Our band came along just when Paul Whiteman and his orchestra had popularized the symphonic style. We came in with a new style. Our playing was stark and wild and tense. That's the way our boys had to play and we planned our music that way. We put the Negro feeling and spirit into our music. We were not the first to do that, but maybe we added some more."

Probably Duke needed no watchdog to keep him working, but had he done so, there was always Irving Mills snapping at his heels, driving him on. No manager ever battled harder for his artists than Mills did. He had been a song plugger, then a singer in cinemas, and finally a megaphone vocalist (like Rudy Vallee) in dance halls before he concentrated on management and music publishing. Mills was almost a parody of his profession: squat, burly, pugnacious, a waver of fat cigars, a fast-talking, excitedly gesturing hustler. His energy broke barrier after barrier for Ellington. Mills insisted that Ellington record only his own music; then he badgered record companies to get his black artist into hitherto all-white catalogues. He secured a Hollywood contract for the band, and in 1930 Duke and his musicians appeared in *Check and Double Check*, with the popular radio team of Amos 'n' Andy. "Ring Dem Bells" was the big Ellington feature as, a year earlier, "Black and Tan Fantasy" had been in a short movie of the same name. In 1929, the band was simultaneously appearing at the Cotton Club and in Florenz Ziegfeld's *Show Girl*, whose score, including "An American in Paris" and "Liza," was by George Gershwin. This prestigious billing was matched by the Mills coup which took Ellington into the same concert as Maurice Chevalier at the Fulton Theatre, New York, in 1930.

Yet the impresario was only beginning his achievements for Ellington, who exulted over Mills's ear and feeling for a song, his trick of amending a lyric so that it came out perfectly. Mills, indeed, is partly credited as lyricist on dozens of early Ellington compositions in the 1930s—"Sophisticated Lady," "Solitude," "Ring Dem Bells," "Caravan," and "Prelude to a Kiss" among them—and he was partly responsible for Ellington's first venture into extended composition.

The band had at last ended its residency at the Cotton Club and was playing a theatre in Chicago in 1931 when Mills breezily announced that a new long work—a rhapsody—would be premiered the next day. This was news to Ellington, but he sat down and wrote "Creole Rhapsody," which turned out so long it filled both sides of a 78 rpm record, a very chancy departure at the time. Mills had to talk very fast indeed even to get Brunswick and Victor (it came out in different versions on both labels) to accept it.

As Ellington was growing in confident daring, so, virtually unknown to him and his musicians, was his reputation outside the United States. The first to sense it was Otto Hardwick, for whom Duke always had a special affection. "God bless him,"

Duke said of Hardwick, "He was a charmer, and he lived the way he played his C melody sax—sweet and straight. Toby was what he liked to be called, and he had this kind of warm, helpless air so that chicks wanted all the time to mother him. Every now and then he'd let it happen, so I never knew quite when he'd skip out of the band for a spell."

Hardwick journeyed in Europe in 1929 because he wanted to travel. In Paris, he played with Noble Sissle, toured a bit, then got a job with Fats Waller and wound up at the club run by their old New York ally, "Bricktop." Hardwick was astonished at the reputation Duke's records had won for the band in Britain and on the Continent. Once back in the U.S.A., he spread the news. No one quite believed him, but when Irving Mills heard about it, the impresario began sending letters and cables. In 1933 his persistence bore fruit. In association with Jack Hylton, the British bandleader, Mills announced that Ellington's band was to play the Palladium in London, then—as now—the premier variety theatre in the world.

In one way, Duke was ready for the trip. He had been playing in American clubs, dance halls, and theatres up and down the East Coast, in the Middle West, and in California for a decade. It was enjoyable up to a point, but the scene had begun to pall. He'd become used to the beautiful showgirls in the clubs, the endless booze, the high wages. Now it was the drunks endlessly making requests, the routine, the commercialism which dominated his thoughts and sometimes depressed him. He would appreciate a change, and already he must have sensed that discerning judges knew he led more than just another dance band. In 1932 the Australian-born composer Percy Grainger had been instrumental in fixing a date for the band to perform a concert at Columbia University in New York, and Duke was also to lecture on jazz at New York University during Grainger's tenure as head of the music department. It's claimed that Duke, having heard Grainger declare how much Ellington had been influenced by Frederick Delius, stopped his cab after the lecture and sauntered into a music store to buy $100 worth of Delius records. He hadn't wanted to tell Grainger he'd never heard of the English composer.

Nevertheless, although the strength of his ambition to increase his own and his band's reputation was powerful, there were drawbacks to a European trip. In the wake of his broken marriage, Ellington had brought his parents, his sister, Ruth, who was almost twoscore years his junior, and his son, Mercer, to New York. From 1930, they lived in a Harlem apartment on Edgecombe Avenue, giving him a home base from which he was, nevertheless, often absent. Both Ruth and Mercer were at high school in New York, and would move on to Columbia University together, before Mercer switched to the Juilliard School and New York University to take particular music courses. Ellington had also met many girls he liked, and his romances formed an integral part of what bound him to New York. One woman particularly, Mildred Dixon, was to become the first of those few who, after Edna Ellington, were to play a significant part in his life.

Mildred Dixon was Ellington's regular companion for several years, and was sometimes thought to be his wife by the new friends Duke swiftly found as his stature grew during these expansive years for him. She was part of a dance duo at the Cotton Club, a small, sweet woman of whom he was very fond—as were practically all of his acquaintances who knew her—until she was supplanted in his affections toward the end of the 1930s by, oddly, another dancer from the Cotton Club, Beatrice Ellis, who came to be known as Evie Ellington.

There were other women, too, around this time, for Duke's reputation as a ladies' man was already well established; so was his renown for that finesse which was to become part of his universal image. He once telephoned Ralph Gleason to ask for a hotel reservation to be made for him, adding, in the gentlest of tones, "and a separate room for the young lady who is travelling parallel to me." It was Gleason, too, who recalled an older lady, minked and diamonded, approaching Ellington in a club to request a tune ("Birmingham Breakdown"). He ignored her. She grew persistent. He ignored her. She reminded him of the place (a girls' school) where their liaison had taken place—and the year: 1928. Duke grew even deafer. He knew who she was, but she reminded him just how old he was. Oh, how he hated that! Whenever anyone asked him for his oldest tunes, he'd smile and tell them they must mean his father's band, since Duke himself was *much* too young to have been in the business so long ago. Anyway, the story goes, this tall and angry lady walked away, paused, then removed her hundred-dollar shoes and hurled them at him, singly, clear across the dance floor.

Apart from his burgeoning romances, there was another reason why Ellington had to be persuaded to go to Europe in 1933. He had a deep-rooted fear of the ocean, arising, he explained, from reading a book about the *Titanic* in his youth. It was a standing joke among his musicians that Ellington wouldn't even take the Hoboken ferry in the Cotton Club days. When he finally ventured on board the S.S. *Olympic* on June 2, 1933, for the transatlantic voyage to Southampton, he stayed awake drinking most nights, his alarm increased even more when he was told that during darkness the ship was often steered by an automatic pilot. "I couldn't understand how an automatic pilot could see an iceberg," he explained.

As Ellington sailed toward his new horizon, he took with him an even stronger orchestra than that which had caught the imagination of a growing army of admirers with its innovations and virtuosity after it began to broadcast from the Cotton Club. The forcefully emotional and sensitive voice of Ivie Anderson was now an established feature. Lawrence Brown had joined "Tricky Sam" and Juan Tizol in the trombone section, so different in style from the other two with his phenomenal speed and his smooth, lightly flowing style, patterned on his love of the cello. Of all Ellington's long-serving musicians, Brown was the one who most emphatically rebuffed the stereotype of jazzmen as fast livers and big drinkers. In the early 1930s, when liquor and marijuana were in vogue among musicians in California, where he was raised, he drank milk or Coke at parties. He had studied in his teens to be a doctor, looked in later life as if he'd make a fine funeral director, and was forever mourning his discovery that music was a business and (in Brown's view) a rotten business. The other musicians called him "Deacon." Yet he played—even when he had to take over the plunger-mute role of "Tricky Sam," which he hated—like an angel.

There was, finally, another change of emphasis within the Ellington camp. Toby Hardwick was back in his saxophone chair after leading his own band at the Hot Feet Club in Greenwich Village, an aggregation that featured Chu Berry on tenor sax and, at different times, Fats Waller, James P. Johnson, or William "Count" Basie on piano—a record of some kind, surely, and one of the reasons why, in a band battle at an Astor Club charity night during Waller's reign, even the Ellington band conceded that Hardwick's had outplayed them. "When I rejoined, it was just like I'd never left. Except this way, maybe. It wasn't *our* thing any longer. It had become Ellington's alone. This was inevitable, I guess. Ten years ago, it was 'We do it this way' and 'We wrote that.' Now the we was *royal*."

Royal, also, was the reception which awaited Ellington when he arrived in England on June 9. Henry Hall, the BBC bandleader, and the symphony conductor, Basil Cameron, were among those who welcomed him in person. His fans included the Prince of Wales (later the Duke of Windsor) and Prince George, the Duke of Kent (killed during the Second World War). It was in London that the other Duke got his first taste of acclaim from the high and the mighty of the Old World. The visit coincided with the International Economic Conference, and between their Palladium appearances the band was invited to appear at a party in Lord Beaverbrook's palatial London home, Stornaway House, set just behind St. James's Street. Jack Hylton's band played waltzes and softer pop until midnight, when the Ellington orchestra took over. Prince George, the Duke of Kent, requested "Swampy River," which Ellington had a hard time remembering. (Just to show he wasn't always consistent, Duke said on one occasion he played it, and on another that, not recognizing who the hell was talking to him, he gave Prince George "the light fluff" and told him "I never do solos.")

In later years, Ellington said Prince George was a good jazz pianist: "We played a lot of four-hand duets together." He was even more emphatic about the Prince of Wales's ability as a drummer. "It wasn't just Little Lord Fauntleroy drumming! He had a hell of a Charleston beat." He also drank gin, which Ellington had hitherto regarded as low-life but now believed to be rather grand! A lot of gin, if Sonny Greer is to be believed, was consumed as the Prince of Wales tried out the drums and stayed close to them, observing Sonny's technique, for most of the evening. "People kept coming up and calling him 'Your Highness,' but he wouldn't move. We both began to get rather high on whatever it was we were drinking. He was calling me 'Sonny' and I was calling him 'The Wale.' " It was said afterwards that the Prince of Wales persisted in introducing Ellington to guests as "The Duke of Hot."

Such anecdotes seem deliberately, even incredibly naïve today—as does Duke's comment on the party when he got back to New York: "It was very ducky. We were way up, feeling

mellow, the result of plenty of nectar." But in those relatively
innocent times, Britain was somewhat bewildered by the prospect of this elegant, black entertainer leading out his impeccable
band. The photographs of their arrival at Southampton show
them looking more like a convention of cheerful visiting busi-
nessmen or academics; they defied all the stereotypes of jazzmen
as rakehellers, although some of them could be wild enough,
and the reaction of Britain was a mixture of surprise, delight,
and ignorance.

Ellington was called "a Negro Bandmaster," "a Negro Genius," "a great man." One of the few discordant notes was struck
by the renowned but petulant critic, Ernest Newman, who
dubbed him "a Harlem Dionysus drunk on bad bootleg liquor."
There were reports in the newspapers that no London hotel
would house the band because the musicians were colored; later
the reports were questioned and Duke himself was comfortably
located in the Dorchester. The *Daily Express* reported Jack Hylton as saying that Duke had been intended for the law and, ig-
noring his studies, had been disinherited by his well-to-do
parents—a quaintly old-fashioned notion about Ellington. Spike
Hughes, the composer and music columnist, wrote reams about
him: "a tall, splendidly built young man with a slow infectious
smile and quick sense of humour . . . yet, curiously, he is a
prophet without honour in this country." Hannen Swaffer,
usually a columnist commenting on politics and general subjects,
wrote an immense piece in the *Daily Herald* under the oddly
patronizing heading :'Hannen Swaffer Listens to the SOUL OF A
NEGRO." It was to Swaffer that Ellington gave what must have
been among the earliest interviews indicating that he shrewdly
knew precisely where he might be going. Explaining to Swaffer
that he was composing a suite telling, in five movements, the
story of his people, Ellington went on:

> If only I can write it down as I feel it. I have gone back to the his-
> tory of my race and tried to express it in rhythm. We used to
> have, in Africa, a "something" we have lost. One day we shall get
> it again. I am expressing in sound the old days in the jungle, the
> cruel journey across the sea and the despair of the landing. And
> then the days of slavery. I trace the growth of a new spiritual
> quality and then the days in Harlem and the cities of the States.
> Then I try to go forward a thousand years. I seek to express the fu-

ture when, emancipated and transformed, the Negro takes his place, a free being, among the peoples of the world.

Not surprisingly, the liberal-minded Swaffer commented after recording Duke's words: "All this was said with a quietness of dignity. I heard, almost, a whisper of prophecy." Less expected was the outcome of his appearance at the Beaverbrook party, which resulted in a reference during the course of a *Daily Express* editorial.

The newspaper tycoon was fascinated that night. "This mob, they'd never heard music like that," one of the band entourage later recalled. "I was standing with Beaverbrook and Lady Mountbatten. We were watching all these dignitaries, all diamonds and medals. Beaverbrook was so taken with the music, and he said the mob was like a bunch of kids. He asked me questions about the band." The questions led to the reference in the *Express*. In an editorial advocating colored colonial MPs, Beaverbrook cited Ellington as a fine example of his race, "a genius of Negro music . . . [who] sat by the side of his host, modest, dignified, delighting all the company with his gay mind and splendid bearing."

Much as a substantial section of London's intelligentsia worshipped Duke's music, his performance didn't draw universal acclaim. The serious fans wanted only to hear the already classic Ellington compositions, and at the Palladium, they were annoyed that they had to wait one and a half hours before the orchestra appeared as the thirteenth act on a bill which also included comedian Max Miller. The show was limited to eight numbers, and "Mood Indigo" was only included as one of two encores. The other was "Some of These Days." One of the biggest hits with the Palladium audiences was the featured trumpeter, Freddie Jenkins. "He takes his bows like a railway signalman," wrote Hannen Swaffer. "He grins twice as big as himself." The biggest sensation of all, however, was the "snake-hips" dancer, Bessie Dudley, waggling her bottom, clad in black satin knickers, while the impeccably dressed musicians—usually in gray tails with gray satin facings or in neat white jackets with shoes to match—stomped along with "Rockin' in Rhythm." That brought the crowd to their feet, spilling into the aisles to applaud.

The intelligentsia weren't so sure about that, nor did they like the repeating of "Some of These Days" (plus Lawrence Brown's solo version of "Trees"!) at the first of two special concerts sponsored by the jazz weekly, *Melody Maker*, at the Trocadero Cinema, Elephant and Castle. This was supposed to be a serious show, played only for 4,500 jazz fans, who travelled to it from all over Europe, with no commercial demands made of Duke. But when Ellington heard some people laughing during "growl" solos by Cootie Williams and Tricky Sam Nanton, and perceived a certain restlessness when the band played slower numbers, he switched to items from his vaudeville routine.

Reaction was mixed. There was the critic, typical of several, who reported after witnessing the scenes at the Palladium: "His music has a true Shakespearian universality and as he sounded the gamut, girls wept and young chaps sank to their knees." But, as so often later in his career, Ellington couldn't please all of the people all of the time, especially those who took his music very seriously indeed. Whilst the influential critic, Spike Hughes, took the audience at the Trocadero to task for applauding at the end of solos, one *Melody Maker* reader, Laurie Lee, whose fame as a poet was still to come, turned his wrath upon Duke. "I had always considered Ellington the prophet of a new art," he wrote, "but on Sunday I found a prophet who continually debased himself." Duke was unaffected. He was doing what he always did, playing in contrasting contexts and enjoying them all equally. Before leaving for a short tour of France and Holland after five weeks in Britain, he played for dancing not only at Beaverbrook's palace but in earthier venues like the Grafton Ballroom in Liverpool and Green's Playhouse in Glasgow. Besides the two concerts at the Trocadero, he had given concerts in Hastings, Harrogate, and Blackpool. His short season at the Liverpool Empire was marked by a further encounter with the Prince of Wales, who followed up a visit to a golf international at Southport with an evening at the music hall. Just before the interval he walked down the aisle at the Empire with Lord Sefton and slipped into a two-shilling seat in the front row of the stalls; the packed house rose and cheered him as well as Duke. After these varied triumphs, the departure of Ellington's band from Liverpool Street Station on July 24 was as lively and emotional as their arrival in Southampton.

The visit was a watershed in Duke's career, by no means the

only one, but important enough. He had got a taste for travel, sensed the inspiration he could draw from it in his music. He knew now at first hand how people outside America, important and ordinary, were devoted to him and would help him. Friendships were formed with great artists and VIPs from other worlds, as well as with younger people like Renee Gertler, the niece of the painter, Mark Gertler. Aged thirteen, she telephoned Duke at the Dorchester and, luckily getting through, explained that even her father couldn't get tickets for his shows. Could Duke oblige? He did, extracting as the price for his largesse that she should ring him daily at the hotel when she came out of school just after noon to make sure he got up. The friendship blossomed down the years, and after her happy marriage to Leslie Diamond, Renee's home—especially their apartment off Park Lane—became Duke's regular London retreat.

Renee Gertler was not his only conquest. Five times in the Palladium audience was a Turkish schoolboy of fourteen, Nesuhi Ertegun, whose father was ambassador to London. He kept sneaking away from his studies at the Lycée in South Kensington to attend. "I'd heard Armstrong and Henderson. I'd heard Lew Stone. But I'd never heard anything like this. It changed my life." Later, with his brother Ahmet, Nesuhi Ertegun founded Atlantic Records, one of the most successful jazz and pop labels of the last thirty years.

Above all, as the band journeyed back to America from Europe, Ellington must have realized that with such dedicatedly serious support for jazz from cultured Europeans, he could afford more often to experiment in his compositions, in form and in length, and to lessen his dependence upon (although never ignore) the commercial demands of the music business.

Little more than a month after his return there was evidence of that. He recorded "Rude Interlude," a number which derived its title from Mrs. Constant Lambert's trick of calling Duke's most renowned piece "Rude Indigo." This dark-textured, reflective composition was virtually bereft of melody, depending for its effect on a sombre harmonic sequence, with Cootie Williams's trumpet and wordless vocal from Louis Bacon (Ivie Anderson's husband) giving it added dimensions. Comparisons between Duke's music and Delius had already been made in the *New Statesman* by Constant Lambert, who also declared: "I know of nothing in Ravel so dextrous in treatment as the varied solos in the middle of the ebullient 'Hot and Bothered,' and nothing in Stravinsky more dynamic than the final section." Among other statements of Lambert's was this: "He gives the same distinction to his genre as Strauss gave to the waltz or Sousa to the march." Percy Grainger, in a New York University lecture, added Bach to the list of comparisons, and soon such conservatoire recognition gained further credibility as a new composition, "Reminiscing in Tempo," arrived a year later.

This was the melancholy tone poem in which Duke mourned his mother, but it also showed how rapidly his musical ambitions were expanding. Throughout its twelve minutes Ellington experimented with harmonies more advanced than in his earlier "Creole Rhapsody," which, by comparison, was dynamically straightforward. Later in life he characterized it as "one of my first ambitious things. It was written in a soliloquizing mood. My mother's death was the greatest shock. I didn't do anything but brood. The music is representative of that. It begins with pleasant thoughts. Then something awful gets you down. Then you snap out of it and it ends affirmatively."

So it must have hurt when some of his allies turned down their thumbs on hearing it. In America, John Hammond, in an article headed "The Tragedy of Duke Ellington," regretted the absence of the composer's peculiar vitality. Ellington never forgot the review in all the long years afterwards; it wounded him deeply that the memory of his mother should thus be indirectly slighted. In Britain, in the *Melody Maker*, Spike Hughes joined the attack, dismissing "Reminiscing in Tempo" as "a long, rambling monstrosity that is as dull as it is pretentious and meaningless."

What some of the critics failed to see—not surprisingly, for hindsight is always marvellously easy compared with the hotter-blooded task of instantaneous comment—was that Ellington was in a most interesting state of evolution. During the 1920s he had gathered around him a smallish band of superb individual musicians. From time to time, their solos were given special coherence and unity by his compositions (as in "Creole Love Call" or "Black and Tan Fantasy"), but he didn't control them as he did later. Mostly he provided a sympathetic background for his star soloists. These were the days when, at the Cotton Club, the flair of the brass could make the pianist, Eddy Duchin, who was in the audience, literally roll under the table in ecstasy. "Creole

Rhapsody," heralded by Spike Hughes as "the first classic of modern dance music," with the individual player completely subservient as never before to the composer's personality, marked the change in emphasis. Duke was moving away from straightforward jungle music—with cymbals sizzling and tom-toms thudding in suggestion of Africa behind wailing horns, all of which so delighted his early admirers—into much more studied compositions.

Inevitably, the increasing maturity and sophistication of Duke's music sprang partly from his own genius; but he was also responsive to new influences. He was beginning to hear music which had previously been outside his knowledge. In 1936, for example, he met for the first time a young New York stockbroker, Edmund Anderson, with whom he formed a warm friendship that lasted until the end of his life. Anderson later worked with Duke occasionally, gave him his biggest non-Ellington hit, "Flamingo," and founded his career in radio production, advertising, and a gamut of show-business activites. At the time, however, Anderson was simply a young man who'd been swept away by enthusiasm for Ellington's sounds and was looking for a way into the music business—preferably as a partner with Ellington. According to Anderson:

> We became very good friends from the start. His father was alive then, a very courtly gentleman, and I met Millie Dixon too at the apartment. We spent many afternoons at my place listening to records. I was intrigued that this man had been compared to Delius and Ravel and Debussy. He'd read all that, of course, but he said that actually he'd not really heard much of that kind of music. So that's what I used to play for him. Do you know that long ascending oboe passage in "Walk to the Paradise Garden"? At first, Duke just gasped and said: *"Man,* listen to him *climb!"* Another time someone was screaming for a rumba to be played when I put on Ravel's "Daphnis and Chloe." "Hey, *that's* a rumba," Duke said. That was part of his fascination. He could be so earthy *or* so sophisticated. He laughed at the idea that he was supposed to be like Delius, but he *loved* that music.

If Anderson could produce sounds to surprise Duke, then Ellington's opinions sometimes astonished the younger man.

> Once I asked him what he considered a typical Negro piece among his compositions. He paused a moment before he came up

with "In a Sentimental Mood." I protested a bit and said I thought that was a very sophisticated white kind of song and people were usually surprised when they learned it was by him. "Ah," he said, "that's because you don't *know* what it's like to be a Negro."

In such exchanges, in the hearing of new music, Ellington was undoubtedly understanding how he might develop. As the 1930s progressed, he became the composer, boss of the band, increasingly concerned with structure and harmony, still a jazzman, but with new horizons which he never allowed other men's ideas of what was proper in jazz to constrain. As Duke put it later in his life: "I told those guys in 1927 they were never going to drive me to the nuthouse. 'We may all go there,' I said, 'but I'm going to be driving the wagon.' " By the mid-1930s he was driving hard, and whereas in 1930 his had been just another band, he was now well on the way to becoming *the* band, the one which would outlast the rest when the orchestra-touring scene crumbled in the 1940s.

Yet the life to which he had returned after his first venture into Europe was superficially much like that of any other bandleader of the time. Afternoons listening to Delius were an occasional but scarcely a typical diversion from the club and theatre dates, the tours from city to city in the United States, the occasional movie-making, which became the pattern of his days. He had also to compose for the needs of tomorrow as much as for the taste of his intellectual fans. "We're not interested in writing for posterity," as he once observed. "We just want it to sound good right now!"

These were the years of travelling all over America for the first time, of grafting for a living in a period when the new white "swing" bands led by Benny Goodman, Tommy and Jimmy Dorsey, and Artie Shaw swiftly grabbed the limelight, and the subtler, more complex music of Ellington (and of other black leaders like Jimmie Lunceford and Count Basie) was less regarded. The Ellington band never suffered during the Depression years, however; they weren't the biggest at the box office, but they were comfortable, even though Mercer Ellington did once recall that money was sometimes short. He was working as a baggage boy with the band at the time, and when they reached Cleveland, Ohio, around breakfast time he complained he was hungry. "What!" said Duke. "Didn't you just eat yesterday?"

Mercer was often on the road during his school holidays, as was Ruth. "We'd jump in a car and follow the band," she said.

Irving Mills was again a savior for the band at this time. He pioneered tours through the Deep South and Texas and overcame the problems which segregation caused by hiring two private Pullman railway coaches for the band, plus a van for baggage. Through most states of the U.S.A. the caravan went, with DUKE ELLINGTON emblazoned on the side of the Pullmans. It was the only band, white or black, which travelled in such style. They lived out of the Pullmans, shunted into station sidings, with automobiles parked alongside to take them to their one-night stands. This often avoided the hassle of looking for hotel rooms and restaurants in what might be, for blacks, hostile territory. The camaraderie of the orchestra continued to blossom. Duke paid them well, looked after them; they really felt they belonged to a unique artistic organization.

The relationship between Ellington and his musicians has always been a fascinating study. Discipline was never intense, but it was much more apparent in the early days when Duke had Arthur Whetsol to help him. "One look from him would straighten those cats out," Ellington observed. At the Palladium in 1933, dress was immaculate, instruments polished, and the curtain rose on a band already positioned to play. "He said we should play pretty and look pretty," Sonny Greer recalled. The semblance of order crumbled progressively until in later years the musicians used to drift on to the stage at concerts one by one, an air of genteel scruffiness about them, with Johnny Hodges, probably the highest-paid member of all, usually the last to arrive and the most casual.

Sometimes there would be absentees. Tubby Hayes, a noted British saxophonist, who died tragically early, once stood in at the last minute for Paul Gonsalves of the Ellington band in 1964 at the Festival Hall, London. The reasons for Gonsalves's absence were never given, but everyone knew he was a big drinker and had at various periods of his life taken soft and hard drugs. It was, incidentally, one of the more shameful aspects of the British scene that on every visit by the Ellington orchestra during the last fifteen years of Duke's life there were always pushers hanging around the stage doors trying to get hold of Gonsalves even when that noble artist had tried very hard to reject drugs.

Yet despite the inevitable though small quota of prima donnas who passed in and out of the Ellington band down the years, and the suspicion that a few of the musicians who stayed resented Duke but loved the money, dates were mostly kept, usually to time, on the most exacting schedule any group of artists was ever called upon to fulfill.

From the earliest days, Duke had problems. "Bubber Miley," he once recalled, "was very temperamental and liked his liquor. He used to get under the piano and go to sleep when he felt like it. In fact, all our horn-blowers were lushes, and I used to have to go around and get them out of bed to see they got to work." Ellington's own evidence of his ability to keep his highly strung crew afloat has been confirmed by a hundred other sources. In the days when Ellington was a drinker, it seems, in retrospect, almost as if he were doing it to win the men he wanted over to his cause. He had, for a spell, to be one of the boys. Sonny Greer said that Duke continually fraternized with his men in these years. He'd talk with them, play cards with them—and for a reason. "He'd never let them lose confidence in themselves," Greer explained. "He'd sit up and ball with them, and he used to be able to drink them under the table." By the 1960s, however, Duke had placed himself at a marked and unmistakable distance from his men, and once delivered a sermon to the pianist, Dave Brubeck, because Brubeck's quartet were sharing the dressing room with their leader. You're the star, Brubeck was told; stars don't share dressing rooms.

The way another musician, Russell Procope, expressed it was that Duke ruled his men "with an iron hand in a mink glove." Duke was very good at using people for his own musical ends and disguising the fact that he was doing so. If you asked him whether he'd ever fired anybody, he'd say he couldn't remember one instance. The iron hand in the mink glove was rather more subtle. One musician who continually turned up to work drunker than even Duke could tolerate was, time after time, called upon to solo at blistering tempo. Tiring of not being able to play the notes, the man finally quit in humiliation. Duke even used to discipline his long-time stars for breaches of the band's code (getting too bigheaded, for example, or too many absences, or too heavy a spell of drunkenness) in similar fashion. He'd announce number after number featuring Gonsalves or Hodges or whoever else might be the object of his displeasure, meantime pouring out praise of the victim to the audience, whipping up the calls for encores. A session like that, especially if the culprit wasn't feeling so good, could be punishment indeed.

Well, it seemed to work out. Most of his musicians repaid Duke with a loyalty and an affection which is a rare commodity in the average boss-employee relationship, as innumerable statements have testified. Sonny Greer used to point out that the kind of concerts which Duke gave in England in 1933 took place years before any other jazz musicians tried them. He was twenty-five years ahead of his time with "Creole Rhapsody" as well, said Greer, and other Ellingtonians proclaimed much the same (as also did Nat "King" Cole among many others), and always, with their lordly ways, acted as if they believed it. Their affection was displayed in less formal fashion, not least in the nicknames they gave their boss. "Dumpy" was Greer's. "Governor" was usual from Rex Stewart, a trumpeter who came in soon after the first European visit. Others called him "Fatso," "Pops," "Phony" (short for Phony Duke), or "Ze Grand" (meaning Ze Grand Duke).

Two other nicknames for Duke, "Piano Red" and "Sandhead," had particular relevance. For most of his life he used a lotion to straighten his hair, a common enough practice before the Afro emphasis of black Americans in the 1960s, and it often used to leave his hair with a reddish tint. His bandsmen impishly picked up the point. Early photographs of Duke show his hair as curly before he began to straighten it, and he was very careful about his hair throughout his life; he might have crumpled (even holed) cashmere sweaters and baggy slacks, but his head was neatly enfolded between shows or when travelling in the bandanna or towel which was almost his hallmark. Slightly sardonic nicknames weren't the only outgrowth of campfire humor among the musicians during the 1930s. Toby Hardwick and Juan Tizol were, reputedly, the pranksters of the band. Stink bombs went off onstage, itching powder was put in band uniforms, soap was rubbed on the bow of one uppity guest violinist so that no sounds resulted, and, once, water was placed in Wellman Braud's tuba by a gang including Barney Bigard; when Braud switched from playing bass to tuba, Bigard was the bandsman who got the water over his head.

Living as closely together as they did during those travelling

years on the railroads, there were inevitably some frictions. Juan
Tizol claimed that his habits of meticulous punctuality and instrumental practice made him something of a butt in the band.
He suffered quite a bit because he couldn't take "all the foolish-
ness." He was a moderate drinker, rejected every kind of dope,
and had his taste for itching-powder-type practical jokes curbed
when, at a party in Irving Mills's office, someone set off a fire-
cracker under his chair. In the circumstances it was not surprising that musicians left the band from time to time, as founder-
member Arthur Whetsol did because of illness in 1937 (he died
three years later), but that so many of them stayed so long. Carney was with Duke for forty years, Hodges (with a five-year
break) for as long, and Brown for thirty-five years; at least half a
dozen other men clocked up twenty years or more with him.
The usual reason for leaving was that the individual simply
couldn't sustain the eternal travelling any longer. That was why
Tizol quit after fifteen years, wanting to live in California, but he
returned to the band in the 1950s. So many of Duke's musicians
left for a spell and then returned, as if they found they couldn't
ever get the Ellington magic out of their blood. Hardwick (in
1946) and Greer (1951) were the last of the original Washingtonians to turn their backs on the road—yet as late as 1969
Hardwick could still say how much he missed the life and that
he still felt he was part of the Ellington band.

In the later 1930s, Ellington was providing still more reasons
for his musicians to stay. He made his music so right for each
one of them, as individuals, to play once they'd got used to his
unusual scores. "He was smart," Bigard said. "Say he was
going to build a number round me. He always studied a
person's style, to make it comfortable for him to play. He knew
the guy's limitations and his exceptional qualities." The art of
presentation seemed to be ingrained in Duke, and as the 1930s
progressed some of his composing talents were concentrated on
building a series of showcases for the individual artists in the
band: "Echoes of Harlem" (Cootie's Concerto) and "Clarinet
Lament" (Barney's Concerto), as well as the less successful vehi-
cles for Rex Stewart—"Trumpet in Spades"—and Lawrence
Brown—"Yearning for Love."

These are, however, not the compositions by which Ellington will be remembered from this decade of his career. Within
a few years he'd achieved "Mood Indigo," "Creole Rhapsody,"

"Drop Me Off in Harlem," "It Don't Mean a Thing (If It Ain't Got That Swing)," and the exquisite "Sophisticated Lady," the last named a particularly redolent piece of Ellingtonia. Written in 1932, it was, according to Duke, a composite portrait of three women schoolteachers he knew in his youth in Washington. "They taught all winter and toured Europe in the summer," he said. "To me, that spelled sophistication." From the time of these early songs and instrumentals, he seemed to achieve high peaks in virtually every year, with the exception of 1935 and 1936, when it is logical to assume that the death of his mother overshadowed his life. He had brought her to New York long before Edna Ellington went back to Washington. He had been mollycoddled by her, and continued to adore her. He bought her furs, a big diamond ring, and sought her advice constantly. She had looked after Mercer, too, from the age of three, and often went with Ellington when he played in other cities.

Ellington was on a one-nighter tour of the South when his mother died; yet, as so often, he was able to shut himself off from his surroundings and brood as the band's Pullman cars headed through the night. "Reminiscing in Tempo" emerged from his reflections, "all caught up in the rhythm and motion of the train dashing through the South." It was in the year his mother died that he took to wearing the gold cross around his neck.

Ellington's father, who was the band's manager for a period, died in 1937, a further blow. But, even in Duke's "down" phase of a year or so, not only "Reminiscing in Tempo," but also "Showboat Shuffle" was written, the latter a bubbling portrait of a Mississippi stern-wheeler—the churning of the paddles captured by staccato brass, with flowing solos from Johnny Hodges's alto saxophone and Rex Stewart's cornet. From other years came "Solitude" (1934), "Harmony in Harlem" (1937), as well as his joint composition with Juan Tizol and Irving Mills, "Caravan" (1936), and the long set of variations on the traditional twelve-bar blues, "Diminuendo and Crescendo in Blue" (1937). The last-named composition gave Irving Mills another round of haggling with the record companies, who still preferred numbers in neat three-minute packages suitable for one side of a 78 rpm disc.

The years of 1938 and 1939 were especially rich, with one of his most singable melodies, "I Let a Song Go out of My Heart," the beautiful "Prelude to a Kiss," a new, better "concerto" to feature Rex Stewart, "Boy Meets Horn," and his homage to one of his great teachers, Willie Smith, "Portrait of the Lion." Besides these new compositions and the recording of them, Ellington was making revised versions of several older tunes, like "East St. Louis Toodle-oo" and the "Black and Tan Fantasy" (to which he added a separately recorded "Prologue"), and small groups drawn from the band were also recording regularly.

The pressures under which this stream of compositions was produced make the achievement all the more remarkable. Late in his life he once told an officious committee man at a Sacred Concert rehearsal that he didn't need time; he needed a deadline. And throughout his life he had enough of those. "Mood Indigo" he wrote in fifteen minutes "while my mother finished cooking dinner." On his way by cab to a recording session, when he'd been drinking all night in an after-hours club, he started and finished "Black and Tan Fantasy." During another session at the RCA Victor recording studio in Chicago, he found he was one number short: "Solitude," completed in twenty minutes leaning against a glass partition, was the result. More than in any other place during the 1930s, however, Duke's compositions were planned and plotted in the Pullman cars of his caravan.

The train was his sanctuary. He could rest all day if he wanted, escape the endless questioning and argument about his music, achieve privacy and isolation, despite the card-playing, chattering, snoring, sometimes boisterous, sometimes boozing companions with whom he travelled. "You'd see him," his sister Ruth once told me, "in a siding somewhere in Texas, the heat at 110, the sweat pouring off him onto a piece of manuscript paper on his knee, catching up on something he wanted to finish." The journeying not only gave Duke time to compose, but also inspired him. He would look out of the window at night in the industrial heartland of Ohio, watching the fires belching from steel furnaces. "I think of music sometimes in terms of color. I like to see the flames licking yellow in the dark and then pushing down to a red glow." He would listen to the chattering of trains at crossings, to the hissing and chuffing as they left stations, and above all the whistles. "Especially in the South. There the firemen play blues on the engine whistle—big, smeary things like a goddam woman singing in the night."

The feeling of trains which lies behind his "Daybreak Express" (almost a scoring of the bounce and the tonal varieties of a rail ride), "Happy-Go-Lucky Local," and many other pieces, is obvious; but what Duke added to the mixture of train-like sounds and rhythms provided the magic in these and also in compositions not directly associated with railroads.

The band were not only touring, of course. They were resident at a Hollywood night spot for a time. They returned in 1937 to the Cotton Club for a season at its new downtown site at Broadway and Forty-eighth Street, and it was here that Duke first met Arthur Logan, who came in one night to treat Otto Hardwick's asthma. The attraction between Ellington and Logan was immediate. This handsome man, with a distinctive mane of silvery hair later in life, became Duke's doctor and the closest of confidants, a black American technically, but with so pale a coloring that he could have "passed" for white, yet never tried to. He was, rather, a powerful fighter for civil rights and other causes—"a civic leader of extraordinary intelligence and devotion," according to Mayor John Lindsay of New York, who, like Governor Nelson Rockefeller of New York State, was to be numbered among Logan's personal friends. Logan became personal physician to the civil rights leader, Dr. Martin Luther King, as well as to Ellington.

Leopold Stokowski often came to hear the band at the Cotton Club. He was enthusiastic at the time about ethnic music, wanting to incorporate Oriental and African styles within symphonic tone poems. "You and I should to to Africa and hear that music," he observed one evening to Ellington, who gave him a sardonic look and replied: "The only thing I could get in Africa that I haven't got now is fever!" He had, perhaps, enough to do without journeying so far.

There was a first season at the most famous Harlem theatre of all, the Apollo on 125th Street. The band appeared in movies: *Murder at the Vanities* and *Belle of the Nineties* in 1934, with "Ebony Rhapsody" (a free adaptation of Liszt's second Hungarian Rhapsody) featured in the first, and Ivie Anderson's emotional and sensitive singing in the second. In 1936, Ivie was also featured in the Marx Brothers' *A Day at the Races*, for which Duke composed some of the music. Then, in the spring of 1939, the orchestra went back to Europe. They played in France at the Palais de Chaillot, a group of buildings, including museums and a theatre, built two years earlier for the great Paris Fair. Overlooking the Seine and the Eiffel Tower, this terraced complex was later the original home of the United Nations under Trygve Lie. In the audience for Duke's concert, Nesuhi Ertegun found himself sitting next to his other idol, Django Reinhardt, who jumped up and down with joy as Ellington played. Later, Django recorded with a trio drawn from the band. Ellington also played in Scandinavia, for which the celebratory "Smorgasbord and Schnapps" was composed before Duke left. After a concert in Copenhagen, Ellington was greeted by a group of German fans who told him that listening to jazz was forbidden under Nazism. So they had risked the consequences of absence from their country by inventing excuses for leaving to make a short visit to Copenhagen. Indicative of the reverence greeting Duke's concerts was the review by a Dutch critic of a performance of "The Mooch" in Utrecht. "I feel in this piece a conflict of two elemental forces: the one the violence of Nature, which is in an eternal struggle with the other, the force of Man, a more melancholy, restrained and mental force." The orchestra missed out Britain on this tour because of a ban by the Musicians' Union on American instrumentalists, which was to last too long.

Yet it was still life on the road—the iron road—which was the dominant factor in the band's existence during the 1930s, and it was important for Ellington. When the train was rolling, as Barney Bigard recalled, Ellington would summon up a phrase which Sidney Bechet had used, and enmesh it into an embryonic theme. Duke's own words—so graphic—were these:

> The memory of things gone is important to a jazz musician. Things like the old folks singing in the moonlight in the back yard on a hot night, or something someone said long ago. I remember I once wrote a 64-bar piece about a memory of when I was a little boy in bed and heard a man whistling on the street outside, his footsteps echoing away. Things like these may be more important to a musician than technique.

That Ellington could frame such sentences and write such music was remarkable not only because of his gypsy life and the sheer pressure of the work schedule. He claimed he was sometimes on the point of giving up because of the rackets of the music business. He was depressed as much by the rubbish which earned fortunes for Tin Pan Alley hacks as by the publishers who brought him ready-made pop numbers, inviting

Duke to put his name on them in exchange for major plugging and a cut of the royalties. His faith in the benevolence of God—and his luck—was shaken by the death of his parents. As blacks, he and his musicians suffered the customary indignities, notably in the South: restaurants refused to serve them, which at times resulted in the band going onstage unfed and ravenous, taxi drivers ignored them, and there were the usual violent and foul remarks on the streets. Even later in his career, Duke met a southern cop who was very friendly, jovial, enthusiastic about the music. "If you'd been a white man, Duke, you'da been a great musician," the cop is supposed to have said, to which Duke replied: "I guess things would have been different if I'd been a white man." Ellington's cool survived a thousand episodes of that kind, which caused Rex Stewart to observe of their transatlantic visit in 1939, and the restorative effect it had on all the musicians, Duke included, "You have to be a Negro to understand why. Europe is a different world. You can go anywhere, do anything, talk to anybody. You are like a guy who has eaten hot dogs all his life and is suddenly offered caviar. You can't believe it."

On another occasion Stewart recalled hearing 5,000 schoolchildren serenade Ellington in Sweden on his birthday during this trip, and he continually stressed the irony that Ellington was more regarded outside his native land than inside it—a fact Stewart attributed to Duke's color. Even greater was the irony that some black Americans didn't rate Duke very highly because they felt his music was too "white."

Duke must have understood all this very well. But had he lost his cool in those years when the band was establishing itself around the world, it would have interfered with his music. And his music was all, he felt, he had to offer the world. So he maintained his dignity, would not be provoked, and stored up what he felt he had to say. It would emerge in music, rather than in banner-waving and street fights—but that is another, and later, story.

Indeed, as the decade of the Depression came to an end, there were several elements of the Ellington story—both personal and artistic—which were beginning to foreshadow his future. Edmund Anderson accompanied Mildred Dixon one night in 1937 to the Cotton Club when Duke was playing there. Mildred had told Anderson's wife that Duke had often been staying out all night, that she knew he had another girl. The band was roaring through a number behind the Cotton Club chorus when Mildred leaned over to Anderson, pointing to one of the girls who were dancing. "There she is, that's the one," she said. Anderson saw then, for the first time, the woman who was to mean more to Ellington than any other for the rest of his life, except perhaps his mother and his sister, Ruth.

The place of Beatrice Ellis, who came to be known as Evie Ellington, in Duke's world is among the most poignant and mysterious parts of his life. She was a strikingly attractive dark-haired woman, part Negro, part Spanish; "The most beautiful child-woman I ever saw," in the words of Herb Hendler, who produced many Ellington records during the 1940s. "Very very lovely," said Anderson. "When she danced, she looked so proud, and rather petulant too." Duke met her when she was a showgirl at the Cotton Club, and she had the lithe legs and the delicate grace of a dancer. He was immediately attracted—infatuated, some of his friends said—and this was the woman who saw more of him than any other from the time they met until the day he died. "Thirty-seven years of my life I gave," she once said simply, and she might appropriately have said "gave up," for their liaison was bizarre.

During the early days, when she created a home for Ellington to return to in another Harlem apartment—this time on St. Nicholas Avenue—they saw a good deal of each other. She would sometimes drive him to dates and would stay for extended periods in the 1930s and 1940s; resident seasons for bands were then still commonplace. Once, in Miami, Florida, she drew out every cent of her savings to pay the band's way when it was stranded without funds or engagements. Later, as the ending of the classic years for the swing bands forced Ellington to become a virtually incessant globe-trotter, their life together was lived for the most part in bursts between his tours. She was alone whenever he was away. Only on rare private occasions—perhaps over a late-night meal with friends—was she seen with him, and she seldom joined in conversations, sitting quietly beside him. She was sometimes introduced as Mrs. Ellington, although she was never his legal wife.

Musically, too, Ellington was already glimpsing other horizons. His sessions listening to symphonic music with his friend Edmund Anderson had changed him. He was reaching out to better himself, intrigued with all kinds of musical experimentation. In 1936, he was interested enough in sound quality to use a microphone planted in a men's lavatory to achieve an echo effect on recordings—a coup to which many others have laid claim since. In 1938, Johnny Hodges's solo on "Empty Ballroom Blues" was recorded with such echo chamber effects, and in the 1940s the RCA record company was still using a converted lavatory for this purpose. Duke was equally fascinated by the new forms of symphonic and conservatoire music being played at the time. As early as 1938—long before he made Carnegie Hall—he was featured in a virtually unreported and definitely socially upgrade soirée at the St. Regis Hotel in New York. It was a white-tie occasion, planned by a committee got together by the composer, Vernon Duke, and attended among others by Mrs. Vincent Astor, undoubtedly a breakthrough at a time when there was still a strict application of the color bar in most leading New York night clubs and restaurants. Duke played one half with a septet drawn from the band, including Hodges, Carney, and Cootie Williams, and the rest of the evening was provided by a dozen or so musicians of the New York Philharmonic, who performed a program by modern French and Russian composers which, at this date, was regarded as ferociously *avant-garde.*

Ellington's program that evening—airy and bouncy short pieces—reflected the direction his band was beginning to take in 1938. The set-piece arrangements of the early 1930s, some of which had a heavy and deliberate feeling, were giving way to lighter, more swinging numbers.

That transition—which didn't change the Ellington band's basic character, but gave it more balance, more range, and more commercial as well as artistic appeal—was hastened by the arrival of a handful of new musicians in 1939, the first major changes which Ellington had made for several years, except for the arrival of Harold "Shorty" Baker in the year after the departure, in 1937, of Arthur Whetsol, whose wistful, light-toned playing had given an edge of melancholy to many of his leader's themes. Baker, however, couldn't by himself achieve the explosive impact which Billy Strayhorn, Ben Webster, and Jimmy Blanton had on the band in a single year, or the influence of Ray Nance and Jimmy Hamilton not too long afterwards. As Europe went once more to war, good times for the Ellington band were just around the corner.

4

1940-1950
Strayhorn on the Team

Billy Strayhorn had never intended to be a jazz musician. Until he heard Ellington's band, he was strictly a classicist, playing in the school orchestra, studying Bach, Beethoven, and Brahms. Then, aged nineteen, he went to a theatre in Pittsburgh, where he was raised, just after Duke had made the film *Murder at the Vanities*. The band played "Ebony Rhapsody," which was a free Ellington treatment for Liszt.

"It really shook me up," Strayhorn recalled. He went back-stage, got to Duke, then could think of nothing to say and just stood with his mouth open. Later he went to a dance to hear the band. This time, in Strayhorn's own words, "I was *lost*." It took him almost five years to gain the confidence to go and see Duke about working for the orchestra. He played Ellington some compositions he'd written for a high-school band, including one song, "Lush Life," which must be one of the most haunting, sophisticated, and unusual songs ever written by so young a musician. It was certainly enough for Duke. Within three months the band had recorded its first piece jointly composed by Strayhorn and Duke, "Something to Live For," and after a brief stay with a band led by Duke's son, Mercer, he joined the main Ellington organization, within which he remained until the day he died.

Oddly, he was primarily hired because Ellington liked his lyrics. But almost immediately, he was put to arranging and playing the piano with several of the small groups from the orchestra. From this beginning grew an unmatched artistic relationship, certainly unique in jazz. It was, as several Ellingtonians have witnessed, a love affair. Duke described it in these words: "Whatever his comment was, I was adjusted. It was like going out with your armor on instead of going out naked." And Strayhorn it was who succinctly spelled out one of the most important artistic facts of all about his unusual partner: "Ellington plays piano, but his real instrument is his band"—a statement to be compared with an equally striking metaphor coined many years later by Alvin Ailey, the distinguished choreographer, who cooperated often with Ellington. "He collected around him a group of superbly gifted musicians who were like his Stradivarius." Certainly the musical and psychological vibrations between the two men were so sympathetic that neither they nor members of the band could accurately say which parts of their many collaborations—from "The Perfume Suite" of the 1940s to the "Far East Suite" of the 1960s—belonged to which composer. Much of Duke's work has to be called Ellington-Strayhorn music.

Strayhorn was a neat, diminutive man, sensitive and intellectual. He hadn't been in the band long when he gained a nickname from Toby Hardwick, who also claimed to have christened "Tricky Sam" Nanton, the trumpeter Roy "Little Jazz" Eldridge, and Ray Nance ("Floorshow," because of Nance's flair for presentation). Hardwick had been reading Popeye in the comics, and Strayhorn was "little and sweet, and everyone crazy about him," with a habit of talking politely and demurely to each member of the band in turn. So Hardwick, observing this, leant over to Greer and whispered: "If that ain't Swee' Pea, *I hope somethin'.*" Greer broke up so much, Strayhorn was Swee' Pea thereafter.

It's doubtful if Ellington could have kept going with such zestful energy throughout the next twenty-five years without Strayhorn around to take so much of the burden of the composing and arranging, and to provide stimulating artistic, intellectual, and personal companionship. Strayhorn was, it's been observed, the female side of an artistically joint *persona*. "I think Duke was a much simpler character before he met Strays," someone who knew him in the 1930s explained. "You could even say he was sweeter. But he was so much more *interesting* once Strays happened along. Duke picked up some of his fine language from the elegant sentences Billy used. He had an ear for sentences. Particular words fascinated him. Billy also filled him in on the tours. Often Duke would be lying in bed while Strays was out pounding round the sights. He'd take what Billy said as gospel—and, to be fair, vice versa. In India, for example, I don't think Duke ever got to the Taj Mahal himself. He let Billy cover it for him." On the other hand, he could be kept so busy writing music in some places, he never got out to visit the sights. As late as 1964, a BBC producer, Steve Allen, took Strayhorn on a whirlwind car tour of London tourist spots, from the Tower of Westminster Abbey, because Billy complained he'd seen little of the city except the Embankment.

Duke's accelerating productivity after Strayhorn's death in 1967 has made some observers doubt if he really needed Swee' Pea. That seems a dubious argument. The sharing of the burden was one boon. And although Ellington never acknowledged to the world in his last decade that he was getting old, he must privately have realized that his life was moving toward its end, and accordingly drove himself to superhuman efforts of solo composition which could scarcely have been sustained at such a pitch throughout the previous thirty years—not even by the iron Duke. Strayhorn's record as a composer in his own right also suggests how valuable was his role in the total achievement of Duke and his musicians.

His peak period came almost immediately after he had joined the organization. Between 1940 and 1942 he composed the exquisitely beautiful "Chelsea Bridge," with its echoes of Ravel, the bouncy "Take the A Train," which became the band's theme, and many other splendid pieces: "Johnny Come Lately," "Passion Flower," "Raincheck," "Midriff," "Day Dream" (officially a joint composition with Ellington), and "After All." The first named was misnamed: Strayhorn was bowled over by a Thames-side painting of Whistler's, which inspired the music. Only later did he learn it was Battersea Bridge he'd been looking at. The "A Train," however, was brilliantly and usefully titled. Strayhorn's feeling for Fletcher Henderson's arrangements led him to write the tune the way he did, right at the beginning of 1941. Suddenly Duke was screaming for new material because a dispute (which would last a year) between the American Society of Composers, Authors, and Publishers (ASCAP) and the radio stations was keeping all ASCAP music off the air—and Duke was in ASCAP, but Strayhorn wasn't. "A Train" was in the library which Strayhorn quickly produced, named as it was because of the confusion caused by the adding of new trains on the expanding New York subway system. Passengers kept on taking the recently introduced D train, whose route visited Harlem at 145th Street, but then shot off to the Bronx. If you wanted to hit Harlem and keep going straight on from 145th to 200th Street, you needed the A train. As Strayhorn explained, he was writing subway directions.

He was part of the spearhead of Ellington's renewed vigor at the start of a new decade. Ben Webster was another part, a graduate of the battling, hard-nosed Kansas City jazz school, where jam sessions and the musical slaughtering of rivals were a way of life. He had been heavily influenced by the rich-toned Coleman Hawkins and produced, if anything, an even lusher color and lighter line from his tenor saxophone, without sacrificing anything of his fast-driving swing. Webster had played on odd recording dates with Ellington since 1935, taking a few solos; when he joined full time from 1939 to 1943, with a brief return in 1948, he provided Duke with a new musical problem, since the leader hadn't regularly used tenors much in solos till then, lacking an outstanding player. Webster also started a tradition. When Paul Gonsalves came in later, he knew all of Ben's solos by heart.

The third newcomer, Jimmy Blanton on double bass, brought a further challenge for Duke, who hitherto had used the instrument in the customary metronomic fashion. Blanton, only eighteen, was first heard in his native city of St. Louis, Missouri, by Strayhorn and Webster, who dashed straight from the club, roused Duke from his hotel bed, and insisted that he accompany them forthwith to hear this prodigy. Ellington wasn't disappointed. Blanton wanted to use the bass as an instrument for themes, improvising tunefully with finger and bow, essaying long runs, and using melodic and harmonic ideas unheard of from his cumbersome instrument until that time. All of this virtuosity did not impair the propulsive beat he gave to the band, or his clear, mellow tone. He was hired at once, and for a time Duke had two double bassists in the band until the regular man, Billy Taylor, sadly but inevitably quit in the middle of a dance in Boston and, lugging his bass away with him, declared he couldn't stand next to someone playing so well any longer; it was too embarrassing. It takes, as Duke observed, a big man to face the facts so honestly.

The arrival of Strayhorn, Webster, and Blanton, and the continued development of the great soloists already present—Hodges, Carney, Stewart, "Tricky Sam," Bigard, and Cootie Williams—drove Ellington to new and different kinds of writing. The band swung harder; it was capable of more moods, more tone colors and imaginative voicings. Many critics view it as the best and most expressive orchestral unit he ever had, although that accolade could also be claimed by the band of the early and middle 1960s, which contained many of the same musicians, but had, of course, an immensely more comprehensive Ellington library to play from. Not that such comparisons matter much, for it's undeniable that the band of 1940 was easily Duke's best yet, and that for it was created a brilliant set of compositions. "Cotton Tail," a fierce swinger which showed the terrific zest brought by Webster to the sax section, "Jack the Bear," "Ko-Ko," "Morning Glory," "Bojangles," "In a Mellotone," "Warm Valley," "Sepia Panorama," "Just Squeeze Me," "C-Jam Blues," "I Got It Bad and That Ain't Good," "Never No Lament" (later, with lyrics, a huge success under the title "Don't Get Around Much Any More"), "All Too Soon," and "Harlem Airshaft" were just a few of the compositions which streamed from Ellington's mind in the years 1940–1942, and Strayhorn's numbers were also available.

Almost every composition has some kind of story attached to it. According to Rex Stewart, "Warm Valley" happened when they were on the train going to California. They were passing a range of soft, undulating hills and Duke exclaimed: "Just look at that! It's a perfect replica of a female reclining in complete relaxation, so unashamedly exposing her warm valley." Completely in contrast was "Don't Get Around Much Any More," which indicated how well Ellington was beginning to do financially.

In 1939 he'd severed, reasonably amicably, most of his connections with Irving Mills. Duke continued to insist that the impresario had done a marvellous job for him, and one reason for the change was that Ellington felt he now wanted to move in directions different from those in which Mills could help him. It was Mills who had been hesitant about Duke performing long, serious concerts in the late 1930s when Edmund Anderson and others were urging this kind of engagement upon him. At the same time, Ellington believed he never got as good a financial deal with Mills as he should have done. One of Duke's friends, puzzled over Mills's joint credit on so many of Ellington's songs, joked in those days: "How is it that Edward flogs himself to death on the road all year and comes out of it at the end owing Mills money?" To which Duke would reply: "I owe him a lot. I can't be ungrateful." He was deeply hurt when, in 1935, Mills refused to advance him $5,000 to pay for his mother's funeral in the style which he felt she merited. Yet Mills continued to receive joint-composer credits on several Ellington songs copyrighted during the late 1940s and even as recently as 1962. The break was, probably, inevitable, and when he heard in later years that Ellington was writing an autobiography, Mills telephoned several of Duke's friends, asking in some anguish what the book would say about him. Duke was, as ever, gracious in what he said.

His new business associates for a long period after 1939 were the William Morris Agency. Four years later, while playing at a Broadway club, he found himself short of cash and popped into the Morris offices to borrow a few hundred dollars. As he waited, an office boy gave him some mail. He opened one letter, from RCA Victor, and found a check. He slid it back into the envelope, congratulating himself on the figure of $2,250 which he saw. Thinking he might now not have to ask for that loan, he jerked the check out again, fearful he could have misread it and only be the owner of $22.50. This time, he took in the real sum: $22,500. It was all royalties for "Don't Get Around Much Any More," which had recently been recorded by the fashionable singing group, the Ink Spots.

Most illustrative of Ellington's development were his innumerable impressionist compositions in the early 1940s. These pieces showed the Ellington who was half painter and half dramatist, expressing himself in delicate and idiosyncratic musical sketches, equally telling whether the subject was a person or a place. Character was caught perfectly in "Bojangles," with Duke's piano nimbly suggesting the footwork of the great tap dancer Bill Robinson; in "Jack the Bear," where the subject was an earthy sporting house pianist; and in "Portrait of Bert Williams," a vaudeville comedian whose stuttering speech was mirrored in Rex Stewart's squeezed tonal effects on cornet. As Duke's railroad pieces reflected his travels, so did "Harlem Airshaft"—the greatest of these musical sketches—foretell his fascination with New York's black quarter, which was to last through his full-scale "Harlem" suite and beyond. There isn't a better passage of Ellingtonian words than that which he produced as the accompanying note for "Airshaft"; it suggests precisely why claims are made that if Duke hadn't taken to music, he could have been a substantial writer or painter.

> So much goes on in a Harlem airshaft. You get the full essence of Harlem in an airshaft. You hear fights, you smell dinner, you hear people making love. You hear intimate gossip floating down. You hear the radio. An airshaft is one great big loudspeaker. You see your neighbors' laundry. You hear the janitor's dogs. The man upstairs' aerial falls down and breaks your window. You smell coffee. A wonderful thing, is that smell. An airshaft has got every contrast. One guy is cooking dried fish and rice and another guy's got a great big turkey. Guy-with-fish's wife is a terrific cooker, but the guy's wife with the turkey is doing a sad job. You hear people praying, fighting, snoring. Jitterbugs are jumping up and down, always over you, never below you. That's a funny thing about jitterbugs. They're always above you, never below you. I tried to put all that in "Harlem Airshaft."

Ellington hadn't changed his ways, only expanded and enriched them. More and more experiences, moods, memories filtered through his imagination and came out in music. Soon he found a different form through which to express them: a musical stage show, *Jump for Joy*.

Oddly, the idea for the show came out of Hollywood, which despite its nature (or maybe because of it) has always had its colony of radical thinkers. *Jump for Joy* was conceived as a propaganda exercise on behalf of civil rights for the blacks. One idea for a scene in it featured a symbolic Uncle Tom on his deathbed, with a chorus dancing around him to send him on his way, while Hollywood and Broadway producer figures desperately tried to keep him going by pumping adrenalin into his arms.

Ellington enthusiastically joined in writing the music for this

"Sun-Tanned Revu-sical," as the bills called it. He felt it was something he could do, ought to do, for the civil rights movement. Throughout his life there were always black activists who criticized Ellington for not playing a more direct role in the race struggle. His music spoke for his people. His example—as artist and human being—shone forth throughout his life, and he was immensely more useful to the cause alive and playing than he would have been as a bloody martyr. He had paid his dues in all those years of living and working in the South, taking the insults and the humiliations, but determined to fight the good fight with his own weapons. Much later in his life he told a television interviewer who was harassing him about the civil rights movement that he'd had his *own* freedom march in the 1930s. "We went down in the South *without* federal troops."

Throughout his life, the very names of so many of his compositions, from "Black Beauty" to "Deep South Suite," spoke clearly of Ellington's pride in and preoccupation with the color of his skin, the destiny of his race. There was one man who wrote to him urging that he should take his jungle music back to Africa with all possible speed. To him Ellington replied, with the gravest and most characteristic courtesy, that this unhappily was not possible, because the blood of the American Negro down the generations had become so mixed with that of the letter writer that he would scarcely be accepted there. If it were all right with his correspondent he would, however, settle for Europe. "There," Ellington observed with barbed irony, "we are accepted." The argument that he would deal with the civil rights issue *his* way was developed by Duke consistently as his career moved on.

"Screaming about it onstage don't make a show," he told me during the 1960s, when he'd done still more in the musical theatre to emphasize his blackness and the role of the black artist in American culture, including the major show, *My People*. "It's all right for some cat on a soapbox to go making speeches and such, but in the theatre you've got to find some way of saying it without saying it, you dig? At the end of *My People*, we've got the song, 'What Color Is Virtue, What Color Is Love?' You know?" Then he shrugged, as if he wasn't certain I understood. "All round the world I've had to answer questions about the race situation in my country, often hostile ones. People asking why Negro artists haven't done more for the cause, that kind of thing. It makes me very angry, and I say that people wouldn't ask questions like that if they knew what they were talking about. But then usually I cool down and tell them of the things since the 1930s, all the shows and concerts and benefits the band have done. There's such ignorance about the subject, and halfway bouncing around of the issues does no one any good if they don't know the whole scene."

For Ellington, *Jump for Joy* was one of "the things" he was talking about. The money for the show came from (mainly white) members of the movie colony, with whom Duke had struck up an acquaintance whilst working on the MGM musical, *Cabin in the Sky*. The most fanatical devotee of all for Ellington's music was Orson Welles, reputed once to have said that (next to Welles) Duke was the only genius he had even known. Other Ellington fans in Hollywood included Mickey Rooney, Lana Turner, Jackie Cooper, John Garfield, Tony Martin, and Joseph Pasternak, and their enthusiasm was justified when *Jump for Joy* ran for over three months in Los Angeles during the summer of 1941. Duke was both actor and musician in the show, which featured the band, Ivie Anderson, and other stars like Dorothy Dandridge and Herb Jeffries; the blues singer, Joe Turner, also joined later.

The shape of the show was always changing, for there were fifteen writers involved, including, surprisingly, Mickey Rooney, with other less unexpected names like that of the novelist and poet, Langston Hughes. Meetings took place almost nightly after curtain fall because everyone wanted to ensure that the tone was right. Ellington insisted on showmanship: no shouting and moaning, with the social demands used to flavor the dish rather than dominate it. Everyone was careful, rightly or wrongly, not to go *too* far in controversy. As a result, some numbers disappeared. "I've Got a Passport from Georgia (and I'm Going to the USA)" was one; but there was plenty of punch left despite that. The finale of the first act, "Uncle Tom's Cabin Is a Drive-In Now," had some fine verses.

> There used to be a chicken shack in Caroline,
> But now they've moved it up to Hollywood and Vine;
> They paid off the mortgage—nobody knows how—
> And Uncle Tom's Cabin is a drive-in now!

Altogether it was another important stage in Duke's career, as well as being one of the rare (if not the first) full-scale theatre musicals to be created and produced on the West Coast. Ellington claimed it couldn't move on later from Los Angeles because the draft for the Second World War (Pearl Harbor was in December 1941) took away so many of the cast; others, however, said with perhaps more realism that *Jump for Joy* was too far ahead of its time to get commerical backing. It certainly failed to get off the ground as late as 1958 when a revival was attempted in Miami. Its particular significance for Duke, however, was that it had aroused the interest of others, as well as his own, in the composition of really long works. Some time after the band returned to New York from its spell on the West Coast, William Morris, Jr., from the agency now looking after Ellington's affairs, suggested that he write at length again with a view to a Carnegie Hall concert, an adventurous plan for a jazz band at that time, even though Benny Goodman had already broken the ice at New York's great centre for classical music in 1938. But he had mostly played his customary band program. The plan for Duke was different, and since their first meeting in 1936, Edmund Anderson had been urging him to play Carnegie.

For much of 1942, on and off, Duke thought about the idea, but he had many other things to preoccupy him. The touring life—New York one day, Connecticut the next, Chicago the next—was again the eternal background for him, and the brilliant band he'd built up in 1939 and 1940 was soon to lose some of its important members. Barney Bigard, Ben Webster, and Jimmy Blanton were all present at the start of the *Jump for Joy* season. One day Blanton, who was rooming with Strayhorn, said he was leaving because he wanted to go and live with a girl. The reality was that he'd found out he had tuberculosis, and didn't want to expose Strayhorn to it. When the truth came out, Duke sent him to the best specialists and he was placed in a ward to await their decision. But after Ellington left town when *Jump for Joy* closed, a friend of Blanton's persuaded the young man to move out into a cheap private nursing home. By the time Ellington returned to see him, the damage had been done. Duke blamed himself greatly for what he considered the waste of Blanton's life. He died in California on July 30, 1942, in only his twenty-fourth year.

Bigard also left the band in 1942, as did Ivie Anderson, who was to die seven years later. Once the war began, the luxury of private Pullman cars was over, and often the musicians even ended up sitting on their instrument cases in gangways. The problems were enough to make Bigard quit and go to California, to be followed a year later by Ben Webster, whose place as soloist Al Sears ultimately filled. Cootie Williams, too, had ended twelve years with Ellington in November 1940, and gone off with Benny Goodman's orchestra, an event which so devastated Duke's fans that the bandleader and composer Raymond Scott wrote a number called "When Cootie Left the Duke."

Most people assumed the trumpet star had betrayed Ellington and simply jumped at the chance of a fatter pay packet. The truth appears to be that Duke understood Cootie's ambition to play with the greatest bands of the day, his admiration for Goodman's outfit, and helped finalize the deal, including Cootie's wages. In return, he told Duke he'd be back in a year, but when the time came Ellington urged him to use his big reputation to set up as a bandleader on his own. He did exactly that, becoming on the way a major discoverer and developer of new talent. Charlie Parker, Bud Powell, Thelonious Monk (who wrote Cootie's band's theme, " 'Round Midnight"), the altoist/blues singer Eddie "Cleanhead" Vinson, and the great singer, Pearl Bailey, were all employed, encouraged, and helped by Williams. He didn't, in fact, come back to Ellington's band until 1962, but then he, too, stayed through until the end, and his gutsy, growling trumpet solos were a major show-stopper during the orchestra's last decade. Cootie also said that his return made a happy man out of him. Not surprisingly, for his orchestra was a casualty of the collapse of the big-band market in the 1950s; he was teetotal with Duke and Goodman, but started drinking whisky heavily when he was a leader. Back with Ellington, he could— and did—go back to Coke-only again.

Despite these grievous losses, Duke's luck held. He'd taken Cootie out of Fletcher Henderson's band back in 1928 (on Chick Webb's advice), and the very day after he and Williams decided to part that November, he heard Ray Nance playing in a club and hired him. This pint-sized musician from Chicago was a huge asset during the twenty-three years he spent with the band. Not only did he play trumpet, and later cornet. He doubled on violin, he could sing, he could dance. No wonder he was called "Floorshow," although the alternative, "Root"—from the jazz-slang era of "all reet" and "all root"—was used by some of his intimates, including Ben Webster, who coined it. Ellington featured him heavily down the years, but it was as a "growl" specialist that he was especially valuable to the over-all band sound, and he learned that art from "Tricky Sam" Nanton, who continued to play with the orchestra until his death in San Francisco in 1946, aged only forty-four. Nanton had taught many of the "growl" tricks to Cootie Williams; now Nance in turn became his pupil and his companion around the gambling and drinking joints whenever the band was on the wide-open West Coast. Nance adored "Tricky Sam," who used to carry a large zipper bag full of mutes, medicines, and whisky; whenever they played a classy venue, Nanton would place a bottle of whisky in his inside pocket and slyly take sips through a straw as the band played on.

Jimmy Hamilton, a clarinet player with a smoothly beautiful tone, and a useful tenor saxophonist, took Bigard's place in 1942, and stayed for a quarter century, leaving unwillingly, but (yet another example) exhausted with the round of band buses and one-night hotel rooms. He was also an exception to Duke's habit of choosing "typed" replacements—musicians with styles as similar as possible to those of their predecessors; Hamilton sounded utterly different from Bigard. Different, too, was the role of Al Sears in place of Ben Webster. He was solid and dependable, but his choppy, staccato phrasing was far removed from Webster's rich and breathy sound. Sears stayed with Duke from 1943 to 1949 and appeared intermittently until 1951. Webster came back for a short spell in 1948, but Duke misssed him sorely until Paul Gonsalves—lush and romantic in style as Ben had been—arrived with the dawning of a new decade. More beneficial was the move which brought Tom Whaley into the fold.

Whaley, as steadfast a character as Carney, was the third of the Ellington Bostonians. He had been conductor, arranger, and pianist at many theatres, including the Apollo in Harlem during the 1930s, and was invited to join the family by Duke in 1941. He quit his Apollo job at once, despite the realization that with Strayhorn around his functions would be limited. One night a falling theatre curtain hit Strayhorn's head; Whaley delighted in recalling Strayhorn's lighthearted accusation that it had been deliberately arranged so that he could take over Swee' Pea's job. In fact, Whaley became the band's music copyist, and as such was more closely involved with Ellington as composer than anyone except Strayhorn.

At first, he queried a lot of the scores: he would point out, maybe, that there was an E natural set against an E flat. Ellington just told him it would sound fine when he heard it in context, and it usually did. He was continually asking Ellington what precisely he was going to do with the music he was racing to complete late in 1942 for the Carnegie Hall concert planned by William Morris, Jr. To Whaley, it seemed like an awful lot of work for one concert. Many years later, in 1963, Duke used parts of "Black, Brown, and Beige," as the Carnegie Hall suite turned out to be called, in a musical staged in Chicago, *My People*. Whaley would shake his head whenever, like others among Ellington's associates, he concluded that the man was as usual a couple of decades ahead of his time.

"Black, Brown, and Beige," which runs for nearly an hour in its original version (though not on record), was composed under the customary conditions of rush and squeeze. Duke may have been thinking about it a long time, but he didn't start putting notes on paper until barely a month before the Carnegie concert was scheduled, on January 23, 1943. Before Christmas he was playing a theatre in Hartford, Connecticut, with, intriguingly enough, Frank Sinatra—then starting out as a single—as his support act. It was one of those movie-plus-stage-show places so common in Britain as well as America in the 1930s and 1940s, and Duke was up against so tight a deadline he used to go on-stage while the movie was showing and compose at the piano in the half-light. The movie was a horror variation on the werewolf theme, *The Cat Woman*, and from time to time Duke would glance up at the screen. He kidded in later years as to whether the woman who turned into a murderous cat, or Frank Sinatra, was the part inspiration of his magnificent composition, which was among the greatest single achievements of his life, if not the greatest of all.

It was planned, in Duke's phrase, as a tone parallel to the history of the American Negro. In it he used some of the material from *Boola*, an unproduced opera devoted to the same theme, upon which he had been working for some time. "Black," the first section of Ellington's suite, contrasted the secular "Work Song"—containing space for grunting within it as well as mel-

The Duke who came to London: One of the portraits produced for the 1933 tour, suggesting that here was no ordinary bandleader.

Daisy Kennedy Ellington: founder of her son's faith

James Edward Ellington: father of elegance

Ruth Ellington: Duke's only sister, aged sixteen

Duke, aged four: no child of the ghetto

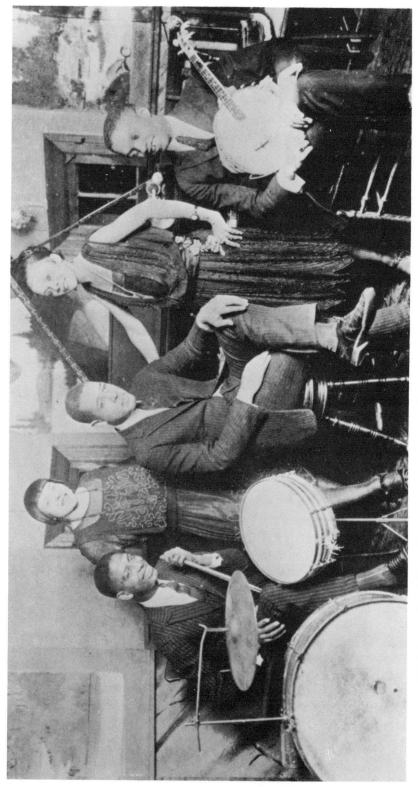

Washington band boss: From 1917 until he went to New York five years later, Duke ran his musical affairs in his home town, often sending out five bands a night. This was one of them, pictured in a Washington cabaret room. Sonny Greer is on drums, Sterling Conway on banjo, next to his wife. Bertha Ricks is the other woman.

ABOVE: The first big break: This was the band Ellington took into the Cotton Club in 1927. Ellington is at piano. At the back are Sonny Greer and Wellman Braud (bass). In the middle row are Joe Nanton, Bubber Miley, Harry Carney, Rudy Jackson, and Nelson Kincaid. In front sit Fred Guy and Ellsworth Reynolds. The major names of Johnny Hodges, Barney Bigard, and Cootie Williams were still to come; Jackson and Kincaid were to go. BELOW: A Cotton Club show in the 1930s: Ellington leads the band, Ethel Waters is the central figure surrounded by showgirls.

ABOVE: Ellington and the elegant band on arrival at Southampton for the first European visit in 1933. Seated in the front row are Derby Wilson, Freddy Jenkins, Jack Hylton, Ellington, Irving Mills, and Arthur Whetsol, with Juan Tizol's head framed between Mills and Whetsol. The women are dancer Bessie Dudley (*left*) and Ivie Anderson. The men behind are (*left to right*) Bill Bailey, Sonny Greer, Fred Guy, Harry Carney, Otto Hardwick, Barney Bigard, Spike Hughes (the British journalist), Cootie Williams, Wellman Braud, Johnny Hodges, Joe Nanton, and Lawrence Brown. BELOW: The same band onstage at the Palladium, 1933.

ABOVE: The composer and pianist, Percy Grainger (*center*), was among the first during the 1930s to compare Ellington to Bach and Delius. This photograph was taken in 1932 after Ellington had played his composition to music-appreciation classes at Columbia University in New York. At the time, Grainger was director of the music department at New York University. On the left is Basil Cameron, then conductor of the Seattle Symphony Orchestra.

ABOVE, RIGHT: Duke composes in a dressing room during the 1930s—a change from the buses, trains, and studios where he usually worked. Often he used menus or paper bags instead of manuscript sheets.

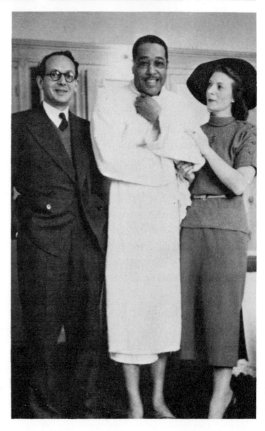

RIGHT: With Renee and Leslie Diamond in Paris, 1950. Later, he gave them a piano and composed one of his loveliest pieces at their London apartment.

RIGHT: Mercer and his mother, Edna Ellington. She rarely appeared at public functions after the breakup of her marriage with Duke. This was an exception, when Mercer was leading a band of his own at a Washington society dance. BELOW: The Ellington band in 1942—a publicity shot for the movie *Cabin in the Sky*. The faces fully in view are (*left to right*): Hardwick (with saxophone), Tizol, Shorty Baker (with trumpet), Ellington, Carney, Ivie Anderson (immediately in front of Carney), Stewart, Hodges, Sears, Webster (with saxophone, immediately below Sears), Nanton, Wallace Jones (with trumpet, below Nanton), Brown, Greer.

ABOVE: Moscow concert, 1971: Duke reacts to the playing of Paul Gonsalves *(left)* and Harold Ashby. BELOW, LEFT: Johnny Hodges solos with the band during a BBC tele-recording in 1964. BELOW, RIGHT: Cootie Williams plays, Duke dances. The place was West Berlin in 1969.

ody, to indicate that labor was involved—with the sacred side of black life, "Come Sunday," constructed around the most exquisitely ethereal solo for Johnny Hodges's alto saxophone. "Brown," the second section, drew its inspiration from the Negro heroes of the Revolutionary War which brought the United States their independence, including the 700 free Negroes from Haiti who aided the Americans at the siege of Savannah. In the third section, "Beige," Duke came right up to date, trying to suggest in music that although Harlem (and all the other Harlems in the U.S.A.) meant singing and dancing, the American blacks did have other concerns: religion, education, advancement. The Negro could be sophisticated, too, Duke seemed to be saying. Of "Sugar Hill Penthouse," one of the "Beige" pieces, he said: "If you ever sat on a beautiful magenta cloud overlooking New York City, you were on 'Sugar Hill.'"

Not everyone jumped for joy when "Black, Brown, and Beige" was premiered, despite the exuberant headline in *Variety:* DUKE KILLS CARNEGIE CATS. But however mixed were the early reactions, it established Ellington as belonging to a different class from other big bands both artistically and financially. The Carnegie Hall concerts were soon regarded as an annual affair; and for Duke they became, in his own words, "social-significance thrusts," although they weren't always that. He had the platform for which he could create throughout the 1940s a series of major compositions. "New World a-Comin'," its title suggested by a book of the same name by Roi Ottley, which anticipated a social revolution for Negroes once the Second World War ended, was premiered in December 1943. It contained a long "concerto" for Duke as pianist, and was afterwards rearranged for symphony orchestra. A year later came the Ellington-Strayhorn "Perfume Suite," in four parts, and the standing of the Carnegie Hall concerts was indicated when the great opera singer, Lauritz Melchior, presented Ellington with his portrait in oils. "The Deep South Suite" (1946), "The Liberian Suite" (1947), commissioned by the black African republic to celebrate its centenary, and "The Tattooed Bride" (1948) all provided major premieres for Ellington during the decade.

By 1950, jazz concerts in venues hitherto reserved for classical music were much more common. Ellington had opened the way for them and firmly established that popular music could, occasionally, grow into extended forms, without ever losing its sense of humor, as Duke never lost his. Visiting another Carnegie Hall in Pittsburgh for a concert, he walked the band through the marble-columned foyer, with inscriptions to Schubert, Bach, Brahms, Mozart, and other composers on its walls, and remarked: "Boys, we're in fast company." Commercially, the pioneering "Black, Brown, and Beige" premiere helped him, too, although its effects were not to last. The William Morris office placed a hustling executive, Cress Courtney, in charge of the orchestra's affairs, and the first result was a six-month season at a New York club, the Hurricane, which with regular broadcasts quadrupled the band's asking price. There were other notable dates, too, including a Broadway season at the Capitol Theatre in the same show as Lena Horne, then a suddenly emerging new star, with whom the band also appeared in the movie, *Cabin in the Sky*.

The partial respite from touring must have pleased the musicians, and even the ambitious Ellington. He basked in a new kind of fame, more serious and prestigious than it had been, and the business side of his artistic life was thriving. He formed Tempo Music to publish his work, and that company was effectively given by him to his sister Ruth, with whom he had an intensely close and loving relationship all his life. "Look after little Ruthie," his mother had said as she died, and Ellington followed her instructions precisely.

In 1939, having majored in biology at Columbia University, Ruth went off to Europe to learn languages, to do a thesis based on a comparison of biology teaching in Paris and New York, and to continue her subsidiary music studies. "I was the only one in the party of thirty-five who had a *personal* chaperone—and she was a friend of my mother, and her grandmother had known my grandmother! And all that was on Edward's insistence. That's how conventional he was! He told me how to powder, what shoes to wear, everything. I only stayed five months in Paris because war broke out, and when I came back I was a student-teacher for a time. I really wanted to be a doctor, but once Edward gave me Tempo to run, I became too involved in music publishing to do anything else.

"I used to play piano a lot in those days, but I had so many giants around me, I couldn't stand the comparison, so I gave up. Tempo was a fascinating business. Do you know its first two compositions were both *not* by Duke? They were 'Flamingo' and Billy's 'A Train.' Mostly we published Duke's music, but we pulled in around thirty composers in the end—some of the musicians in the band, and people like Harry James, Luther Henderson, Randy Weston."

Duke not only trusted his sister implicitly. He was greatly influenced by her throughout his life, and wherever he was in the world, he rang her most days, as he also did Evie Ellington. He bought a four-story house for her at 333 Riverside Drive, an area of the greatest and, before the ascendancy of Park Avenue, the most fashionable homes in New York City. Ruth continued to live there, as well as in an apartment at Central Park South, on and off for years. It was a great place for parties and contained the Ellington trophy room, where, in a space around thirty feet square, he kept all the medals, ribbons, degree robes, certificates, and other bonuses which the world was to shower upon him. The neighboring house, No. 331, he gave to Mercer Ellington.

Duke's relationship with Edmund Anderson was also prospering around this time. In 1943, Anderson had given Duke perhaps his biggest non-Ellingtonian hit—the beautiful song, "Flamingo," written in partnership with Ted Grouya, and later to be a million-selling record in 1952 for the saxophonist-bandleader Earl Bostic and others. At the apartment on St. Nicholas Avenue, with Billy Strayhorn looking on, Anderson taught it to Herb Jeffries, the band's singer. When Duke came to form Tempo Music, he wanted to give Anderson a minor interest, which was refused. Next, Duke suggested that Anderson should write the lyrics for a musical based on Aesop's Fables, and they spent six months working on the idea. Lena Horne was to be featured and Rex Stewart, the trumpeter, was to star as the Jackass. Anderson recalled:

> William Morris, Jr., wanted the show to be full of social significance, like *Jump for Joy*. He used to say "Duke Ellington can't turn his back on the world!" I'd deliberately kept social significance out of it, because I felt that wasn't the way to keep on presenting Edward. I think Duke was rather awed by Morris and all the attention he was getting, and we couldn't make it work out. Well, I guess you could say I was young and stupid and I said to hell with it, I'm not having Duke on a soapbox, so the whole thing

never came off. But I'm glad we did it. I enjoyed it all, except getting Duke to wake up. It would take an hour sometimes to drag him out of sleep.

Anderson's memories of the period are particularly vivid. One night in 1940 he discovered Ellington's doctor, Arthur Logan, in Duke's dressing room at the Lafayette Theatre in Harlem.

Joe Louis was there—he was the heavyweight champion of the world at the time—and he adored Ellington. He was just standing there and mooning at Ellington and all three were stuffing themselves with vanilla ice cream—at Duke's suggestion, of course. He was pretty fat at the time. When he was playing the Capitol Theatre in 1944, while we were still working on Aesop's Fables, I went down to see him and met Dizzy Gillespie. Very few people remember that Dizzy played trumpet with Duke. I asked him how he liked it and he said: "It's the nearest to being in heaven."

Over thirty years later, the jovial, balloon-cheeked trumpeter—perhaps the greatest survivor of the bebop age—didn't disagree with his earlier assessment.

Man, what a month that was! I was in there because Ray Nance had union card trouble. I looked at the music, and I couldn't play it! Did I read! None of them, not Rex nor nobody, would give me any help. So I used to sit there each time the curtain came down and I'd play and play to myself. It took me two weeks before I'd got into it. And one day Sonny Greer, he comes up to me and he says: "Hey, *nigger*. What you doin' there practicin' all the time when you s'posed to be restin'?" So I look him straight down the eye and I say: "Hey, *old man!* What you doin' sleepin' behind them drums when you s'posed to be playin'?"

Of course I was full of shit in those days. Still am, baby—but Sonny, umm, he was getting to be real mean by then. I loved Duke, though. Who didn't? My man, Duke. I made a record with him later, kind of accidental. I just happened along one day with my horn and we blew and they taped it and they put it out. And when I got no money, I mentioned it, very gently—to Duke, and he smiled and he says, "Well, Diz, I can't pay you what you're really worth." Whee, was that a cunning, elegant man! So I smile and I says, "Don't give it no mind, Duke. Just so long as you *pay* me!" And maybe a year later, he did. He was surely *the* greatest!

Even in those Capitol Theatre days, that opinion was becoming widespread. Edmund Anderson remembered that Ellington's Capitol billing was:

> The Genius of Jazz—and he sure hated that! Lena Horne was on the bill, too, and it was a tremendous show. One night he was just complaining to me that $900 had been stolen from his trunk—he didn't mind the loss, but was worried that someone in the organization had taken it—when there was this great booming voice outside asking if Mr. Ellington was in. Somebody announced the man as Mr. Robeson, and Ellington drew back and said "My God, that's my tailor. I'm not in, tell them I'm not in. I owe him lots of money." So the message went back and the voice said. "Pity. Well, I'll go up and see Lena." Then we realized it was Paul Robeson who had a big hit on Broadway in *Othello*, with Jose Ferrer as Iago. So Duke jumped up and let him in and they were embracing and laughing. They respected each other a lot.

These years of the middle 1940s were some of his happiest with Evie Ellington, for the long periods of absence by Duke which marked his later years had not yet begun. They were together a great deal, living happily in the pleasant apartment on St. Nicholas Avenue, and Evie tried hard—but without success—to turn him into a family man, for she had already developed a friendly relationship with Mercer Ellington, often taking his side in arguments with his father. Rightly or wrongly, Evie believed that Ruth Ellington looked coolly on her relationship with Duke. Later in her life, Ruth was noncommittal about it. "I approved of everyone who made Edward happy. But you know how reticent he was. As a family, we kept our private affairs to ourselves."

Mercer, however, became openly attached to Evie and he even called her "Ma" as she grew older. At this time, in her early thirties, Evie was still at the height of her beauty, elegant in growing maturity. Duke's London friends, the Diamonds, said that when they first met her in 1950—tall, svelte, wearing a black velvet fitted coat over a split long skirt in the same material, rounded off with white Cossack hat and muff, both in ermine—they were stunned with her looks. At the same time, Evie must have been already deeply sensible of the painful insecurity of her position. While Duke was around, the edge was taken off the pain in their strange liaison, a life together which was increasingly subjugated to the demands of his music.

Evie loved him very much, understanding and accepting the rules of the game even if she must have prayed they could be otherwise, and this uneasy situation again illustrates the paradox of Ellington, the man with thousands of friends around the world—musicians, a select crew of business associates, dignitaries, fans young and old, many girl friends and some mistresses—yet essentially a solitary man at the heart of all the worship and affection. Closest to him were Mercer, Ruth, and their families, of whom younger members like Ruth's son, Stephen James, might work with the band in various back-up capacities. Men like Strayhorn and Ellington's doctor, Arthur Logan, formed another segment of his circle, only a little less intimate; further off stood the musicians in the band and their wives; still further away were the multifarious collection of international friends.

Duke was graced with the gift to make almost anyone in these various groups feel that, at a given moment, he or she was the most important person in the world to him. Everyone was in the "family," but some were more equal than others. Evie was the odd woman out, the one example of a person who had a piece of his life completely to herself; and she was gradually to become the loneliest friend of all.

During the 1940s, Duke's relationship with his son was also settling into the unusual pattern it followed over the next twenty-five years or so. In some ways they were close, and particular Ellington traits rubbed off on Mercer—the habit of irony, for instance, where the observer was always in doubt whether the shading of the words used indicated feelings that ran deep or shallow. But there was always the suspicion that Mercer found the shadow of the paternal image oppressive whilst his father was alive. I talked with him once in the 1960s, soon after he'd taken over the role of manager of the band—much, it appeared, to Duke's delighted relief—and was astonished to hear him call his father "Ellington" in every sentence he used.

I always wanted to be an individual. That's why I stayed out of the organization. And of course Ellington and I don't agree on everything. Like in music he basically believes all rules are made to be broken. I just think you've got to do some things by the rules. Sure, we've had a lot of differences. Yet there's been this father-image thing, too. I've always wanted to write scores like Ellington. If anything we're too much alike. It just took a little maturity to understand him.

The understanding, it seems, was never perfect. Part of it was the classic problem of sons living in the shadows of very famous fathers. Mercer was also distressed by what had happened long ago in Washington between his father and his mother, although Duke's treatment of Edna Ellington was scrupulously generous. She lived in considerable comfort in the capital at Ellington's expense, until the end. But the strains of his parents' separation were inevitably felt. "In his childhood," Duke wrote of Mercer in his autobiography, "he had to go from one household to the other, his mother's and mine, alternatively, so he had absorbed the full range of love and discipline." Yet there are few men, once he has been persuaded to start talking, who can explain, interpret, and illuminate Duke's music better than Mercer. It has been part of him for so long. When he was eleven or twelve, he would often, around four in the morning, wake up in the New York apartment where Duke's mother looked after him and hear his father, back from the Cotton Club, playing the piano. He'd be half asleep as he listened, but these were the sounds which he would later try to emulate. He called those nights his first lessons in composition.

As Mercer grew older, Duke pushed him toward music. The teen-ager would be left with a harmony Ellington had written on a sheet and instructed to write two melodies, one fast and one slow, to fit; no note used in the harmony was to appear in the melody. In this way, Mercer began to teach himself, before attempting formal music studies at Columbia University, New York University, and Juilliard. Around the time that Ellington was pulling Strayhorn and Webster into his orbit, Mercer was forming his own first band, using many Strayhorn arrangements and musicians as promising as Dizzy Gillespie and Clark Terry. He had other bands down the years (as well as jobs as a whisky salesman, musical director to the singer, Della Reese, a successful disc jockey, and a semi-pro footballer), but none of them made much of a hit.

His father, wryly remembering Mercer as a young bandleader, could say to me in 1965: "He's always fought against being little Duke Ellington. He's built up this resistance. When he first got his own band I said, 'There's a lot of territory we haven't played in ten years. Go out and give them "A Train" and make a lot of money.' And people were telling him, 'Sure, print the "Ellington" big and the "Mercer" small. A great idea.' But he was fresh off that football team, full of that old school spirit and that fair play, and he just wouldn't. Which is one reason he hasn't made a big name for himself." And which is also a reason, in retrospect, for feeling that Mercer took an extremely honorable decision under considerable pressures in those early days.

Before he went off into the U.S. Army in 1943, where he played for part of his two years in a band under Sy Oliver, the outstanding arranger for Jimmy Lunceford and Tommy Dorsey, Mercer had already begun his contributions to the Ellington library. His easy-swinging number, "Things Ain't What They Used to Be," dates from 1941 and was still being played as part of the most repeated Ellington repertoire in the 1970s. "Moon Mist" and "Blue Serge," also by Mercer, were less often heard but are both fine themes.

The band needed such material, for long stays (like that at the Hurricane Club) and prestigious one-nighters at Carnegie Hall were only the cream on the cake; in the 1940s, as at most other times, Ellington was still leading a band which went from dance halls to theatres, wherever the money and the conditions were attractive enough. These venues usually demanded swing and sway rather than suites. So, if there was "Black, Brown, and Beige," there was also "What Am I Here For?," "Just a-Sittin' and a-Rockin'," "Do Nothin' till You Hear from Me" (a vocal version of "Concerto for Cootie"), "I Didn't Know about You," "I'm Beginning to See the Light," "Everything but You," and "I'm Just a Lucky So and So," all of them Ellington classics from the period 1943–1946, and some of them curiosities. "I'm Beginning to See the Light" had Don George, Johnny Hodges, and Harry James on the compositional credits, as—with the exception of Hodges's name—did "Everything but You." Ellington had some unlikely collaborators on odd songs down the years, including Frankie Laine and Tony Bennett. Equally, there were rare examples of more expected names, notably Mel Tormé (in 1946) and the great Johnny Mercer, whose joint lyrics with Strayhorn for "Satin Doll" (1953) helped create yet another all-time Ellington standard.

Yet even during this longish period of relative stability in New

York, and the happy days he spent with Evie, Duke had still to exist for long periods on trains, by day and by night. He worked out the essence of "New World a-Comin' " at night in an open railroad coach heading back to the East Coast while around him four men (not from the band) were playing a kind of gin rummy, a baby was bawling, GIs were talking to girls, and kids were eating oranges. Duke, according to an eyewitness, was impervious to every interruption, from his own musicians or outsiders. He just sat there working, cursing whenever the swaying of the coach made his pencil jump across the paper from the series of notations he was writing, until at last he called out insistently "Swee' Pea, Swee' Pea," and Billy Strayhorn, aroused from a light doze, came uncertainly to join him.

The story goes that, excitedly, he asked his companion to listen. "Dah dee dah dah, deedle dee deedle dee boom, bah bah bah, boom, boom," he chanted, then laughed. "Boy, that son of a bitch has got a million twists."

Strayhorn appeared uninterested, finally suggesting sleepily that a particular piece of musical phrasing might be reversed. Duke tried out a further variation; they deedle-dee'd and dah-dah'd to each other a bit before Strayhorn went off to sleep, realizing that he was just as likely to hear his friend shouting deedle-dee through the wall of their adjoining rooms in whatever hotel they hit next. Then Duke went back to scribbling until dawn, before he himself collapsed into slumber. Ellington may have reversed the normal hours of waking and sleeping, but once he went into oblivion he could be the hardest of cases to bring back to the world again. Weary of the gruelling battle to get the recumbent Ellington off trains in time, his road manager in the 1940s, Jack Boyd, once allowed his boss to be shunted off into a siding five miles from the depot at Tacoma in the state of Washington. The walk back still didn't cure Ellington. On another occasion, Ellington stumbled blearily from a train in San Francisco and inadvertently followed a line of men into a van. They were prisoners, still in everyday clothes, on their way to start jail sentences at San Quentin. Boyd had to rescue him from a guard who wasn't easily convinced.

Other incidents were no less bizarre. There were times, out in the sticks, when ballroom temperatures were so low that many of the band played with their gloves on: according to Ben Webster, the aptly named Crystal Ballroom in the tough-sounding town of Fargo, North Dakota, was such a venue. In the hot-blooded South, Duke experienced gentlemen who backed up requests for a diet strictly confined to their favorite tunes with guns; in Texas, drunken cowboys were known to round off the evening by firing their guns at the ceiling. Off the train, there were offensive people to be dealt with; like the woman in the saloon at St. Louis, Missouri, who turned to Jack Boyd (white) and expressed her surprise when she saw one of Duke's musicians entering a cab. Boyd explained that the man was regarded as a great artist. "I always say that the worst white man is better than the best nigra," observed the woman. On the trains, there were nice people who just wanted to talk, and to them Duke and his musicians gave freely of themselves. In such circumstances, Ellington is reputed to have explained to a couple of GIs how he composed "In a Sentimental Mood" at a private party given for him after a dance in Durham, North Carolina. Two girls were having a fight over a man. He sat at the piano, a girl on each side of him, and to patch up the quarrel said he'd make a song for them. "Sentimental Mood" was what came out; and the girls kissed and made up. On another occasion, explaining to a German refugee how he wrote his music for the individual tones and traits of the particular men in the band, he observed: "You can't write music right unless you know how the man that'll play it plays poker."

That was, for Ellington, a natural comparison, for although he was increasingly embraced by intellectuals of every shape and size, and revered as a culture hero, Duke never looked down his nose at the workaday end of his business. He loved the excitement of clubs and dance halls, and around this time, when jitterbugging to jazz rather than shaking to rock 'n' roll was what the young did, the frenzy at dances he played was often intense. In a hall in Arkansas in 1942, the proceedings had to be stopped when the floor started to collapse under the stomping of the dancers, and another time, in West Virginia, the stage caved in. Ellington smiled through it all, both then and in later years as he recounted the stories, and when beetle-browed intellectual fans at one such event aired their disapproval of the whirling bodies, Duke responded with the most benign tolerance. "If they'd been told it was a Balkan folk dance, they'd think it was wonderful." Out in the sticks, his audiences would often be sparse, especially if the snows had come. Surveying one small gathering on a wintry night, Duke's usual gallantry came to his aid. "We may not have the biggest audience in the world, but we surely have the most beautiful." And if he ever felt down-hearted, well, there was always a good meal just around the corner.

With the amount of energy he expended, he needed fuel, and these were the years of Ellington the gourmand rather than the gourmet. Many descriptions of typical Ellington menus exist from this period, revealing, so often, a man whose virtuous resolution to keep his weight down collapsed in stages so that he ended up eating three or four separate meals in succession. Maybe he started well, with breakfast cereal and black tea, proclaiming that this would be enough. Then, viewing companions carving at steaks, he would add, straight-faced, a plain steak. Several minutes might elapse before the will to resist finally disintegrated. A second steak, onions, French fries, salad, with a Maine lobster on the side might next appear. Then fruit and cheese, and, with coffee, a specially concocted Ellingtonian dessert, for which he was renowned; chocolate cake, custard, ice cream, jelly, apple sauce, and whipped cream. He adored ham and eggs, so that might be added as an afterthought, with pancakes and syrup, of course. The after-afterthought would be a resumption of the diet: cereal and black tea to finish with.

Even in the last twenty years of his life, when he stopped all this stuffing and existed mostly on steaks and salads—with occasional forays into ham and eggs and Chinese food, which he loved—in a rigorous regimen, he'd delight in recalling places all over the world where in the old days you could eat well: there was a Mrs. Wagner at Old Orchard Beach in Maine whose hot dogs, he said, had two dogs to a bun. "I ate thirty-two one night." In the 1930s it was said he could drink any of his band under the table, but by the 1940s he was slowing down, and by the 1960s he'd virtually given up alcohol. "I retired undefeated champ," he claimed, preferring to sip a little coffee with lemon in his older age, alternating with weak tea and plain old hot water.

Apart from touring in the middle 1940s, the band was continuing to make records, and it was in the studios that, so often, the magical event of collective composition and arranging by Duke and his musicians would take place. Even with Strayhorn and Whaley to help him, the pace was so intense that a recording session might arrive with nothing properly prepared or scored for it. Ray Nance was one who criticized Ellington for such slapdash behavior, believing the band might often have done better with less chaos; but he admitted that it was probably deliberate policy by Duke, wanting to gamble on his men being able to cope in order to catch the feeling of spontaneity. So if Ellington gave himself to his men, they gave inspiration back to him continually.

Many descriptions by Duke's musicians exist of typical recording sessions, which would usually start with Duke arriving late and sitting at the piano doodling for fifteen minutes as he warmed up. If the tempo was fast, the band knew the first number would be swinging; if slow, they were prepared for a lament. Once Duke's humming and strumming was over, he'd suggest they see if the piano was in tune, which meant that the band should tune up. They'd already done so, but Ellington wanted to hear the tones before he'd go any further. This, in the words of Rex Stewart, is what happened next.

> Then the fun begins as Duke reaches into his pocket, and with the air of a magician produces some scraggly pieces of manuscript paper—about one-eighth of a page on which he's scribbled some notes. I recall one occasion when he'd jotted some notes for the saxophones, but there was nothing for Johnny Hodges. Duke had the saxes run the sequence down twice, while Johnny sat nonchalantly smoking. Then Duke called to Hodges, "Hey Rabbit, give me a long slow glissando against that progression. Yeah! That's it!" Next he said to Cootie Williams, "Hey, Coots, you come in on the second bar, in a subtle manner growling softly like a hungry little lion cub that wants his dinner but can't find his mother. Try that, okay?" Following that, he'd say, "Deacon" (how Lawrence Brown hated that nickname), "you are cast in the role of the sun beating down on the scene. What kind of a sound do you feel that could be? You don't know? Well, try a high B-flat in a felt hat, play it legato, and sustain it for eight bars. Come on, let's all hit this together," and that's the way things went—sometimes.

Duke was a great one for hats in music. He liked derby (bowler) hats—real ones, not aluminum—because, used on trombones, they gave him big, round, hollow effects. He loved it when Ray Nance varied the effect by stuffing a sweater into a derby, which increased the mellowness of his trumpet tone.

There was always this kind of improvisation at recording sessions, with musicians calling out suggestions, sometimes arguing with him, and at the end of it all Ellington and Strayhorn putting the mishmash together, Duke encouraging them at the final rehearsal with cries of "Get sincere! Give your heart! Let go your soul!"

Ellington's methods made him a nightmare for a music publisher to handle, and for a period the sufferer was Jack Robbins, a plump Broadway operator of the old show-business school and head of the Robbins Music Corporation. Plaintive telegrams used to flow from Robbins to Duke as he toured the country asking for lead sheets of new compositions already recorded by the band. Mostly Duke ignored them. Sometimes he would advise his publisher to put an arranger to work to pick the melodies off the records. One arranger, trained at Juilliard, failed because he couldn't separate the melody from the unusual harmonies. Robbins sent some of his men to a Philadelphia theatre to persuade Duke to give them a lead sheet on another occasion. Ellington had no manuscript paper with him, so, a witness recalled, he scribbled out the notes on an empty paper bag in which his valet had brought him a quart of ice cream.

All this slapdash behavior must have cost Ellington tens of thousands of dollars because of the slowness with which his music became available on sheets. It was estimated at this time that he was paying his musicians at least $2,500 a week and was grossing only around $200,000 a year at the box office, by no means a large sum when another bandleader, Kay Kyser, was pulling in well over $1,200,000 and Glenn Miller, before he joined the U.S. armed forces, was at around $1,000,000. Duke probably netted no more than $30,000 a year, and that was spent as fast as he made it. He economized on nothing; and especially not on his musicians, an understandable priority.

Further confirmation of such descriptions comes from Herb Hendler, who as Artists and Recording (A. and R.) Manager for RCA Records at that time had charge of many leading bands and singers contracted to the label. He arranged Ellington's studio sessions, and hearing on the grapevine that Harry James had recorded one of Duke's numbers with the word "light" somewhere in the title, he pressed Duke to do the same. "Ellington said he knew of no such tune, but after I'd kept asking him, he remembered that Don George had written a lyric something like that. The song was 'I'm Beginning to See the Light,' and we did a rush job. We got it out in a week from studio to shellac. Usually it was a month to six weeks. It sold almost a quarter of a million copies.

"It was always a rush job with Ellington. In a way he was like some of today's rock bands. It was all done on the spot. Other bands came in with parts all neatly written out. When Duke was coming in, I used to set up tables in the studio for his copyists. He'd sit at the piano and bang away. Then he'd give a lead sheet to the copyists, and an arrangement would be done there and then, with Duke adding odd phrases as he went along." Later, Hendler produced the recording of "The Perfume Suite" as well as a little-known single which features Ellington playing one of his own tunes with Tommy Dorsey's band on one side ("Tonight I Shall Sleep") and vice versa on the other ("Minor Goes a'Muggin' ").

That Duke's continuity of collective creation could be kept up required that key players like Hodges, Carney, and Brown should remain with the band. The surprise was that the musicians who joined from time to time during the middle and later 1940s fitted in so well: very little changed, except that with the band's repertoire growing all the time, there wasn't the same pressure for new material. And people began to get sloppy about scores. So much was in the heads of the older members, they didn't need music in front of them. Very late in Duke's career there were still tattered saxophone scores around which had "Otto" (Hardwick) scribbled across the top of them. The most notable recruits during the middle years of the decade were the withdrawn, solemn-faced alto saxophonist and clarinet player, Russell Procope, who came in 1946, not too long after Hardwick's departure, and the trumpeter, William Alonzo "Cat" Anderson, who first played with the band in 1944 and whose stratospheric ability on the trumpet was to provide such exciting distinction to the Ellington sound.

Both had long careers with the band, virtually until Duke's death. Procope had grown up in the same New York environment as Freddie Jenkins, Bubber Miley, and "Trickey Sam" Nanton, and he was a natural Ellingtonian from the start, as his comment about Duke's "iron hand in a mink glove" illustrates. He'd already played professionally for many years, with Fletcher Henderson and John Kirby among others, when he joined. Cat

Anderson was also richly experienced. Unlike most of those who'd preceded him, he wasn't a replacement. Like Ben Webster, he joined on his own merits, and for a time Duke had a five-strong trumpet section, with Rex Stewart, Ray Nance, Taft Jordan, and Shelton Hemphill. Cat's arrival—he got his name from fighting like a cat against the school bully at the orphanage in Charleston, South Carolina, where he was raised—caused problems in the band, though. As he tells the story, he took over a solo by Rex Stewart at a theatre show one night when Stewart was late—only he played it an octave higher. Stewart arrived at the stage door in the middle of Cat's solo and was furious. "He didn't speak to me for fifteen years," Cat has claimed. "He was highly strung, and so am I." When Stewart left Ellington in 1944, the trumpet section grew even bigger for a time with the addition of Harold "Shorty" Baker and Francis Williams, and one of the most famous Ellington specialties, "Trumpets No End," a fast version of Irving Berlin's "Blue Skies," was born.

Oscar Pettiford came in during 1945 to play bass for three years, but he and Duke didn't get on well—a real clash of personalities in musical and other senses. Pettiford was one of the early converts in the bebop revolution which transformed jazz in the 1940s. As a bopper, he persisted in trying to bring boppers into the band. Significantly, he is one of the few Ellingtonians not given a section of his own in Ellington's autobiography. Oddly, however, Pettiford returned to the band for short spells during the 1950s when Duke needed a bassist. According to Clark Terry, one of Duke's trumpeters later on, Pettiford leapt from the band bus during one trip when Ellington was riding along with the musicians (unusually for that period) through hazardous mountain territory. He disappeared into the forest shouting "I'm an Indian" (he'd been born on an Indian reservation). "I understand the wolves and animals of the forest. They talk with me." It took twenty minutes to retrieve him, but once back on the bus he continued to rage and finally picked on Duke, who told him to talk with Al Celley, the band manager of that time, if the subject was to be money. Pettiford became even more furious, whereupon Duke closed his eyes and simply went to sleep. "He has this phenomenal knack of being able to exclude himself when he wants to," Terry commented. Wendell Marshall, bassist cousin of Jimmy Blanton, and Tyree Glenn, the trombonist who later played a lot with Louis Armstrong, were happier newcomers. Glenn stayed five years on and off and played a lot in the wah-wah plunger style of Nanton, whom he effectively replaced following Tricky Sam's death in 1946. Marshall, arriving in that same year to follow Pettiford, was with the band until 1955.

Ellington sailed on with apparent serenity as the decade moved into its final three years, but there were ominous signs. Not everything he touched was successful. With his reputation enhanced by the Carnegie Hall concerts, he was commissioned to write the music for *Beggar's Holiday*, an updated version of John Gay's *The Beggar's Opera*, with Alfred Drake cast as Macheath (a mobster) and black artists playing the parts of the chief of police and his daughter. Even the production team was biracial. Maybe it was still ahead of its time; maybe it was just too long—three and a half hours when it was out on its pre-Broadway tour; maybe the clash between the show's musical director and Duke was too fierce. The man kept asking for more songs, even though Duke had already produced seventy-eight of them, of which thirty-nine were ultimately used in the show! On Broadway, it was a flop, despite being welcomed by the intellectual establishment.

Far happier was Duke's return, after fifteen years, to the Palladium in London. He couldn't bring the whole band because of the long-standing quarrel between the British and American musicians' unions. But with Ray Nance and Kay Davis, the singer, plus a British rhythm section (Tony Crombie on drums, Jack Fallon on bass, and Malcolm Mitchell on guitar) he was able to play as a "variety artist." Although it was a mini-representation of Duke's musical talent, the British visit was a great pleasure for many people—myself included—who had longed to see Ellington in the flesh. Ellington played his magical songs at the piano, smiling and urbane. Kay Davis, a completely legitimate soprano voice, was pleasant enough. ("Transblucency" in 1946 had fused her voice with the band most beautifully in a wordless vocal reminiscent of Adelaide Hall in 1927.) But Nance was really the star. He repeatedly had the audience on their feet cheering with his singing, his tap dancing, and his extraordinary humor on both trumpet and violin. Pearl Bailey, too, contributed as much to the show as Ellington. The British band of the time, the Skyrockets, struggled manfully to interpret Duke's music during their spot.

Duke spent his spare time happily in a Curzon Street apartment, indulging himself at shops like Turnbull and Asser, where he bought shirts by the dozen down the years that followed in keeping with his reputation as a dandy dresser. The Diamonds saw a lot of him. Once, breakfasting with them, he began dancing to his 1933 tune, "Merry-Go-Round," which was on the gramophone. Suddenly he stopped and shook his head. "Kids, did I ever play *that* good?"

He travelled around the provinces to do concerts as well, but, interestingly, he wasn't welcomed everywhere. The plan for him to give a concert at the Albert Hall in Nottingham was thwarted when the trustees of the Hall, the Wesleyan Methodist Mission, refused to allow the Hall to be used. To the musician who was later to play his Sacred Concerts in cathedrals of every denomination all over the world, the Reverend Frank T. Copplestone, the superintendent minister at the time, said: "We allow its use for social functions and high-class concerts, but *jazz.* . . ." Other incidents during Duke's travels were just as fascinating. The troupe was on its way by train to Bournemouth when Ray Nance, who'd just bought himself a portable gramophone, put on a record by Thelonious Monk. Duke, passing in the corridor, heard it, came into Nance's compartment, and sat down to listen. "Sounds like he's stealing some of my stuff," he observed. Nance later commented cryptically: "He was very interested. He understood what Monk was doing."

He did indeed. Monk was one sign of a new threat to Ellington—new music and smaller bands. There were other threats. Throughout the decade there had been continual outbreaks of squabbling between American unions and both radio and record companies leading to periods, as in 1943, when Duke's band wasn't in the studios. In 1947, a trouble-free year, the band recorded for Columbia (they'd done their 1940–1941 classics for Victor) a most beautiful set of compositions, with interesting themes and outstanding solos and ensemble colorings. Kay Davis was blended exquisitely with trombones and reeds in "On a Turquoise Cloud," and Johnny Hodges's alto was the voice on another impressionistic piece, "Lady of the Lavender Mist." There was a kind of concerto for Jimmy Hamilton's clarinet on "Air-Conditioned Jungle," features for the rich open tone of Tyree Glenn ("Sultry Serenade") and for Lawrence Brown's light-as-a-feather slide technique ("Golden Cress"). Fine piano features for Ellington—"New York City Blues" and "The

Clothed Woman"—were another part of the rich mixture, and this was also the year when "The Liberian Suite" was recorded.

By 1948, however, a renewed union ban on recording robbed the world of anything by Ellington, and in 1949, when the ban was lifted, some crass Columbia executives insisted that Duke record what with charity could be called "pop" material, including a piece entitled "Cowboy Rumba." In Ellington's autobiography, there is a horrendous gap of five years, no less—between 1947 and 1952—in the huge list of his compositions, whose dates are given in their order of copyright. Although the years when Duke's compositions were copyrighted do not always match the years when he created the works, the hiatus is notable. From 1923 to 1975, with the exception of 1947–1952, Duke always has annual entries, often at the length of many dozens of compositions. Obviously, something was seriously wrong.

Partly, it was the general state of the music business. Big bands were no longer wanted. The bebop revolution in jazz had happened; and the combos in which Dizzy Gillespie, Charlie Parker, Thelonious Monk, and others featured used only five or six musicians. They were cheaper, and promoters were looking to save money in a poor economic situation, with Wall Street on the slide. Solo singers had broken free from the bands and now stood as performers in their own right. There were any number of small "jazz-pop" combos, like Louis Jordan's, and in some places trad-jazz revivalist bands were the rage. Ballrooms were closing as the postwar good-time mood faded and leisure pursuits became more sophisticated. Managements of cinemas could now get away with a policy of films-only; they didn't need stage acts to flesh out the bill. One by one the big bands of the swing age broke up; even Woody Herman and Count Basie were driven to cut the number of musicians in their bands drastically. Indeed, when Ellington was presented with his *Down Beat* magazine poll awards in Chicago early in 1950, they added a special parchment scroll to mark the fact that his was the sole winning band from the 1949 voting lists still working.

So 1949 was not a happy year for Duke, even though he made another breakthrough by playing with the Philadelphia Symphony Orchestra, one amongst almost fifty such orchestras whose platform the band (or its leader) shared in the years that followed. Economically, he was shaky, for his concert tours had begun to need subsidizing out of record royalties; there were fewer royalties than before with the studios so often closed to the band. His trumpet section was weak. Cat Anderson had gone temporarily elsewhere; the lead man, Al Killian, had lip trouble. The reeds were fine—the old team of Hodges, Procope, Hamilton, and Carney—but no total replacement for Webster had yet been found, despite the employment of Al Sears and occasional sessions by Charlie Rouse and Don Byas. Sonny Greer was inconsistent, drinking and in indifferent health. A deputy, Butch Ballard, was often used. And when there was talk of a European tour in 1950, Tyree Glenn's wife put her foot down and refused to let her husband go, doubtless because of an affair he'd had with a French girl while touring with Don Redman in 1946. Glenn continued to play on and off with the band, but he couldn't be counted on. An increasing number of the musicians were in a similar position. They could see very little future in the big-band game, Duke's composing flair seemed temporarily to have deserted him, and in buses and hotel rooms they talked continually of leaving to set up on their own.

5

1951-1959
Swing Low, Swing High

Whenever he was asked how old he was in the 1960s, Duke Ellington tended to give a mock scowl and say: "That's a dangerous question. I was born in 1956 at the Newport Festival."

The quip was more than an uneasy evasion. Although Ellington had an aversion to discussing death, it was not primarily a dislike of stating his age which made him answer questions concerning it so flippantly. He was talking about artistic birth and death when he mentioned Newport, Rhode Island, once the site of America's most prestigious annual jazz festival and in 1956 the occasion of a triumph for his orchestra which heralded a new era of activity, composition, and travelling unprecedented even in Ellington's already flamboyant career. If he wasn't born at Newport, then he was, artistically, undoubtedly reborn there; for in the five years preceding it, he had almost died an artistic death.

Popular music is, apart from an art form, also a commercial business. America in 1950 wasn't beginning to turn its back on Ellington specifically, but on the big-band business in general. With solo singers dominating the stage in theatres, combos taking over the clubs, and a few hustlers already glimpsing the possibilities of turning black rhythm-and-blues into the gold mine called rock 'n' roll, Ellington was just one of the casualties.

He, however, didn't die. While bands all around him were breaking up, he kept the faith. But with engagements scarcer than usual and public interest at a low ebb, it was a dispiriting time for his musicians, many of whom were already feeling exhausted after years of travelling around. Public adulation helped to keep them going, and without it they grew demoralized. It couldn't have been easy for Duke, either, to maintain or increase his high salaries for the more renowned sidemen he employed.

Typically, as he had done before in 1933 and 1939, Duke sought an escape route. If America didn't want him, then perhaps Europe would. In the spring of 1950 he set off on a lengthy tour through Scandinavia and France, with a few new faces riding the bandwagon, trumpeter Ernie Royal and tenor saxist Don Byas among them. Obviously, too, Duke still needed Butch Ballard as relief drummer because of Sonny Greer's poor health and drinking excursions.

As a tour, it was a very mixed experience. One important personal factor for Duke was that Evie accompanied him, and she brought along her friend, Eve Celley, wife of Al Celley, a key man in Duke's management team. After a few days in Paris, Eve Celley was all for roaring off to London for a day or so, but Evie wasn't interested. This was the first time she'd been abroad with Duke and, apart from a flying visit to Japan in the 1960s, the last. She savored every moment of his company.

Duke's London friends, the Diamonds, came to Paris too, and Leslie Diamond took the opportunity to reprimand Ellington for having allowed his band to deteriorate so much in appearance. "At the Palladium in 1933, they were all in tails—now they come on in crumpled suits, stained and shabby. Your instruments used to be all silver or all brass-gold. Now they're mixed up—you take them from whoever gives them to you free. And this habit you've slipped into of letting the musicians drift on one by one—why?"

Perhaps the description of the band was one of the symptoms of its decline and demoralization at the time, although some traits—the drifting-on habit, for instance—had come to stay. Duke did not explode in face of such frankness. Sadly, he agreed, claiming he'd no time to do much about it. He always seemed to be hiding behind the excuse that he had better things to do whenever the question of band discipline arose. Maybe the only way he *could* handle his unpredictable virtuosi was to let them do as they pleased, so long as they played most of the time to their limit. But there was, too, always the suspicion that he wanted to be all things to all men, and that he could play roles as it suited him. When the band came to leave Paris, everyone was looking for him, afraid he'd miss the boat train. Suddenly he was spotted, darting behind pillars in the hotel. "He practiced stage entrances all the time," one of his companions commented.

There was little wrong with the music during the tour, and the concerts at the Palais de Chaillot in Paris were a notable success. The band seemed to retain its fire and humor onstage, and audiences were enthusiastic. The musicians adored Paris; it was a city where blacks were welcomed on equal terms, where musicians like Sidney Bechet and Coleman Hawkins had already found a haven in the 1930s, and no one wanted to leave. Of the future, however, the band were less certain. Offstage, some of the musicians freely said they'd leave if they had anywhere else to go. Al Killian, to die later that year in a shooting affray, was so depressed by his persistent lip trouble he vowed to quit the music business altogether. The programs they played in Europe consisted entirely of old favorites, although Duke later claimed that this was because the audiences demanded the numbers and wouldn't let the band get on to newer stuff like "The Liberian Suite." Whatever the reasons, Ellington seemed to be glimpsing no new musical horizons, and back in America more and more critics, bedazzled by bebop, were writing him off as over the hill.

The tour had an unhappy climax, casting the shadow of things to come. Sonny Greer, who'd missed several concerts and was drinking heavily, approached Duke outside the Hotel Claridge in the Champs Elysées and demanded money. Duke tried to evade him, told him to "talk to Cells" (Celley). Greer persisted as Ellington continued to back off, and suddenly spat out "You son of a bitch."

To Ellington, the word had at that time fewer of the connotations of everyday jargon it later developed. He chose to take it as an insult to his mother. With two dull red spots in his cheeks he said to Greer: "That does it, that's the end of us." Then he turned sharply and walked away. It wasn't quite the end, but the quarrel emphasized the unhappiness within the Ellington camp as the band sailed westwards on the *Ile de France*.

Once he returned to the States, Duke cut some small-group recordings for the new Mercer label, operated by his son and the jazz critic, Leonard Feather. They were interesting because the various combos included musicians from different traditions, including the bop drummer Max Roach and trumpeter Red Rodney. But this wasn't music which displayed Ellington knowing where he was going, obviously moving forward. There were a series of duets with Strayhorn; a moving tribute to the lost double bass genius, "Blues for Blanton"; and one number, "New Piano Roll Blues," on which Ellington used a piano fitted with a "mandolin" attachment, a popular gimmick at the time, and played so percussively that his points of similarity with Thelonious Monk were more obvious. When the full band went into the Columbia studios, after a year's absence, the result was again not of great musical significance, although in one way the horizons for Duke and other sophisticated musicians were expanding. Columbia was experimenting with long-playing records, and this gave Duke the chance to do a version of "The Tattooed Bride," two years old and important among his suites, as well as extended arrangements of "Sophisticated Lady," "Mood Indigo," and "Solitude."

These tunes were a vehicle for long solos and experiments in unusual tempos, but the most encouraging sign for the future was the debut of Paul Gonsalves, who was to remain with the band for more than two decades. A shy, easygoing man, he filled the gap which Ben Webster had left in the saxophone ranks. He could unleash fast solos for chorus after chorus, but it was his warm, rhapsodic treatments of ballads which revealed him at his creative peak. Breathily rich-toned, he was really a master. Coleman Hawkins was his early model, and he played with Count Basie and Dizzy Gillespie in the 1940s. But Ellington was his god. He knew every Webster solo by heart, confessed that all through his early days as a pro, he tried to keep a tone which would suit the Ellington sound. In September 1950, with no fixed job after the Gillespie band folded, and around seven dollars left of his savings, he went one night to Birdland, the New York jazz club named after Charlie "Bird" Parker. Duke was there, but Gonsalves was too shy to greet him until Ellington got up to leave. The sight of Gonsalves must have struck a chord in Ellington's memory. He invited the saxophonist to the office next day, and offered him a job. "If I die tomorrow," Gonsalves was later to confess, "I'll consider I've been successful, because when I began to study music it was with the idea of being with that band."

Yet the coming of Gonsalves as 1950 drifted to a close could scarcely compensate for what was to come in the disastrous year of 1951. It began promisingly. On his way back from Europe on the *Ile de France*, Duke had begun to write his "Harlem" suite, commissioned by the NBC Symphony Orchestra, then conducted by Arturo Toscanini. It was premiered in January at the Metropolitan Opera House during a long concert in aid of the National Association for the Advancement of Colored People, and it proved that he could compose very effectively for a large-scale orchestra, although he once proclaimed to a questioner who wanted him to do more such writing: "Strings? Positively no! What could I do with strings that hasn't been done wonderfully for hundreds of years?" Apart from the suite, the program contained Ellingtonia as varied as "Ring Dem Bells," "The Mooch," and "Coloratura" (from "The Perfume Suite") mixed in with songs like (believe it or not) "Danny Boy" and "Trees" sung by Al Hibbler. The *Down Beat* magazine critic, Mike Levin, was kind about most aspects of the concert, but even he had to say: "Something important and vital is missing from the Ellington band. Exactly what, it is hard to say." The answer, probably, was a sense of commitment and belief on the part of several members of the orchestra. Within a month of the concert, Johnny Hodges, Lawrence Brown, and Sonny Greer handed in their notices. The event dumfounded the music world and, however he glossed it over later, must have profoundly shocked even the phlegmatic Ellington.

Greer had been with him since the beginning. He was a fine drummer, whom Duke used to say kept time with everything from trotting horses and windshield wipers to bells clanging and people sweeping. The quarrel in Paris made his departure less surprising, of course, and he had also been growing less reliable; but Ellington had obviously enjoyed a special relationship with Greer through the years, valuing his spunkily humorous companionship until the break came. "Bread cast upon the sea comes back buttered toast" was one of Greer's aphorisms which Duke, oddly, was always quoting. Greer, however, was probably less difficult to replace than Johnny Hodges and Lawrence Brown, both of them unique melodic voices. Between them the three musicians had already clocked up well over seventy years' service with the band, and for many observers an Ellington orchestra without them appeared a travesty. It must have hurt Duke, too, that the trio were going to stay together, as the heart of a small band led by Hodges. The band also included other Ellingtonians—Al Sears on tenor saxophone and the bassist, Joe Benjamin—and was signed up for recording and other purposes with Norman Granz, the increasingly powerful promoter of "Jazz at the Philharmonic" concerts, which were the most crowd-pulling and important jazz presentations of the late 1940s and 1950s all over the world. Hodges told the newspapers he was going to play a lot of Duke's tunes. "We didn't like the tone poems too much. The boys like to stick to the old stuff."

Norman Granz's role in the departure of Ellington's musicians was, it turned out, crucial and in later years he made no bones about it. "Sure, I pulled Johnny and the others out of the band. I'd been very close to him ever since 1941 when *Jump for Joy* was in Los Angeles and I was doing my first jam sessions out there. I'd used him on jam sessions, and from time to time after the war I'd presented Duke's band in concerts. I felt Johnny was kept down in the band. I wanted to record him outside of the Ellington context, and that's why he and the others came out. Harry Carney almost came too, but he was afraid to quit, and anyway we didn't need him. Johnny's band had one big hit with "Castle Rock," which was like a Louis Jordan thing with no singing. After a time Greer didn't want to travel, so we used Sam Woodyard on drums and Aaron Bell on bass. It was a good band."

According to Granz, Duke didn't speak to him for a year, and the episode was the start of a curiously up-and-down relationship between the two men for the rest of Ellington's life. Granz was very involved with Duke for long periods, yet has always expressed significant reservations about the calibre of Ellington's genius and the niceness of his character. Of the Hodges business, Granz said: "Duke liked life to go smoothly. If anything disturbed his equanimity, then that was a great drag to him. He was incredibly *égoiste* in the French sense. It disturbed him equally if the room service didn't work somewhere, or if Johnny Hodges quit the band. Both upset his life, and he hated it. So he was really piqued when I took Johnny away."

For a few weeks after the bombshell, Duke's stock was at zero with those who thought he could never recover. He'd even been robbed of his copyist, Tom Whaley, who'd gone off to South America to lead a band when he couldn't squeeze more money out of Duke. Yet at this darkest hour, Ellington's pragmatism came brilliantly to his rescue. This aspect of his character, often overlooked, has been emphasized several times already in these pages. His reaction now underlined his faith, his essential toughness and determination; rarely again had he to justify so dramatically what he later told the critic, Nat Hentoff, during an interview for *Down Beat:* "The only reason we're still in it is mainly artistic interest. We're not one of those people who stay in the business only so long as business is good. We stay in it fifty-two weeks a year."

Ellington hesitated only momentarily before he showed how he was going to stay in business. Then, ruthlessly, he carried out what was later dubbed the Great James Robbery. From the band of the trumpeter, Harry James, Duke enticed away (with money and flattery, presumably) three of his cornerstone musicians: altoist Willie Smith, to replace Hodges; the drummer Louis Bellson as Greer's successor; and, to take over Brown's chair, his old companion Juan Tizol, who had been fifteen years with him before moving to the James band in 1944. Nor was this all. Before 1951 was out, the trombonist Britt Woodman and two excellent trumpet players, Clark Terry and Willie Cook, were also recruited.

Duke simultaneously sought to strengthen the management of the band. He approached Leslie Diamond, remembering their conversation in Paris; but Diamond, established as a pharmacist in London, wasn't interested. He also put propositions continually to Herb Hendler, who had moved from producing records for RCA to band management, and had made the Ralph Flanagan band, as well as Buddy Morrow's, into top attractions. "One night in Cincinnati, Ralph had just played to 5,000 people, and Ellington was also in town. I went to his show and there were a few hundred people present, that was all, and Edward was crying the blues and asking me to come with him. He started ringing me in New York from wherever he was around the country. Swee' Pea always came on first, sweet-talking. Then Edward . . . and he really nagged me. And I used to say, 'Do you want a manager—or a friend?' But he wouldn't give up, so at last I went down to see him in Philadelphia and I looked seriously into his business.

"At that time, Flanagan was grossing more than half a million dollars a year, and I insisted he had a very tight payroll, around $2,500 a week. With over $10,000 a week coming in, there was plenty of money left after paying the band. Edward was paying *his* musicians $4,500 a week and some weeks he was only taking $3,000 or so from his dates. He was using his personal money, out of royalties and so on, to take care of the band. So I told him the situation was ridiculous. The only way he could survive was to cut his guys' pay in half. And he smiled at me and he said: 'Listen, Herb. I have to stand out in front of that band for five shows a day, sometimes. The band you run has got to please the audience. The band I run has got to please *me*. So that's why I've got to have them, no matter what they cost.' Well, that was the last time I heard about being manager. It would have been impossible. We just stayed friends."

Hendler was also the man who once inveigled Ellington to go horseracing with him at the Belmont track in New York. "First, though, I had to wake him up. Have you ever heard about those scenes? He was always *impossible* to wake. It was around noon and Evie was there, and she showed me what to do. We had to drag him from the bed—and he was a heavy guy, around two hundred pounds then—and dump him on the floor and keep pushing him. So finally we get to the track and I tell him which horse will win the first race, but he takes no notice and goes off on his own. Every race I ask how he's done, and every time he says he's got the winner and he goes off to collect his money. I'm mystified, because my horses are losing and I was a pretty good handicapper in those days."

Ellington had indeed kept winning that afternoon. He invented his own system. He backed every horse in every race, so that he could say with justice he'd been on the winner. "That was like Duke," a friend observed. "He always had to be a winner."

His ruthlessness over the James gang proved that too; and he was right about paying top money for the best as well, for in retrospect the musicians he won were a lifesaving transfusion for the orchestra, even though Willie Smith stayed scarcely eighteen months and Louis Bellson departed at the beginning of 1953 following his marriage to the singer, Pearl Bailey. They got Duke through a desperately difficult time, presented him with new challenges, recharged his own enthusiasm. True, the music the band made during the next couple of years was of variable quality, but Ellington was delighted with his new-look ensemble, both as interpreters of his compositions and as a collection of creative soloists.

It was tremendously important at this particular stage of Ellington's career that most of the new men had *not* played with him before, a reversal of the usual observation about his orchestra. They weren't blasé about roaring into old standbys, and Ellington was even encouraged to sort out older scores on which the dust of disuse had begun to settle. In an interview at the time, this feeling came through very strongly. "The guys call their own rehearsals. That hasn't happened for years in our band. Another thing, there's no rudeness on the stand. When the guys stay together too long, they're apt to get tired of looking at each other. Not this crew!"

Clark Terry, born in St. Louis, Missouri, who had already played with the bands of Count Basie and Charlie Barnet, summed up the invigorating spirit of the band at that time when he later declared that everything he'd experienced before was like elementary school; with Ellington, he was going to college. Not all the critics were so impressed, however. Some said that Louis Bellson was a show-off, because he was featured in exhibitionistic drum solos, like "Skin Deep." He was certainly flamboyant, of which his use of two bass drums was an obvious sign. The antagonists didn't say, however, that the solo features were only a small part of what he did or that, more important, he'd learned how to drive along a big band during his years with Benny Goodman, Tommy Dorsey, Harry James, and others. He uplifted the Ellington band rather better than Sonny Greer had often done in his last year ot two. Willie Smith was criticized because he wasn't Hodges, because he, too, was something of an exhibitionist. Again, the judgment had some point to it, but was exaggerated. Smith hadn't the stamina and invention of Hodges in longer solos; but he was good, often inspired, in most of his work, and he was a fine leader of the reed section which, at the time, needed the authority he'd brought to the Jimmie Lunceford band in the 1930s.

Duke, as was his wont, ignored such attacks. He went on saying that he'd got a great band with a great drive and a great bunch of soloists, and the musicians acted for much of the time as if they believed him. The orchestra, even in this relatively down period, had its successes. There was an enthusiastically received season at Birdland and a charity concert in New York when, after the NBC Symphony Orchestra had played "New World a-Comin' " and "Harlem" with Duke's musicians, a remarkable jam session developed. "Finally," the *Down Beat* review proclaimed, "the longhairs leaped in, the bass men plucking frenziedly, the violinists sawing with vigor."

Moreover, after a long hiatus, Duke was beginning to compose again. It wasn't his greatest music—although 1953 was the year of "Satin Doll," one of his finest and most often played pop songs, with lyrics by Strayhorn and Johnny Mercer—but it was useful as a prelude to what was to come later. Duke rode the departure of Willie Smith (replaced by Hilton Jefferson) in 1952, and of Bellson (for whom the old standby, Butch Ballard, eventually substituted) in 1953, and was still able to make some highly interesting records with the Capitol label, for whom he signed three months after Bellson's departure. These included eight titles which brilliantly revealed Ellington as a solo pianist, backed only by bass and drums, playing new compositions like the beautiful "Reflections in D" and quirky, often highly percussive versions of established favorites. The orchestra's recordings in 1953 and 1954 were much more mixed in quality. The long-playing record entitled "Ellington '55" was old material played with flair and power and praised with faint damns by most critics at the time, but from today's distance seeming full of enjoyable music. The attacks on other recordings made of non-Ellington material, with a commercial craze of the time reflected in "Twelfth Street Rag Mambo" and "Bunny Hop Mambo," were much more justified.

When Duke signed up for the whole summer of 1955 to play in the "Aquacades" show at Flushing Meadows, Long Island, site of the 1939 World's Fair, the critical storm reached a furore. Five men in the band, including Paul Gonsalves and Willie Cook, were temporarily dropped from the lineup because they didn't hold cards with the right branch of the union. A string section, an extra pianist, and two girl harpists (doing water effects which went with the swimming angle of the show) augmented the thinned-out Ellingtonians. It really did seem as if the end might be in sight.

In later years Duke always evaded too many questions about the year of 1955. The reason why he went to be a backing band to a summer show must have been primarily economic. He hadn't been drawing large audiences for some time. Around the college circuit, which was now an important factor in jazzmen's finances, the kids wanted small groups like those of Miles Davis and Dave Brubeck. Norman Granz was concentrating increasingly on Oscar Peterson and Ella Fitzgerald. Count Basie, too, was making a comeback and getting the dates which Duke was missing. Duke was even left out in the cold by the aqua-show format. They allowed a piano solo by him, and then his musicians took over with a house conductor in charge.

Ellington laconically observed that at least he used to get home early; and when he got there he worked. He wrote a play, *Man with Four Sides*, and 1955 was also the year of his composition, "Night Creature," commissioned for the radio orchestra, Symphony of the Air, and played by them in concert at Carnegie Hall with Duke's band. A lot of other symphony orchestras—Buffalo, Detroit, New Haven, the National—liked it and played it, but no one wanted to record it. The albums he'd made within the "jazz" slot which he was considered by record companies to inhabit hadn't been outstanding either artistically or commercially for some time. Who, the label executives argued, needed the expensive aggravation of paying for well over one hundred musicians playing Ellington's music "out of category"? Duke must have felt frustrated by this, and not until 1963 was "Night Creature" recorded: the first and second movements by the Stockholm Symphony Orchestra, and the third by the Paris Symphony—yet another example of Ellington's being nurtured by Europe rather than his own country.

This was the lowest point in Ellington's progress. His music *was* well below his best; he did appear to have lost some of his enthusiasm and drive. His responses, however, seemed in good order, and so was his luck. While parts of the music world bewailed his demise, he was already preparing his renaissance. The first step was the return of Johnny Hodges, whose band conveniently broke up while Duke was playing in the aqua show. An alert and powerhouse drummer, Sam Woodyard, joined the band to form a remarkable partnership with Duke's new bassist, Jimmy Woode, and to stay longer than any percussionist apart from Sonny Greer. Next, with the Capitol contract ended, Duke produced one album for a small label—"Historically Speaking, the Duke"—which ran through some of his tunes down the years and demonstrated, for those who wanted to hear, that the band (if not the composer) was on the climb once more. Finally, in early 1956, he moved back to Columbia Records and had the good fortune to be given Irving Townsend as his executive producer. Townsend wanted to make money for Columbia if he could, but there was also a side to his character which accepted that some part of the millions of dollars rolling in from Mitch Miller and other pop hit makers of the 1950s should be used to record distinguished contemporary composers; for Townsend that group included Ellington.

The two men met alone for the first time in a tent on July 7 at Newport, Rhode Island. The occasion couldn't have been more dramatic. It was among the most important tests of Ellington's whole life. The signs that he was coming back still hadn't convinced many of the doubters. The promoter of the Newport Jazz Festival, George Wein, hesitated to make Duke the star attraction, uncertain of his drawing power. Now, Ellington waited to take the stage, aware that he needed to succeed. Yet still, according to Townsend's account of the meeting, he could talk calmly about music—and business.

Duke wanted money up front for his recordings; he needed it to meet his payroll. He emphasized another point to Townsend: "But *my* loot comes from publishing. We have to make new music. Don't talk to me about no 'Sophisticated Ladies.' " Onstage, the band began playing "A Train." Duke would go on, as usual, in around a couple of minutes' time to catch the final few bars. He asked Townsend: "Did you know that a drum is a woman?"

"Is that the first album?"

Ellington laughed. "Man, that's not only the first album, that's the mother of all albums. That's the story of Madam Zajj." He repeated the phrase as he rose to leave. "Madam Zajj. She was always a lady, you know, but she was also a drum."

"Do we have a deal?" asked Townsend.

"Record companies don't like me. Are you sure I won't get fired?"

Townsend was emphatic he wouldn't. Ellington promised to see his visitor in New York the following week and sauntered toward the stage for the start of his opening set. He found an orchestra four musicians short of its full complement—a dire and inexcusable beginning for a band hoping for a comeback—played only a few numbers, and gave way to three hours of music by a host of other stars including Teddy Wilson, Anita O'Day, and Chico Hamilton. It was coming up to midnight, cold and moonless, when the full-strength Ellingtonians got back on the stand. Duke, believing he'd now be playing to a going-home crowd, had already complained to George Wein: "What are we, the animal act?" He opened up with his specially composed "Newport Jazz Festival Suite," played a couple more tunes, and, with some of the 10,000 crowd already leaving, coolly announced a piece he had written in Chicago in 1937, "Diminuendo and Crescendo in Blue." The sound was exotic. It proceeded for some minutes and suddenly—for no one knows quite how these moments of emotional artistry happen—the crowds had stopped at the exits, people were getting to their feet, fingers were beginning to snap on the offbeats.

Paul Gonsalves was the man at the solo mike, tearing off a fast but smoothly running passage on his tenor saxophone. He didn't stop. The offbeats became handclaps from the audience. At the side of the stage, drummer Jo Jones was pushing Gonsalves in his own way by shouting and hammering out a rhythm on the boards with a rolled-up newspaper. Gonsalves kept blowing. Soon everyone in the crowd was handclapping in a sweeping percussive chorus. They screamed "More, more!" Before long, hundreds were dancing and officials uneasily eyed the scene, fearing a riot. One man, urging Ellington to cool it from the wings, was reproved by Duke with a mild smile. "Don't be rude to the artists." And still Gonsalves played on through (if you believe the lowest, and probably correct, estimate) twenty-seven choruses or, according to Townsend 128 choruses. Gonsalves himself lost count, but he recalled that one night in Des Moines, Iowa, an offensive patron kept twitting him about the Newport feat. "I don't believe you can play that long like on the record," said the menace. So Gonsalves obliged with sixty-six choruses.

When Duke at last brought in the whole band that Newport night to sweep through the closing "Crescendo" section, the crowd exploded. He had to play four encores, and this remarkable emotional happening ended at past one in the morning. Thanks to the Columbia engineers, it all got safely recorded. The music, in a sense, wasn't the point. This was an event, a turning point, what Duke called "another of those major intersections" in his career. *Time* magazine put him on its cover, and splashed his achievement over several pages. Ellington was back with a vengeance, and the world knew it.

Oddly, although the bookings flowed in much more readily after Newport, the next major composition by Ellington, premiered on color television in 1957, was not among his best. This was "A Drum Is a Woman"—hence his typically bizarre conversation with Irving Townsend. It is a fantastic allegory endeavoring to span around half a century of music, tracing the history of jazz from its African origins, through the Caribbean to New Orleans, then to New York, and ultimately—for some odd reason—to the moon. "The Ballet of the Flying Saucers" is the title of one of the movements, which indicates how madly Ellington's imagination was moving at the time. The story line features jazz in the person of a beautiful woman, "Madam Zajj," who'd started life as an elaborately constructed drum before, magically, the transformation occurred. Ellington always thought "Drum" to be one of his supreme works. When I asked him in 1966 which music had given him most satisfaction in his life, I was told: "Of the big things, 'A Drum Is a Woman,' and some of my early songs. They're not big pop successes, you know, but in all of them you feel the weight of the joy." Most critics have, with some justice, felt differently about "Drum." The script, written by Duke, shows the naïve rather than the inspired side of his word-spinning, which often tended to be highly colorful and finely balanced somewhere between the beautiful and the banal. The humor is labored and the whole concept—originally suggested in 1941 by Orson Welles, according to Townsend— rather self-indulgent. The later products of his recording deal with Townsend were infinitely more rewarding.

The first, and most welcome, came also in 1957, hard on the heels of "A Drum Is a Woman." The work was a suite entitled "Such Sweet Thunder," musical vignettes based on Shakespearian characters "in miniature and caricature," including Lady Macbeth, Hamlet, Romeo and Juliet, Henry V, and Puck. It was important because it restored faith in Ellington both as composer and bandleader. There was wit, lush beauty, and evocative invention in every one of these portraits. The highly idiosyncratic nature of Ellington's writing for varied instrumental ensembles was the most striking aspect of the work, typified in the representation of Iago and the *Macbeth* witches (The Telecasters) by Harry Carney's baritone saxophone mixed with the trombones of Britt Woodman, John Sanders, and Quentin Jackson. At the same time, Ellington's soloists were triumphantly back in form, with the contrasting saxophones of Johnny Hodges and Paul Gonsalves warmly fluent in the roles of Juliet and Romeo on "The Star-Crossed Lovers," and Jimmy Hamilton playing rich-toned clarinet in the gravely imperial piece, "Sonnet for Caesar."

The genesis of the work was a typical example of the inspiration Ellington always drew from particular events and experiences in his life. He had seen Ann Hathaway's cottage, at Stratford-on-Avon in England, as long ago as 1933, but that was incidental. It was an invitation for the band to play at the Shakespeare Theatre in Stratford, Ontario, which fired his imagination. He saw many Shakespearian plays performed there, and afterwards Strayhorn and he read and reread all the plays as thoroughly as Duke had once gone through the Bible. They took their title from a line in *A Midsummer Night's Dream*—"I never heard so musical a discord, such sweet thunder"—a gloriously apt description of so many passages of their own music, and the inspiration which Shakespeare's words gave to Ellington was caught in the program notes he wrote. For provocative insight and relevance, Ellington's prose was rarely more persuasive, nor closer to a definitive statement of his personal musical philosophy:

> I have a great sympathy with Shakespeare because it seems to me that strong similarities can be established between a jazz performance and the production of a Shakespeare play—similarities between the producers, the artists, and the audiences. Basically, both groups face comparable problems in the reluctance of some participants to expose themselves and join the audience. Their hesitance is due, in both cases, to a misconception that the major supporters of both these artistic manifestations—Shakespeare and jazz—are people who have invested time and money in becoming experts.
>
> Many people feel this way about chamber music, too; they fear that as members of an audience, whether for Shakespeare, jazz, or chamber music, their reaction will reveal them as insufficiently informed, or possibly unaware of the sensitivities one must acquire to savor completely the subtleties of a performance. In the case of a jazz listener, he may be caught sitting next to an enthusiast and will be ashamed to admit his lack of familiarity with the names of the exponents. In all cases, the newcomer is afraid he will be looked upon as a square. (Nobody knows what a square is—it's just that nobody wants to *be* one.)

Anybody who listens to a beautifully performed symphony for the first time gains something from it. The next time he hears it, he gains more; when he hears the symphony for the hundredth time, he is benefited to the hundredth power. So it is with Shakespeare. The spectator can't get it all the first time; repeated viewings multiply the satisfaction.

There is a perfect parallel with jazz, where repeated listening makes for enjoyment. The Stratford Festival, by tying in top-grade jazz with its Shakespeare productions each season, is showing awareness of this.

There is an increasing interrelationship between the adherents to art forms in various fields. Contemporary jazz, for instance, has many enthusiastic listeners in its audience who are classical musicians of heroic stature. Indeed, some classical musicians in recent years have involved themselves with jazz as composers, soloists, or both. I am not pointing this out in any attempt to plead for tolerance, for jazz is not in need of tolerance, but of understanding and intelligent appreciation. Moreover, it is becoming increasingly difficult to decide where jazz starts or where it stops, where Tin Pan Alley begins and jazz ends, or even where the borderline lies between classical music and jazz. I feel there is no boundary line, and I see no place for one if my own feelings tell me a performance is good.

Any musician will agree that the final judgment of a musical performance lies in its immediate impact on the human ear, rather than in previous knowledge or academic study.

In the final analysis, whether it be Shakespeare or jazz, the only thing that counts is the emotional effect on the listener. Somehow, I suspect that if Shakespeare were alive today, he might be a jazz fan himself—he'd appreciate the combination of team spirit and informality, of academic knowledge and humor, of all the elements that go into a great jazz performance. And I am sure he would agree with the simple and axiomatic statement that is so important to all of us—when it sounds good, it *is* good.

The success of "Such Sweet Thunder" heralded a three-year period of most intensive activity for Ellington, either as sole composer or in formal association with Strayhorn. The lengthy copyright lists of his compositions show a number of variations on the Ellington/Strayhorn formula, often within a single suite or linked collection of pieces. The Shakespearian pieces are all jointly credited, as was "Royal Ancestry," written in 1957—a portrait, in three movements, of Ella Fitzgerald, with whom the orchestra recorded during the same year. Most numbers in *Jump for Joy* are given to Ellington alone, but in a couple Strayhorn is named as co-composer. By contrast, when Duke was invited by Otto Preminger to write his first complete movie score—for *Anatomy of a Murder* in 1959—Strayhorn's name was missing from the credits. He didn't, in fact, accompany Duke on location in Michigan for the film, but as Ellington observed later: "It all boiled down to the same thing whether he was there or not. He was always my consultant." Interestingly, the movie theme, called "I'm Gonna Go Fishin'," was a collaboration between Ellington and the songwriter and singer, Peggy Lee, who composed the lyrics.

As, in the 1940s, the annual Carnegie Hall concerts spurred Ellington to write a new major composition each year, so his regular appearances at festivals in the late 1950s provided another incentive. The public expected him to produce something special at these occasions. "Toot Suite" and "Idiom '59," both written for the Newport Festival, were examples of such works, excellent in their way, but scarcely among the greatest Ellingtonia. A strange example of petulant independence (or artistic bloody-mindedness) occurred at the Monterey Festival in California, which was the great rival of Newport on the East Coast. The Monterey coordinator, Jimmy Lyons, visited Duke in the Ellington band bus to discuss the music he'd be playing that night. Please, he asked Duke, would he *not* play the "Newport Festival Suite." Newport and Monterey were, after all, in hot competition as jazz venues. Ellington silently went on selecting clothes from his travelling wardrobe and later, once "A Train" had been played, announced a section of the "Newport Suite" as his very first selection. "Ellington," as Irving Townsend noted, "heard the advice of many, listened to the advice of few, took almost nobody's."

He made handsome amends to Monterey, however, with "Suite Thursday," commissioned for the festival and presented there on September 23, 1960. This four-part work runs at around half the length of "Such Sweet Thunder," but as an evocation of literary mood and character it's undoubtedly in the same class. Receiving indifferent critical notices at the festival itself, the later recording has increasingly come to be seen as one of Ellington's most attractive. For swing, coloring, and wit, it seems a perfectly acceptable musical parallel of John Steinbeck's story, *Sweet Thursday*, set in the novelist's favorite habitat: the smelly, shabby world of Monterey's declining fishery quarter, Cannery Row.

Today, Cannery Row is a smartened-up hook for tourists, full of clubs and boutiques. For Steinbeck, it was the habitat of "down and outs," individuals who often possessed hearts of gold and sturdily independent characters. Ellington picked up the point, explaining that as Steinbeck's chief character, Doc, had a theory that the octopus changed color depending on how the creature was feeling, so Cannery Row's denizens changed color too. The bum could turn out to be an angel, especially if given a decent suit of clean clothes. "Misfit Blues," "Schwipti," "Zweet Zurzday," and "Lay-By," the four parts of the suite, showed that Duke was as much a romantic as Steinbeck. The notes he made on the book, which he was apt to read aloud to visitors, shows the care he gave to understanding his author as, earlier, he had tried to understand Shakespeare.

> After the pilchards have been caught, the canneries shut down and the characters, judged by conventional standards, are a lot of social misfits who stay on for lack of anything else to do or any place to go. Steinbeck brings them alive and the mood evoked here is, I would say, gay and funny, sad and tragic, conveying through simple people and incidents the essence of human nobility touched with the ridiculous, which gives it reality.

With "Suite Thursday," however, Duke was inviting trouble. Program music—sounds intended to mirror and evoke particular scenes and situations—is always a difficult area for musical criticism. Rattling snare drums become the musical cliché for armies; electronic wind sounds in rock music today are similarly the stereotype that suggests outer space. Move away from these obvious effects, however, and musical patterns may conjure up totally idiosyncratic pictures in the mind of the listener. And when the light, swinging sounds of "Suite Thursday" were first heard at Monterey, they failed to impress any of the heavy critics with their relevance to Steinbeck or their relationship to each other. The leading magazines—*Time, Down Beat, Metronome*—all panned the suite in varying degrees.

Within months, such discord had turned into torrential praise once the recorded version was issued, which led the critic and Ellington chronicler, Stanley Dance, to observe tartly that jazz critics who clamor for more extended works still appear to lack the qualities needed to judge them at first hearing. He also pointed out that the word "suite" did not imply the formal development and variation of themes to be found in symphonies; from way back in classical music, suites had often consisted of varied and contrasting dance forms—just like Ellington's. Irving Townsend magisterially pointed out to the (*Down Beat*) critic who had failed to see any relationship between the four movements that "Suite Thursday" begins and ends with a minor-sixth interval, which recurs dozens of times throughout, "forming a striking theme for the suite."

Yet, to be fair to the critics, there were changes in "Suite Thursday" between its premiere at the festival and the recording of it a couple of weeks later. Ralph Gleason for one attested that every night for two weeks at a San Francisco night club, once the festival was over, Duke opened his program with the suite, and it could be heard changing and developing with each performance. That was the problem for critics; Ellington's music often didn't stay the same. He was re-creating it as he went along.

He loved nothing better at times than to mislead and mystify the world about his music, another way in which he retained as much of his privacy as he could. At the Monterey festival he held up a sheet of music in front of Ray Nance during a longish violin solo (a trick he performed on other occasions) and *Time* magazine made the obvious comment about last-minute music scribbled on scraps of paper, which was actually true of so many bits of Ellingtonia. In this case, however, the suite had been rehearsed for weeks before the premiere (even though it was later, as we've seen, to be changed again), and Ralph Gleason suspected that Nance had his eyes shut during the whole joke. Ellington enjoyed this kind of spoofery immensely; an Artful Dodger indeed.

All this musicological debate, and the swift volte-face of critical views, were indicative of the several ways in which "Suite Thursday" remains one of the most attractive curiosities in Ellington's career. The lineup for the recording, in October 1960, missed Johnny Hodges (ill at the time) and Britt Woodman, who were replaced by Paul Horn and Matthew Gee; the musical variety of pick-up men who have entered the band from time to time is remarkable. More significantly, Lawrence Brown, who had been free-lancing and playing as a CBS staff musician since the Hodges band broke up five years earlier, had rejoined Duke in 1960 during a season at the Riviera Hotel in Las Vegas which set new attendance records for the place. He took his place in a trombone section already strengthened by the acquisition of Mitchell "Booty" Wood, a former section man with Count Basie, in 1951. Brown was featured in "Zweet Zurzday," for which Duke provided a note describing the clarinet solo as "the beautiful dream . . . the fuzz of imagination" and Paul Gonsalves's tenor excursion as "the fog that clouds it." "Lay-By" consists almost entirely of Ray Nance playing violin, bowed and pizzicato, in one of his greatest solos. And the final surprise is that the original album came out with "Suite Thursday" backed by selections from Grieg's "Peer Gynt Suites, Nos. 1 and 2" in arrangements by Ellington and Strayhorn. "Swinging Suites by Edward E. and Edward G.," proclaimed the title on the sleeve.

At the time, that was less of a surprise, for the album had been closely preceded by another—recorded like the Grieg in mid-1960—on which Ellington and Strayhorn produced their inspired versions of Tchaikovsky's "Nutcracker Suite," the first time Duke had ever devoted an entire LP to arrangements of another composer's work. Alumni who'd been away for relatively short spells—Juan Tizol, Willie Cook on trumpet, and Sam Woodyard, now teamed with Aaron Bell on bass—were back in the band, as well as Brown, and all the musicians worked with great spirit to make a triumph out of humorously translating a classical composer into the Ellington style. The fun extended to the titles: "The Volga Vouty" (Russian Dance), "Sugar Rum Cherry" (Dance of the Sugar Plum Fairy), and "Arabesque Cookie" (Arabian Dance), which featured Russell Procope on bamboo flute, Juan Tizol on tambourine, and Harry Carney on bass clarinet.

Such bizarre instrumental combinations indicated the regal bravado with which Ellington and his orchestra approached the business of music-making. It was as if, since the renaissance at Newport four years earlier, they gave not a damn for anyone. Their worries were over; they could let their hair down; they were relaxed, easy, untroubled. Ellington may never have cared much what others thought about his music, as long as he felt it sounded right, but it was still necessary to be popular if he were to pay the bills and achieve his only priority—to keep his band together. That he could risk drawing the wrath of the uncomprehending upon his head by fiddling with the classics was indicative of his supreme self-confidence, as was his reaction to the blatant plagiarism of his train tune, "Happy-Go-Lucky Local," which suddenly appeared as a fast-earning rhythm-and-blues hit under another's name and title during this period. When he was urged to sue the offender, he said mildly: "We must be flattered, and just go and write something better."

In the event, most people loved his Tchaikovsky; his "Peer Gynt" adaptation made less of an impact, but it was as sympathetic and true to the spirit of the original as "The Nutcracker." One section, "Ase's Death," with the sombre beat of Sam Woodyard's drums underlining unique Ellington voicings for brass and reeds, movingly captures the mood of both composers.

It would be quite wrong, however, to see Ellington in this period only as a composer or re-creator of suites. He was churning out a string of more minor pieces all through the later 1950s and early 1960s. The titles are too many to list, but although most were credited to Duke alone, occasionally he "officially" collaborated with his musicians, as he had done back in the 1930s with Juan Tizol (on "Caravan") and Harry Carney (on "Rockin' in Rhythm"). Now, around the turn of the decade, there were joint creations with Johnny Hodges ("Without a Word of Complaint"), Clark Terry ("Dual Fuel" and "Launching Pad"), Paul Gonsalves ("The Line-Up"), and even with fairly short-term members like Matthew Gee ("The Swingers Get the Blues Too").

Apart from the creative spur which refound success seemed to have brought him since Newport, there was another change of emphasis in Ellington's life. He was travelling again, with renewed intensity. He'd never ceased travelling, of course, but the tempo had slowed down in the middle of the decade. Now the movement between engagements within the United States was becoming continual; soon, he was to move once more beyond America's frontiers. No longer, however, was he living in the age of ships and his beloved steam trains. As he once observed: "There's no romance in diesels." Since around 1950, he'd taken to travelling almost everywhere by car in America with Harry Carney, one of the pleasantest of men, and a sheet anchor of Duke's band, who took his duties as chauffeur very seriously indeed, keeping a notebook into which he entered

every expense—including ten-cent tolls on bridges and highways—all of which he later expected the boss to settle.

These drives with Carney were often made in the early hours,
straight after they had finished playing. They would travel at
least two hundred miles before they stopped, and sometimes the
distance would be as much as six hundred miles non-stop. Ellington used to call himself "The World's Greatest Navigator,"
but even he couldn't always guide the car to private dances; so
they would call up the local newspaper or keep on asking police
and service station attendants. Sometimes Duke would sleep,
sometimes he'd stay awake and scribble notes from time to time
or talk to Carney to keep him awake. He would also open up the
car window occasionally to make sure Carney never got too
drowsy. Duke must have worried when he did that, for Ellington's aversion to fresh air—he used to shut every window in a
room as soon as he entered—was as well known as his dislike of
standing up. "Never stand if you can sit," he'd say, "and never
sit if you can lie down—and don't ever cross your legs."

These endless car journeys yet again demonstrated the sheer
physical toughness of Ellington. He was coming up to his six-
tieth year as he continued to live at what might seem to most people a recklessly punishing pace. It's easy to smile tolerantly at
Ellington's symptoms of hypochondria—"I'm a doctor freak," he
used to put it—but in retrospect, his carefulness seems to have
been completely necessary were he to survive the stresses under
which he placed himself. He had above average health, of which
his renowned lowish pulse rate (a mere 47) was a symptom, and
his efforts to keep himself in good shape were a favorite topic for
more perceptive reporters down the years.

He travelled everywhere with a large bag stuffed with protein
and vitamin pills and various other potions, frequently administered. The bag, a present from Billy Strayhorn, was marked
"DR. E.K.E." "Duke," as one observer noted, "tends to mis-
trust his ability to stay well." His habit of telling people he never
knew how he felt till he'd asked his doctor, which extended to
stopping in the middle of a rehearsal to have his pulse taken,
was an idiosyncrasy with, sometimes, a serious side to it. Dr.
Arthur Logan, who was the man Duke called up through most of
his working life from every corner of the globe, caught planes
out of New York on several occasions to reach his patient fast

when Ellington sounded the alarm bells, rightly or wrongly. Duke was as wary of air conditioning as of open windows. "You know, I'm delicate," he explained. "My hair gets wet, the air conditioning hits it, and I get a sharp pain right down the middle of my back." He even worried about his feet; at odd moments he'd lie on his back and exercise them against any handy wall.

Ellington's relationship with Arthur Logan had developed remarkably since their first meeting in 1937. Logan and his wife, Marion, were closer to Duke than anyone except Ellington's family and, perhaps, Strayhorn. To Ellington he was a doctor, confessor, friend, and family. There can't be many autobiographies, like Duke's, which contain a chapter entitled "Doctors and Surgeons," devoted to the writer's operations and the medicos who had dealt with them. He was fond of quoting Logan, sometimes half seriously. "He said that the bug disease kills more people than any other disease in the world, and that it is therefore important not to let anything bug you. This is very closely related to one of my pet theories: that selfishness can be a virtue." As Ellington further explained to a fellow guest, a woman, at dinner one night in San Francisco, "Selfishness is essential to survival, and without survival we cannot protect those whom we love more than ourselves."

Ellington had few serious illnesses apart from that which ended his life, but such problems as he faced were treated with his customary briskness. He hadn't time to be ill for long. It was during the period of the band's revival, in 1958, that he began to get abdominal pains. Logan diagnosed gall bladder trouble and advised its removal. Within nine days of the operation, Ellington was back on the road with the band. Meeting one of the doctors who had been on the operating team some years later, Duke was told that patients were always overloaded with large doses of vitamin C after major surgery. Thereafter, Duke fed himself vitamin C daily. He was as pragmatic about his health as about most other things. With the program he faced as the decade was ending, he needed to be.

In October 1958, after an interval of eight years, Duke began to travel abroad again. He went, by sea as usual up to this time, to Britain to perform at an international arts festival in Leeds, which the Earl of Harewood, a cousin of Queen Elizabeth, had organized to put the Yorkshire city on the map culturally. For his brother, the Honorable Gerald Lascelles, a great jazz lover, Duke was an obvious choice and the visit was arranged. His concert was a great success and Duke resumed his acquaintance with the British Royal Family, being presented to the Queen and others, including Princess Margaret, for whom he had already composed a special piece, "Princess Blue," which was performed earlier that same year at the ball in Stratford, Ontario, which the Princess had attended. The Queen had not been able to attend the Ellington concert, but Prince Philip had. The Queen was quoted in the newspapers at the time as having told Duke, "I was so sorry I couldn't come to any of your concerts, but my husband tells me he thoroughly enjoyed himself when he listened to you this afternoon." Duke was charmed by all this, and when asked by the Queen how long it was since he'd been in Britain, he gave one of his most gallant replies: "1933, Your Majesty, years before you were born"—and he followed this by promising to write some music especially for the Queen, as he had already done for Princess Margaret. At a gracious party by candlelight during the same weekend, both Ellington and Strayhorn played piano solos in gratitude to their hosts.

The happiness of the occasion deeply affected Duke. After this meeting with the Queen and Prince Philip he said: "My impression of them was that of a very handsome couple, and Her Majesty's tone and demeanor were a reflection of great inner contentment." He also didn't forget his promise. In due course he created "The Queen's Suite," including the exquisite piano piece "Single Petal of a Rose," which was the only one of the suite's six sections ever played in public until Duke was close to his death.

The circumstances under which "Single Petal" was first conceived were typically Ellingtonian. His old friends, the Diamonds, had just moved into a new apartment off Park Lane as he arrived to play at Leeds. Later that month, an Allison baby grand piano arrived at the apartment—their housewarming present from Duke with a note, written by him from the Dorchester, which was (unusually) signed "Evie and Eddie." At a party given by the Diamonds for him, Duke sat at the piano to play. Observing that one petal had fallen from the bunch of roses on the piano, Duke produced the beautiful melody of "Single Petal" for the enraptured guests. Whether it was a genuine piece of instantaneous composition, or a theme which had been haunting him for some time, we'll never know; but as a piece of artistic drama, it was superb. He didn't compose it for the Queen, therefore, but for the Diamonds, although it was later placed with "The Queen's Suite." Other sections of the suite had their birth in experiences Ellington had on the road with Harry Carney which, sometimes, he relayed to Billy Strayhorn, who helped with the pieces and, indeed, is credited as co-composer. "Sunset and the Mocking Bird" was based on a phrase of birdsong heard whilst driving in Florida. "Lightning Bugs and Frogs" came from a nighttime view of insects in the sky, with frogs croaking on the banks of the Ohio River. "Northern Lights" reflected the majesty of the title's phenomenon, seen by Ellington and Carney while driving through Ontario.

"The Queen's Suite" was recorded at Ellington's own expense in April 1959, and pressed as a unique copy before being presented at Buckingham Palace for the Queen's ears alone. During the years which followed, Ellington always refused to allow the music to be issued despite continual pressure. Not until 1976 was it available on album, and the world heard for the first time just how brilliant it was—among Ellington's minor masterpieces, filled with the strange harmonies and felicitous reed colorings of his greatest years. "Single Petal" remains my favorite Ellington piano piece, a most beautiful vignette fit to be placed with the best of Chopin or Debussy.

During that 1958 visit, Duke played other public concerts, both in Britain and on the Continent, under the aegis of Norman Granz, with whom he now had a business association, perhaps surprisingly after the Hodges furore at the beginning of the decade. "There was nothing special about it," Granz explained. "Duke wanted to tour. 'How much?' was the only question. I gave him the right answer." For Britain, the visit was very special indeed, because the appalling Musicians' Union ban on Americans had finally been lifted after nearly twenty years. So dozens of journalists interviewed him, from the time he arrived on the *Ile de France* at Plymouth until his departure. They were fascinated by his lordliness and his style. Much was written about his glossy waved hair, the silk turbans which protected it, his wardrobe of 60 suits, 70 shirts, and 25 pairs of shoes, his travelling valet and barber. He favored initials on both the pockets and cuffs of his shirts and pajamas, as well as on his handkerchiefs. His trousers sometimes had three-inch turnups, and they often seemed not to fit him too well; he was forever hitching them up. He used to change his clothes down to the skin four times a night when he was playing, which was most nights, of course.

These details were engagingly recorded in 1958, as in other years, but the music critics were not so easily conquered. Some of them were very offhand about his programs because so many of the pieces chosen were "showcases" for soloists; they wanted, after so many years, to hear the orchestra more often as an ensemble. At least they were to be well satisfied in later years, for Duke produced a great deal of variety in his presentations of the 1960s and 1970s, and although his visits were not quite annual, there were very few years indeed between 1958 and his death when Britain and Europe did not see and hear the band. Duke was back again on tour in Europe in 1959, and in 1960 he came for a very specific reason. He had accepted his second assignment to write the score for a movie, *Paris Blues*, and, while he was in the French capital, he gained a further commission—to compose and record with French musicians the music for a classic play by Alain Lesage, *Turcaret*, which had not been performed since 1709.

He spent eight weeks in Paris. The city was, as always, a delight for him, and Duke appeared in high good humor most of the time. One contributory factor was certainly that he had recently met—during his Las Vegas season—a woman who was to become a frequent companion during the 1960s and a powerful influence upon his taste in many respects. Fernanda de Castro Monte was around forty when he met her, a tall, arrogantly striking blonde of great sophistication whom he always introduced as "Countess." She had seen a lot of the world, having lived in Algeria and Brazil and been a featured *chanteuse* for much of her life around Europe—she was, indeed, singing in Las Vegas when she and Duke bumped into each other. She spoke five languages (Duke was always impressed by multilingualism and by titles), and from the time he knew her, the sound of her voice frequently echoed around the various hotel suites he inhabited. His life style felt her impact. He dressed more casually. He took to drinking vodka, which she thought a smart beverage, and to eating caviar, which he used to say was good for anyone's virility. He was, indeed, rather a food faddist in his later years, beginning every day with a glass of plain hot water, but basically his tastes were ordinary. His enthusiasm over Chinese food was for Cantonese rather than Peking style: egg rolls, sweet and sour pork, and so forth. Steak, ham and eggs, English jams were what he really enjoyed—mixed with oddities like lettuce sprinkled with sugar—but for Fernanda he would at first eat or drink almost anything. In Britain, in France, in Spain, in Japan she would be found with him in the 1960s, one of his most constant (and, he later declared, expensive) followers.

"She did a lot for Edward," his sister, Ruth, said after his death. "She interpreted for him. She did research. She was very intellectual. I certainly liked her, as I liked anyone who could make Edward happy. She left New York after he died, and even when he was alive she wasn't here *all* the time. She was always going off to the Caribbean visiting with friends." Norman Granz's view is equally positive. "She was," said Granz, who often met her as she toured with Duke, "a very cultured woman. I took her shopping once in Madrid, and she knew the city intimately. She could introduce you to art dealers and such, and she was certainly very cognizant with art. I guess it was Johnny Hodges who first started calling her Contessa. Duke did well to have her, I think. It was much better than having some old groupie hanging around."

Meanwhile, as Duke travelled more and more, Evie Ellington lived her increasingly solitary life in the New York home she had made for him. By now they had an apartment which overlooked the Hudson River from the twenty-second floor of a fine new building on West End Avenue, with a layout of exotic plants and a fountain in the entrance hall. It was comfortable and spacious. Plates outside the front door bore both their names—Ellington and Ellis—without pretense to the world. An unusual room within their home, next to one of the bedrooms, was totally devoted to storing gifts which Ellington had received at various times down the years. They were catalogued in his mind so well that when intimates visited him, he would often dart into it and produce a present he'd been given years before to prove to the callers he hadn't forgotten their gesture. There was one offering he didn't leave in that room, however. Every day of his life he wore gold cuff links in the design of a heart pierced by an arrow. They came from Evie. He lost or had stolen from him many of these cuff links; until he died, Evie replaced them for Duke upon his birthday.

He was just as meticulous in many ways with Evie. As he moved around the world or dashed in and out of New York, he would telephone her, leave her beautiful notes, send mountains of flowers and fruit and candy. But the pattern of their life was beginning to change with Duke's longer absences, and Evie became more of a hermit, subject to bouts of depression. Very few people visited the apartment, for Duke had mostly kept her from the world. She was not used to giving parties, was an indifferent housekeeper—even the piano at the apartment wasn't good—and Ruth Ellington became more markedly her brother's public companion and hostess. The appearance of Fernanda de Castro Monte was only one more symptom of the changing scene.

Still, however, Fernanda was not the most important happening in Duke's life during 1960. That event was, oddly, the least expected. He was invited to play in the Palais de la Defense, the spacious exhibition centre of Paris, at a special Christmas Eve mass organized to raise funds for the renovation of two churches. Charles Trenet was among the many French artists taking part. For the occasion, attended by an estimated 100,000 people, Duke chose "Come Sunday," the spiritual section of "Black, Brown, and Beige." Never before had anyone conceived of placing Ellington's music in a formal religious context. He was moved and delighted. The consequences of that invitation during the last decade or so of his life were to be immense.

1960-1967
Unto All Nations

Mahalia Jackson, the great American gospel singer, always refused to sing in night clubs or to work with jazz groups. She
made an exception of the Ellington orchestra, however, recording an expanded version of "Black, Brown, and Beige" with him
in 1958 and, later that year, performing it at Newport. Asked
why, she explained that she did not view Duke's musicians as a
jazz band, but as a sacred institution.

The next decade was to provide an explanation of her words
which was both literal and metaphorical. Indeed, the careers of
few great artists can have had so explosive and so late a climactic
flowering as did Ellington's in that incredible ten years from
1960. It was a period crammed with so much artistic activity that
only the broadest brushstrokes can encompass it. He was past
sixty, and he acted in every way as though he realized the time
he had left was limited and he had to achieve everything which
was important to him quickly: to play in every country which
wanted him, to compose at forest-fire pace, to proclaim for the
first time openly to the world his faith in God, as well as to
emphasize again, in his own way, his powerful feelings about the
role and destiny of those who happened to be born with black
(or brown or beige) skins.

Time after time in these years, one would be invited to meet him in England or the United States, and find him slumped out on a couch in shorts or dressing gown, towel wound around his head, his handsome face pouched with fatigue. The reaction in the visitor on such occasions would be a mixture of concern and unease; one often felt like saying hello and disappearing again, not wanting to burden him any further. But he would usually insist you stay, then would sidle into an exposition on the latest piece of music he was writing—or pick up stray fragments of history from the past—and ultimately one would hazard the question of when he was going to give up this mad race around the globe. Then he would smile lazily and say, in many variants: "We do it because that's what we want to do. We continue to enjoy our greatest experience: to write music one day and to hear the band play it the next."

The use of the plural personal pronoun continued to be one of Duke's most misleadingly grandiose traits. In his mouth, it always seemed appropriate rather than vain; sometimes the "we" was royal, sometimes a form of modesty, sometimes it meant the orchestra or Strayhorn and himself. You could never be quite sure, for its inflection and significance could change within a sentence. It was another veil behind which Ellington could mischievously shelter. Similarly, the apparent modesty with which he called himself "the piano player" was double-edged; he knew, none better, that his audiences would regard it as exaggeration more than understatement.

During the 1960s, Ellington travelled incessantly; to Europe, to South America, to Africa, and all over the East, from Turkey to Japan. Not just quick hops, these journeys, but gruelling affairs from city to city, often occupying many weeks. His travels can virtually be traced by the music he wrote, for like the fiery tail of a comet compositions streamed from him to illuminate practically every trip. "The Far East Suite" (1964), "The Virgin Islands Suite" (1965), and "The Latin-American Suite" (1968) were such musical reflections. A less major undertaking, but still one of the most perfect compositions he ever wrote, was "La Plus Belle Africaine," created in the same year he represented the United States at the World Festival of Negro Arts in Dakar, Senegal, and in this case written *before* he went, not afterwards. No artist said with more succinctness, yet with typical individuality: Black is Beautiful.

Within the same period he continued to compose for movies

and for plays, to write the less considered melodies which had always been his hallmarks. The world, as if realizing that it ought to mark his genius while there was still time, began to bestow honors upon him, culminating in a gigantic celebration at the White House on his seventieth birthday. Ellington himself, however, was for long periods thinking only of the work which was in his view the most important of his life: the music for the Sacred Concerts which he started to perform in 1965 and continued until a few months before his death.

Duke could scarcely have faced this artistic Everest had he not been certain of his supporting team. There will forever be arguments about what was Ellington's "greatest" period, but he never led so settled a band with so many great musicians in its ranks as for most of the 1960s. Inevitably, it played badly on occasions. Ellington's music is so complex, so often verging on dissonance and exoticism, that one slightly off-key instrument can spoil it; several off-key instruments, or lax timekeeping, can wreck it. The band was very tired at times, its discipline fragile. Yet as the jazz chronicler, Joachim Berendt, observed: "Even a weak Ellington band was more impressive than other famous jazz bands at the top of their form." And at their customary best, the Ellingtonians remained unapproachable by any other orchestra in the world. Its record in the 1960s was scintillating.

The year of 1962 was important, for that great artist and idiosyncratic trumpeter, Cootie Williams, returned to the band after many adventures, including most recently a stint with Benny Goodman and Teddy Wilson. The warm brilliance of his playing, the way he could almost make the trumpet talk when he used a plunger mute, made him an audience-winning part of Ellington performances for the remainder of the band's history. George "Buster" Cooper joined the trombone section in the same year as Cootie Williams returned, and when Mercer Ellington took over one of the trumpet chairs in 1964, the band assumed the final shape of its later years.

Mercer was always a section man; he never took a solo. His value to his father was as organizer, a role which by this time, with the band's increasingly heavy schedules, was vital. Running this collection of wayward geniuses was in many ways a nightmare. The manager had, for example, to carry large sums of money with him around the world, usually in dollar bills, to pay the musicians as they travelled. Johnny Hodges insisted that he be paid on a daily basis, explaining to a questioner on one occasion: "I don't trust myself or anyone else. When I was pickin' cotton I used to get paid at the end of every day. I want to owe nothin' to anyone and have nothin' owed to me either." The cotton-picking reference was doubtless metaphorical, but Hodges's philosophy about money was just one instance of the problems Mercer faced. He turned out to be a very efficient manager, keeping the band to its timetables, getting cross with men who were late, controlling the exchequer firmly, and often making himself unpopular with some of the musicians as a result. His close proximity to his father, however, threw the ambivalent nature of their relationship into a sharper light.

Uneasy and rather strange it was, a juxtaposition which has inevitably been a cause of speculation and of exaggerated claims from protagonists on both sides. It was impossible at the time not to feel considerable sympathy for Mercer, who down the years had always seemed undecided whether to help maintain the band or to take his own directions. One suspects that Duke, a calculated dandy and a man dedicated to maintaining his youthful image, never quite knew how to handle the fact that he had a handsome but comparatively elderly-looking son. He once introduced Mercer to a visitor as "my father, Mercer," and the joke had too hard an edge to it to be funny.

Shortly after he'd talked Mercer out of being a successful disc jockey in New York and into the job of full-time band manager, Ellington explained it to me in these terms.

> It's not the easiest thing in the world leading this band. Other bands, they have books, they just call numbers and turn pages. This band's so highly personalized, so much of the character of the music's dictated by the men. There's no attitude, no discipline, nothing. I can't waste my energies being a disciplinarian. Outrageous things happen, and then they come back and blow their ass off, play like angels, and I forget about it. So you can see we *need* Mercer. I knew he'd been off his horn for a long time and he'd lost his chops, but he can get by, and you know I've had so many managers turn left on me. I thought if anyone else is going to steal money off me, I'd keep it in the family. This band's such a big investment—in time and everything—and we want it to go on.

Again, the attempt at humor—considering it's his son he's referring to—is strained and ill-judged. Ellington said something similar in the autobiography he completed not long before he died, but simultaneously he pays a straightforward tribute to Mercer, a son "dedicated to maintaining the lustre of his father's image," proud of the band, a great discoverer of instrumental and vocal talent. Duke was, in fact, always praising Mercer's part in helping to develop musicians for him, from Billy Strayhorn in the early days to Harold Ashby, Norris Turney, and Harold Minerve (all reedmen), drummer Rufus Jones, and bassist Joe Benjamin during the last years of the orchestra's existence.

Why did Mercer decide to join the band permanently in 1964? A few months after taking the step, he had this to say:

> I just decided to put an end to going upstream, and for the first time I decided I could be useful to the band. My own band had been playing Ellington's stuff all the time, anyway, and I suppose there's a little fear involved here. I just couldn't stand the comparison. Now my future lies in helping the band. I'm here to stay.

So it proved. Mercer never let the band down, spent a great deal of time copying out the tattered old band parts in the latter 1960s, and was generally so useful that Duke undoubtedly owed him a debt for getting the band through the tremendous years which remained, although he seemed eternally to defer the decision on how to treat their relationship. He never mentioned Mercer's presence within the band from the stage. Ellington, as was his later wont, would stay apart from his musicians when travelling—in the Dorchester in London, whilst his men were around the corner at the Washington—and Mercer would be found with the band rather than with his father.

Duke said different things at different times, but in retrospect the truth may be that Ellington would sooner not have had Mercer in the music business at all. On more than one occasion he said that Mercer shouldn't be "scratching around" in music when he could have built an independent career for himself in electrical engineering. He disliked Mercer's being a disc jockey, feeling that it wasn't good enough for an Ellington, and it's likely that Duke's behavior toward Mercer ultimately sprang from the fact that his son wasn't as brilliant a musician (or, perhaps, was *almost* as brilliant a musician) as he was. He'd pushed Mercer toward music, and now his son hadn't reached the standards

Duke demanded. Ellington was forever impatient of anything but the absolute best. Once he simply upped and left the room immediately his teen-aged nephew, Stephen James, started playing a tape, made by some of the band, featuring a composition by James. He was roundly scolded by his sister, Ruth, Stephen's mother, for that instance of unconcern.

Yet, once Mercer came to him as road manager, Duke must have been grateful in many ways. The loser was Evie Ellington. She was close to Mercer, he to her; now she would be even lonelier in the apartment overlooking the Hudson River on West End Avenue whilst Duke was free to steam through the crowded years from 1964 with a family lieutenant and a virtually settled lineup. Only in the rhythm section of the band did many changes occur; for the rest, the typical Ellington team during the 1960s was this:

Reeds: Johnny Hodges (alto saxophone), Russell Procope (alto saxophone/clarinet), Jimmy Hamilton (tenor saxophone/clarinet), Paul Gonsalves (tenor saxophone), Harry Carney (baritone saxophone/clarinet/bass clarinet).

Trumpets: Cootie Williams, Cat Anderson, Mercer Ellington, Herbie Jones—with, for a period, Ray Nance (trumpet/violin).

Trombones: Lawrence Brown, Buster Cooper, Chuck Connors.

Sam Woodyard was the long-serving drummer of the period, with Rufus Jones, alias "Speedy," appearing in the later 1960s. John Lamb, the bassist, was ultimately succeeded by Jeff Castleman and Joe Benjamin.

Ellington spent the opening years of the decade limbering up, as it were, for the main events to come. To 1961 and 1962 belong a number of delightful recording curiosities: a joint endeavor between Duke and the Count Basie band; two albums by Louis Armstrong's band with Duke on piano; a trio album ("Money Jungle") with the leading modern musicians, Charlie Mingus (bass) and Max Roach (drums); a session with the father of jazz tenor sax, Coleman Hawkins, and another in which Duke and the more modern tenor saxist, John Coltrane, alternated with each other's rhythm sections. There was an immensely successful European tour organized by Norman Granz in 1962, a year in which Duke also gave a piano recital at the Museum of Modern Art in New York. The band was back in Europe in 1963, and these were, in a sense, vintage Ellington years, when so many people formed their impressions of this incredible artistic phenomenon.

"Going to his hotel suite was like visiting a medieval court," recalled Steve Allen of the BBC. "There'd be all these punters milling about, dropping in off the street, and as soon as they arrived Duke would ask them if they were hungry, and steaks would keep pouring into the room like there was no tomorrow. And then a copyist would arrive, and Duke would say something like 'Hey—say hello to Steve Allen, and show him the size of your feet.' The guy would sit down and get to work, and the copying was *so* slow because Duke would always be calling out 'let me hear that.' God knows how anything ever got done—it was an absolute pantomime. Tubby Hayes once told me that very few correct Ellington parts ever seemed to be around the stands. Often the guys were just shuffling bits of paper."

During his 1963 visit, Ellington—as usual—couldn't please all the people all the time. During an interview, Humphrey Lyttelton raised with Duke the accusations of some people that at times he was "commercial." To which Ellington, with finely majestic irony, answered: "I don't understand how this thing that people call 'jazz' takes precedence over me." Lyttelton also asked him if he had lost sleep over what the critics said, and again the reply was typically Ellingtonian. "I wish I did—I'd love to enjoy some of that exquisite suffering. But I'm too busy thinking about what I'm doing tomorrow." More serious was his reply to a university student, who asked him about his special likes and dislikes in jazz and other music. "I like 100 percent of Tatum, 100 percent of Bechet, about 100 percent of Oscar Peterson, 100 percent of Delius, Stravinsky, Debussy. If I don't like 100 percent of Ravel, I guess it's because I haven't listened too well to some things."

In artistic terms, 1963 was a watershed—the year when it became obvious that something quite special was beginning to happen to Ellington. Within a relatively short period he conceived and composed a major show, *My People,* wrote the music for a production of *Timon of Athens* at the Stratford, Ontario, Shakespearian festival, and led his band on the longest and most bizarre tour it had yet undertaken through the Middle East, Afghanistan, India, Pakistan, and Ceylon. And even these events were only the surface signs of what Ellington was involved in. Norman Granz was pushing the idea of a film of Duke's life, with Sidney Poitier as the likely star. "We had people in Hollywood very excited," said Granz. "It was to be a story which paralleled the gangster era—when the kind of clubs he played in were controlled by the gangs. The big problem was to get Duke to sit down and tell the story! I kept urging him to take a three-month layoff and do it. I tried for six months, but then it fell apart. He had this terrible side to him. Don't take that myth of graciousness like some people tell it. He could be the very opposite." Duke also wrote around this time a version of a quaint fantasy, *Queenie Pie*, which verged on opera. "I have a script of it," said Granz, "so although it may have been worked on further later in his life, it originated far earlier. It was written with Ella Fitzgerald in mind, so it never happened." In retrospect, it's hard to see how Duke could have fitted in much more, anyway, for *My People* alone was a huge task.

In 1963 the hundredth anniversary year of the Emancipation Proclamation which ended slavery in the United States was reached, and it was marked by a major exposition, "A Century of Negro Progress," held in Chicago. President John F. Kennedy sounded its keynote in a letter which might have been written to express Ellington's own philosophy: "It will expose for all to see the significant contribution of the American Negro to the cultural, scientific, and political growth of the Nation at home and in the world over the past century. It will further interracial understanding and hasten the coming time of equal opportunity for all citizens of these United States." When Duke was invited to stage, in Chicago, the show which turned into *My People*, he regarded it as an immensely important honor. Yet he was also committed to *Timon of Athens*.

So, for a spell, Ellington bounced backwards and forwards between Chicago, New York, and Stratford, speeding off between-times to lead the band on one-night stands. While his musicians rehearsed the *Timon* music at Stratford, Duke would be in the theatre watching the actors at work—a valuable exercise for him since he was doing everything for *My People*. He composed all the music, words, and orchestrations, as well as directing the show and appearing in it. He even ended up choreographing the opening sequence on the gigantic stage, 90 feet by 60 feet. Ellington recalled how he did it:

For the opening, I would have a boy and a girl dancing at the extreme back end of the elevation—a sort of Afro dance. Then black out, fade up to green as backdrop silhouettes the dancers; fade up amber cross lights at the point where the boy is doing the head-rolling thing à la Geoffrey Holder; slow fade to black, and first slowly cross orchestra pit with ambers, purples, and reds, and then quickly bright up. Instead of two tiny figures in the distance, the audience was suddenly looking at forty-eight giant hands rising up out of the dark, towering over them on the orchestra pit elevator. Some were shocked by the silhouette and even cried out in fright.

The music was a development of Ellington's renowned suite of 1943, "Black, Brown, and Beige," with the shape of the show split roughly into two sections representative of the spirituals and the blues, before two pieces—"King Fit the Battle of Alabam" and "What Color Is Virtue?"—created a climax by referring in direct terms to the modern struggle for civil rights. The "Virtue" song was especially beautiful, its meaning poignantly obvious: "King Fit" was a comment on the racial struggle in Birmingham, Alabama, and the famous intervention there by Martin Luther King. First recited by Ellington at the Newport Festival, it became a choral work in *My People*. The biblical walls of Jericho, which of course fell down, were equated in the show with the white police chief, Bull Connor, and the fire hoses and police dogs he directed against blacks claiming their rights in schools and buses. "Bull jumped nasty, ghastly, nasty" proclaimed the words before other verses, of which these are typical:

> Bull turned the hoses on the church people,
> Church people, ol' church people,
> Bull turned the hoses on the church people,
> And the water came splashing, dashing, crashing.

> Freedom rider, ride,
> Freedom rider, go to town,
> Y'all and us gonna git on the bus,
> Y'all aboard, sit down, sit tight, sit down!

> Sit down, baby,
> Sit down and sit tight,
> Go to that school, don't be no fool,
> Sit down, be cool, be cool.

Ellington may have seemed, as Alistair Cooke once pointed out, a man "strangely apart from the troubles and recent turmoil of his race," but no one could have jumped feet first into the arena more emphatically than he in *My People*. Musically, it was a beautiful and dramatic piece of work, with well-known pieces like "Come Sunday" set alongside newer themes. It was performed by four solo singers, including the gorgeous Joya Sherrill, a choir, two companies of dancers, and a sixteen-piece band led by Jimmy Jones and containing nine past or present Ellingtonians. Duke himself appeared at one stage as a soapbox orator, addressing the audience on the subject of *My People*, and, significantly for the Sacred Concerts in the future, there was a fantastic fast tap dance by Bunny Briggs, "David Danced," to illustrate the reference in the Second Book of Samuel, "David danced before the Lord with all his might."

The show was not intended to be a long-runner, for Duke had other huge commitments to fulfill. It opened on August 16, 1963, won a wide measure of critical acclaim—"a show that dovetailed music, dance, theatre, and social criticism in a unique and stimulating fashion," said the *Saturday Review*—and played only until September 2. Ellington thus had only a few days to prepare for a major tour which the State Department had requested him to make. On September 6 the band headed for Damascus. During the next two months or so, playing around four concerts a week, attending receptions, press conferences, lectures, the Ellington caravan passed through Amman, Jerusalem, Beirut, Kabul (Afghanistan), Delhi, Hyderabad, Bangalore, Madras, Bombay, Calcutta, Colombo, Dacca, Lahore, Karachi, Teheran, Isfahan, Abadan, Kuwait, Baghdad, and Ankara. In cultural or any other terms, it was one of the most remarkable journeys ever made.

The Ellington musicians played their repertoire, concentrating chiefly for these new audiences on well-tried material like "Mood Indigo," "Caravan," "A Train," "Things Ain't What They Used to Be," "Diminuendo and Crescendo in Blue," in a bizarre collection of settings: a racecourse in Colombo, a hotel courtyard in Calcutta, a polo field in Kabul (where Duke heard wolves howling outside the city), a 6,000-seat Roman amphitheatre in Amman. In general they were greeted with warmth and great acclaim, and Ellington was especially intrigued that a dozen members of the Royal Family turned out to greet him in Kabul, including the Victor of Kabul, Lemar-i-Ali Marshal Shah Wali, whose finger-snapping, according to Duke, kept time with his own. Some of the reporting of the tour had an exotic freshness about it which is very appealing to Western minds. The *Indian Express* said of the visit to Madras, which Duke missed because of illness:

> All music is praise of the Lord. Jazz, which some people cannot or will not understand, the real jazz form of a spiritual soil, is truly the musical psalms of the twentieth-century man's torment in the tigerish growl of the trumpet. God's wrath and mercy are in the demonic drumbeat and the milk-smooth sound of the saxophone. . . . The Ellingtonians played with startling existentialistic freshness, heartfelt profundity, and an interlinked unity of various individual skills. They played for people in love. The performance at Madras was a triumph for the band in its high-pressure harmony and hallelujah of groin-grinding surrealistic tension.

It was in Madras that Ellington met Arthur Logan, who flew out with medicines to see his patient after Duke had spent some days in the hospital with a temperature probably induced by sunstroke. The change from climate to climate must have strained him as it did the band, who were rushing around shopping in every place they touched. Duke never spared himself at any stage of the tour. He gave lecture-demonstrations as well as concerts, and visited many of the sights—from a display of ancient Indian instruments in Delhi to a ruined palace in Ctesiphon, near Baghdad, where he not only did the usual tourist thing of drinking coffee and smoking a water pipe, but performed the less common trick of pushing a large cogged wheel used for grinding corn. As was his custom, however, he relied upon Billy Strayhorn to feed him information on what he failed to see.

Occasionally the harmony of the tour was marred. A tart questioner at a press conference in Delhi pressed him heavily about America's racial problems. Ellington went along with him for a time, pointing out that America at least had a society which allowed the news of its racial incidents to reach the world outside, and then—with the memory of "King Fit the Battle of Alabam" and *My People* fresh in his mind—delivered this anecdote on the subject of Martin Luther King:

> When I saw him just before I left Chicago a few weeks ago, he was coming down Michigan Avenue. I waved to him, and in order for

him to say hello to me, he had to have his chauffeur stop this long Cadillac. An aide got out and opened the door, and two motor policemen in front of the car, and two more behind, had to stop so that he could get out and shake hands with me. This is the way the man lives and travels who is representing that oppressed race, so the standards are not the same every place in the world. They vary according to where you are.

As Ellington was speaking, he may also have recalled that around this time—October 1963—his granddaughter, Mercedes, was making history of a kind in the United States. At the age of twenty-four, Mercer Ellington's daughter became the first black woman to dance in a showgirl line during a nationwide TV show.

In Baghdad, Ellington and the band were hustled back to their hotel after their concert. During the night, jets strafed the presidential palace and the homes of some government officials, troops moved, and in the morning there was a new regime, with the border closed. When it opened again, the party flew via Beirut and Cyprus to Ankara, arriving on November 22, with concerts in Turkey, Cyprus, Egypt, and Greece still to come. Ellington went to an Embassy reception and retired with Strayhorn to have dinner in his hotel room. He had, he recalled, just said grace when a telephone call announced an urgent visitor. Within a minute or so, Ellington knew that John Kennedy had been assassinated. Like the rest of the world, Duke was numbed. The remainder of the tour was called off and the caravan returned mournfully to New York.

When I met him early the next year during yet another tour of Europe, Ellington was still filled with enthusiasm and awe for his oriental travels. True to his artistic methods, it was the people he knew, the places he saw, the sounds he heard, the books and plays he was moved by which inspired his major compositions. The East was no exception, yet he was in no hurry to complete his musical reflections on the subject, even though he was playing at his concerts some of the sketches he was working on, as well as extracts from "Harlem" and his *Timon of Athens* music. Asking him how far he'd got with the suite based on his oriental travels, this was his reply:

> We did nothing while we were out there. We thought we'd be too strongly influenced by the exact melodies of Eastern music. So we waited till we got back, let it roll around, undergo a chemical

> change, and then seep out on paper. It's seeping right now, but I've no idea how long it will be. We've got too many ideas, really—it's confusing after going to all those old cities. The Taj Mahal—have you ever seen those lizards on the roof? They're there to protect you from the insects. But when you first look up and see them, you don't think a damn thing about music. All you can think is, Man! There are lizards on that roof!

Did Ellington actually *see* the Taj? Perhaps not, if several of those on the tour are to be believed. It was quite possibly another case of Strayhorn acting as his eyes and ears. Duke was helped a great deal during his whole career; he swept up ideas, statements, descriptions into his imagination, and it came out as pure Ellingtonia. Together, he and Strayhorn worked on their reflections of the East during 1964 and 1965, but it was not until December 1966 that he recorded "The Far East Suite," and by this time he'd visited Japan as well—in both 1964 and 1966—and rounded off his impressions of that 1963 tour with a section paralleling later travels, "Ad Lib on Nippon." The East, however, had certainly been good for Ellington. "Sometimes," he said, "I felt it was *this* world upside down. The look of the natural country is so unlike ours and the very contours of the earth seem to be different. The smell, the vastness, the birds, and the exotic beauty of all these countries make a great inspiration." He confessed to finding a certain monotony and sameness in the music, all the way from Arabia to Ceylon, and he didn't want to copy either rhythms or scales, but rather to *suggest* them.

His method was obviously right. The suite finally produced by Ellington and Strayhorn is among the finest and wittiest of all their major compositions, especially for the sureness with which the music suggests the feeling of each place or incident they are recalling, and the masterly choice of solos. When they began playing the suite at concerts, Duke delighted in introducing the piece called "Bluebird of Delhi," originally called "Mynah," with the story that it was named in memory of the bird which used to sing a pretty lick (now given to Jimmy Hamilton's clarinet) in Strayhorn's room. Strayhorn would talk to the bird every day, but got nowhere until he was leaving the room and the city, when he received from the mynah a low raspberry (fruitily played by trombone in the suite, inevitably) to speed him on his way. In total contrast was an exquisite solo from the alto sax-

ophone of Johnny Hodges on "Isfahan," a city called the Pearl of
Persia. "It is a place where everything is poetry," said Duke.
"They meet you at the airport with poetry and you go away with
poetry."

Interestingly, an incident in the East showed very clearly the
character of Ellington and the problems of taking his particular
caravan around the world. During their 1966 tour of Japan,
Mercer came in alarm to his father one afternoon in Fukuoka to
report that $7,500 in bills had vanished from his hotel room.
Duke later claimed he'd been expecting bad news because a few
minutes earlier he'd heard the public square carillon playing
"Way Down upon the Swanee River." Laughing the incident off,
he joked: " 'Way Down upon the Swanee River' in Fukuoka? I
just knew something had to be wrong!"

The loss of the money was no joke, however. Stephen James,
Duke's nephew, recalled how in the plane on the way home he
noticed a large bulge under the shirt of one of the party—not a
musician. So he told Ellington. When they landed at Kennedy
Airport, Duke asked immigration officials to search the man, and
most of the payroll was found on him. Ellington refused to
prefer charges, and didn't even dismiss the offender. Duke was,
indeed, infinitely tolerant of many of the people around him. At
least two of the entourage at various times down the years,
Cress Courtney and Al Celley—neither involved in the payroll
incident—departed from the family and were, later, brought
back into the fold.

The journeys to the East only whetted Ellington's appetite for
more travel and more work. He was back in Europe early in
1965, and to everyone's delight was playing "Black, Brown, and
Beige" in a thirty-minute version—short of the original forty-
five-minute score, but still a substantial restatement of his masterpiece. He wrote, almost as an afterthought, a shorter four-
part work, "The Virgin Islands Suite," after the band played
there in April 1965. "The people get into a comfortable groove,
never aggressive—no theatrical-type animation is needed. I
hope we have expressed some of these attitudes in our music,"
Duke observed when he presented the suite, which favors ca-
lypso-flavored rhythms in "Island Virgin," a stunning violin obbligato from Ray Nance set against the rich sound of the sax
section in "Fiddle on the Diddle," and, in "Jungle Kitty," a very
unusual role for Cat Anderson, who ignores the stratosphere in

favor of moody, choked half-valve trumpet effects; a witty and evocative, rather than fearsome, jungle prowler he is. In a less major fashion, Duke was turning out versions of Beatles hits, salutes to Walt Disney and to his fellow big-band leaders, and selections of all kinds for the band, of which "Afro-Bossa," belonging to 1963, was another outstanding piece of work.

Representative of his crowded program was a period of a few days during the summer of 1965. A fortunate meeting in Stockholm one January with Arthur Fiedler, conductor of the Boston Pops Orchestra, led to a collaboration on July 28 when Duke, supported by his former sideman, Louis Bellson, on drums, and John Lamb on bass, played with Fiedler and the orchestra at the annual festival held on the 210-acre Tanglewood estate in Massachusetts. Happily, the concert, with Ellington in scintillating form as featured pianist, was recorded. He went through versions of tunes from the early days, like "Mood Indigo," and thence down the years all the way up to the march from his *Timon of Athens* suite. Within three days he was very deeply involved in a concert at Lincoln Center in New York. He premiered "The Golden Broom and the Green Apple," a "modern allegory" in three parts specially written for the New York Philharmonic Orchestra, also played piano in his "New World a-Comin'," and was the narrator in Aaron Copland's "Preamble for a Solemn Occasion," performed that night in memory of Adlai Stevenson, the Democratic statesman who had twice run against Dwight D. Eisenhower for the presidency.

As he performed at this concert, Ellington was already planning what was to him the most important event of the year and of his life. He had been invited by the Dean of Grace Cathedral in San Francisco to play a concert of sacred music there as a contribution to the Episcopalian cathedral's year of events celebrating its completion and consecration, and he jumped at the chance.

Sacred music to him it was, but it had little to do with sixteenth-century psalmery, nor was it a jazzed-up traditional mass, a form which at the time was coming into fashion. At the Antibes Jazz Festival earlier in the summer, for example, Catholic priests had joined a black gospel choir in the celebration of mass. Instead, Duke's thoughts reached back to the medieval juggler who offered up his praise to God by putting on a performance of his skills in front of a statue of the Virgin Mary. And so what he produced beneath the high-vaulted roof of the big church on Nob Hill on the evening of September 16 was modern American music, Negro folk music, above all Ellington music, and inevitably he reached back to the seedbed of *My People* for much of it.

There were no fewer than three versions of "Come Sunday"— the usual solo from Johnny Hodges, then a choral arrangement, and, finally, a completely new setting for the young Detroit gospel singer, Esther Merrill, for whom the concert was a triumph. Bunny Briggs danced his mighty "David" piece at a blistering pace, with the rhythm section sprinting and the saxes pacing a softly chanting choir. Duke played "New World a-Comin'," and among many other delights was a new Ellington composition, "In the Beginning God," springing from the phrase which opens the King James version of the Bible. I was, unhappily, not there that first night, but later I often heard Harry Carney's baritone saxophone announce the six tones which match the syllables of the phrase, the notes reverberating majestically around the arches and domes of several cathedrals. It's an awesome sound which genuinely combines reverence, dignity, and wonder, a song of praise strictly in Ellington's own terms, yet with a universality that has no category.

For Stanley Dance it seemed like a miracle to see Hodges and Cootie and Cat and Gonsalves sitting there in the cathedral chancel, and then to hear them playing just the way they always did. In a way it was a miracle. That first concert was to be repeated many times thereafter—including English performances at Coventry Cathedral and at Cambridge—in churches of many denominations until, later in the decade, Duke produced an entirely new set of works for further Sacred Concerts. The seriousness with which he viewed these occasions was unmistakable. I remember him standing admiringly before that stunning altar tapestry of Graham Sutherland's when he came to Coventry in the following year first to perform a Sacred Concert in England. "This music," he said, very simply, "is the most important thing I've ever done or am ever likely to do. This is personal, not career. Now I can say out loud to all the world what I've been saying to myself for years on my knees." Yet whatever he was to say or to write for church occasions later, nothing better expressed what he had in his mind than the moving foreword he produced for the Grace Cathedral concert program that night of Thursday, September 16, 1965.

In this world we presume many ambitions. We make many observations such as (a) everyone's aloneness (there really are no categories, you know. Everyone is so alone—the basic, essential state of humankind); (b) the paradox that is communication—the built-in answer to that feeling of aloneness.

Communication itself is what baffles the multitude. It is both so difficult and so simple. Of all man's fears, I think men are most afraid of being what they are—in direct communication with the world at large. They fear reprisals, the most personal of which is that they "won't be understood."

How can anyone expect to be understood unless he presents his thoughts with complete honesty? This situation is unfair because it asks too much of the world. In effect, we say, "I don't dare show you what I am because I don't trust you for a minute but please love me anyway because I do need you to. And, of course, if you don't love me anyway, you're a dirty dog, just as I suspected, so I was right in the first place." Yet, every time God's children have thrown away fear in pursuit of honesty—trying to communicate themselves, understood or not—miracles have happened.

As I travel from place to place by car, bus, train, plane . . . taking rhythm to the dancers, harmony to the romantic, melody to the nostalgic, gratitude to the listener . . . receiving praise, applause, and handshakes, and at the same time, doing the thing I like to do, I feel that I am most fortunate because I know that God has blessed my timing, without which nothing could have happened—the right time or place or with the right people. The four must converge. Thank God.

For instance, my being invited by Dean Bartlett and the Reverend John S. Yaryan to participate at Grace Cathedral.

I am not concerned with what it costs. I want the best of everything possible. I want the best musicians, the best singers and coaches—amateur or professional—and I want them to give the best they have. I want all the help I can get and to say what I hope I am good enough to say because this is the performance of all performances—God willing.

Wisdom is something that man partially enjoys—One and only One has all the wisdom. God has total understanding. There are some people who speak one language and some who speak many languages. Every man prays in his own language, and there is no language that God does not understand.

The great organ here accompanies worship—sometimes the symphony or part of the symphony—and what could seem more suitable than a harp solo? It has been said once that a man, who could not play the organ or any of the instruments of the symphony, accompanied his worship by juggling. He was not the world's greatest juggler but it was the one thing he did best. And so it was accepted by God.

I believe that no matter how highly skilled a drummer or saxophonist might be, that if this is the thing he does best, and he offers it sincerely from the heart in—or as accompaniment to—his worship, he will not be unacceptable because of lack of skill or of the instrument upon which he makes his demonstration, be it pipe or tom-tom.

If a man is troubled, he moans and cries when he worships. When a man feels that that which he enjoys in this life is only because of the grace of God, he rejoices, he sings, and sometimes dances (and so it was with David in spite of his wife's prudishness).

In this program, you may hear a wide variety of statements without words, and I think you should know that if it is phrase with six tones, it symbolizes the six syllables in the first four words of the Bible, "In the beginning God," which is our theme. We say it many times . . . many ways.

There was a perfect coda to that Grace Cathedral concert, which illustrated that, as Ellington denied categories in music, so, too, there were for him no categories in occasions either. The following Saturday, the orchestra was the star turn at the final night of the Monterey Festival, and by the time their program was moving toward its close after ninety minutes of music, it was early Sunday morning. Esther Merrill took the stage with the band to sing "Tell Me It's the Truth," "Come Sunday," and "The Lord's Prayer," and her gospel zeal so seized the audience that, with the police pushing for the occasion to end, they insisted that Bunny Briggs dance his "David," and a final joyous jam on "Rockin' in Rhythm" saw ex-Ellingtonians like Clark Terry, Rex Stewart, and Dizzy Gillespie playing along with the band.

Ellington must have been sublimely happy at this stage of his career. Apart from having achieved so many of his musical and spiritual ambitions, Duke was receiving honors of every kind. Yet he was also missing some, and he could still be hurt. During May of the same year there had occurred a national furore when the Advisory Board of the Pulitzer Prize Committee rejected a unanimous recommendation from its music jury for Duke to be awarded a special citation. Two members of the jury, Winthrop Sargeant and Ronald Eyer, immediately resigned amid widespread mutterings about racial prejudice. Rather than racialism, one suspects the likelier reason was either straightforward obtuseness or pure ignorance about Duke's true stature. Perhaps the Advisory Board felt they couldn't seriously countenance the claims of a musician who, around the same time he was composing "Black, Brown, and Beige," turned out a minor piece called "Hit Me with a Hot Note and Watch Me Bounce," successor to "You Gave Me the Gate and I'm Swinging," "I'm Slappin' Seventh Avenue with the Sole of My Shoe," "I've Got to Be a Rug Cutter," and several hundred less epic ditties; who entitled one of his Shakespearian pieces "Sonnet to Hank Cinq" and another "Lady Mac," observing when he produced it: "Though she was a lady of noble birth, we suspect there was a little ragtime in her soul."

Whatever the reasons, the Ellington reaction which the world observed was characteristic of his wit, his cool, his apparently infinite tolerance for human failings and follies, and of the impossibility of ever putting him down. "Fate is being kind to me," he said. "Fate doesn't want me to be too famous too young." Yet that suave shrug-of-the-shoulders disguised the very real wounds which the incident inflicted upon Ellington. He could be very touchy indeed about his image at this period, as an incident in New York demonstrated.

Duke was booked into a night club, Basin Street East, for a three-week season late in the year on the same bill as the singer Mel Tormé, himself a peerless artist with a tendency to be controversial, and co-composer with Duke of a song, "You Gotta Crawl before You Walk," twenty years earlier. Tormé's manager had negotiated to get Tormé top billing, which surprised even the singer himself. At rehearsal, five of the Ellington band, including Cootie Williams and Paul Gonsalves, were not present, which distressed Tormé and contributed to an indifferent performance on opening night, when Tormé arrived to find a huge row in progress about the billing. Tormé suggested he talk to Ellington about the problem and found Duke extremely angry. Tormé's contract covered the top-billing point; Ellington's did not.

According to Tormé, Ellington and he did not quarrel personally. But Duke insisted that the situation was ridiculous. "I won't appear. I'll walk out. The band will play without me," Ellington fumed. "Man, I almost just won the Pulitzer Prize!"

Tormé, anxious for his own rights, suggested a compromise. Duke could have top billing on two of the three sides of the marquee outside the club. Ellington refused. Finally it was agreed that for two weeks Ellington should get prime billing in newspaper ads, with Tormé taking the third. In the event, Tormé never got his one week. In the spring of the following year, Tormé and Ellington met again in Tokyo, and Ellington embraced and kissed Tormé as if there had never been any incident at all.

The row upset Tormé enormously. Sometimes, he says, the band played brilliantly for him; one night, however, it was so bad that even Mercer Ellington apologized for the performance. Ellington was his idol. Recalling how he first heard "Reminiscing in Tempo," Tormé—a public performer since he was seven, and a white man raised in poverty in the black section of Chicago— says it convinced him that Ellington was the greatest musician in the world, a view which has never changed. "To me, that piece of music said it all. It was every backstair in Chicago, all the frustration and misery and beauty of the black friends I'd had in my youth. It was eight years before its time." His row with Ellington was massively misreported (in Ellington's favor) by some of the New York papers. In retrospect, the views of both men are understandable. Tormé had contractual right on his side and Ellington was justifiably hurt that the point had been given away. Yet considering that he often took second billing to singers in later years (including Tony Bennett and Ella Fitzgerald), it's hard not to conclude that a factor in his anger at Basin Street East was his sense of injury over the Pulitzer rejection. Fortunately, there were numerous other honors being bestowed on him.

He topped the various jazz polls run by the big magazines— *Down Beat, Esquire, Playboy,* and the British *Melody Maker* and *Jazz Journal*—with awesome frequency down the years. Additionally, there was now recognition from the world at large. In 1965 and 1966, to instance only two years, he received the President's Gold Medal from Lyndon Johnson (he also played at the White House in a Festival of the Arts); other medals from Paris, Chicago, and New York, which named him "Musician of Every Year"; honorary degrees from two American colleges; a scroll from the bishop and trustees of Grace Cathedral, and a Paul Revere plaque from the city of Boston; and he had a Duke

Ellington Day proclaimed in his honor by Oakland, California. As long ago as 1955, he'd been made marshal of Dodge City, an honor peculiar to that metropolis in Kansas.

Even his happiness was, however, becoming overshadowed. During the preparations for the Grace Cathedral concert, Billy Strayhorn had gone into a New York hospital for the first of several long and painful cancer operations. Duke's writing and arranging companion, then only forty-nine, was never able to move with any freedom on the orchestra's journeys again. In the printed program for the Sacred Concert at Grace Cathedral, Ellington glowingly recorded Strayhorn's contribution toward "In the Beginning God" and sought the prayers of the congregation for him. The remarkable rapport between the two men was attested in a story which Ellington often told about the prelude to this occasion. He was 3,000 miles away from Strayhorn's hospital bed, preparing for the Sacred Concert, when they talked on the telephone. Duke gave Swee' Pea a few verbal instructions and the name of the composition, but no clue about the musical theme. Soon, Strayhorn sent out to California music which started and finished on the same notes as Ellington's—F natural and A flat a tenth higher. The key phrase of six notes had only two which were different.

The telephone remained a crucial link between Ellington and the companion he always denied was his alter ego, but preferred to describe as "my right arm, my left arm, all the eyes in the back of my head, my brain waves in his head, and his in mine." While Strayhorn remained behind, Ellington plunged into 1966, a year as busy as 1964 and 1965 had been.

He steamed into Britain early in the year with a new format, as part of a double bill with Ella Fitzgerald. Not everyone liked the idea, for it meant that the orchestra could play alone for only an hour before Ella took over the spotlight. However disgruntled were the true-blue Fllington fans, the collaboration seemed to be one which history demanded and which was certainly not unsuccessful. The backing given Ella by the band memorably enhanced her sweet and flexible voice. In "Something to Live For," the thick, sensuous textures of the reeds enfolded her; in "Cotton Tail" she brilliantly traded jazz phrases with the tenor sax of Paul Gonsalves. Above all, there was a relaxed and easy atmosphere about the band and its entourage at the time. I remember remarking on it to Mercer Ellington, who nodded and pointed to the stage. "Every night," he said, "a contagion of happiness takes place out there." Yet he was under a great deal of pressure. Half an hour before the Festival Hall concert in London, I found him blowing a few notes on his trumpet. Then he was called, as so often, to the telephone. "One of these days," he said, reluctantly putting down the horn, "I'll have the chance to warm up properly. If I miss the high G on 'Black and Tan,' I don't want any dirty looks from the old man." Mercer didn't look like he was joking.

The concerts were also notable for the performance of Duke's beautiful new work, "La Plus Belle Africaine"—first printed in the *Sunday Times* "La Bluebell Africaine," owing doubtless to the emotion-choked sound of my voice over the telephone after the concert. Ellington at this time still hadn't been to Africa, yet here he was offering a piece which, like his "jungle" sounds of almost forty years earlier, and his "Far East Suite," immediately suggested the atmosphere of the place it represented. Duke, as he'd emphasized again and again, always stood at several removes from his influences. "Written his way," the piece I did for the *Sunday Times* observed, "the imitation somehow sounds more authentic than the original."

Few of Duke's compositions have been more effective at first hearing. Perfect in shape, it sets a quiet, simple figure played by piano, bass, and fingered drums against fiercely spurting ensemble passages from the full orchestra. Haunting solos spring from Jimmy Hamilton's clarinet, Harry Carney's baritone sax, and, above all, from the bowed bass of John Lamb. Ellington's cries and groans exotically enhance a superb tone poem.

Duke had himself asked if he might be allowed to perform his sacred music in Coventry Cathedral between concerts, and that outstandingly successful event took place on February 21, the orchestra playing from the chancel steps before the high altar, losing some of their faster passages within the pillowing acoustics, but gaining in stature from the setting each time a quieter, slower mood was demanded. Cat Anderson's high notes arrowing to the roof past the symbolic Crown of Thorns above the choir stalls made as indelible an impression for me as the sight of Duke, exhausted from the preparations for the concert, sleeping earlier on a chair in the bishop's room. The week of Coventry was crowded for him. Two days later he was in Madrid to receive President Johnson's gold medal (for outstanding perfor-

mances and creation of goodwill) and on February 25 he had a
further experience which affected him so profoundly that later
he wrote several pages about it. He was asked to inaugurate the
second wing of the Castle of Goutelas in France, a thirteenth-
century building restored from pitiful dilapidation as a symbolic
act by artists and artisans, and used thereafter for musical festivals and art shows. Ellington arrived on a bitterly cold and
windy night for this celebration of what had become known as
"The Miracle of Goutelas" to find fifty children with burning
torches waiting to guide him to the château. In the music room
stood a nine-foot Steinway concert grand, especially brought
there for him to play.

The doors remained opened to the snowy night air as he
spoke in silence.

> To be accepted as a brother by these heroic human beings leaves
> me breathless. To my newfound brothers, their families and
> friends, I should like to dedicate one of my compositions—"New
> World a-Comin'." The title refers to a future place, on earth, at
> sea, or in the air, where there will be no war, no greed, no cat-
> egorization, and where love is unconditional, and where there is
> no pronoun good enough for God.

Ellington played, the hands of the crowd hammered together,
many people wept. He told me later that he had been more
moved by this friendly occasion in the countryside than even
that night in 1960 when 100,000 people had heard him play
"Come Sunday" at the Christmas mass in Paris. Later he wrote a
suite for Goutelas and was himself honored for his attachment to
the place when he received an award in the opera house at
Lyons. On the night he was to get it, he fell and hurt his knee,
tearing his trousers in the process. Leslie Diamond, who was
with him, put antiseptic on the knee, bound it up, and was (only
mildly) surprised to see Duke pull on his torn trousers again. He
wore them as, with Mrs. Diamond supporting him, he limped
down a long Gothic-ceilinged and chandeliered room to receive
his award.

This routine with the trousers was another of the many facets
of Ellington's superstition. He told the Diamonds it would have
been unlucky to change them. He would, similarly, wear
sweaters and underpants with holes in them as a matter of
course, and his wardrobe was full of such garments. He had a

habit of throwing clothes over lampshades in his various hotel suites as he disrobed before putting on dressing gowns and towels between concerts and journeys. Electric bulbs burned holes in innumerable, and costly, cashmere sweaters. Conversely, he would never again wear clothes from which the buttons fell off, an expensive foible. He needed the scores of suits and hundreds of shirts he owned at any one time, as well as the shoes which he had handmade at McAfee's in Mayfair. Once he was offered a present of several pairs of shoes by a friend, but refused them. "I never give or accept shoes," he explained. "It means that you will walk away from me."

Duke was five weeks in Europe during February and March of 1966. The next month, by invitation, he and the band travelled as America's representatives to the first World Festival of Negro Arts in Dakar, Senegal. Apart from the excitement of his first visit to Africa and the highly emotional reception at his concert from the "cats in the bleachers," as Duke put it, he was insistent that he should play for a party at the American Ambassador's residence. The ambassador, Mercer Cook, was the son of Will Marion Cook, who Duke claimed gave him the equivalent of a conservatoire education back in the 1920s, usually while riding through Central Park in taxis. Cook was a virtuoso, reputed to have broken his violin into pieces after reading a story in the *New York Times* which described him as the greatest Negro violinist in the world. He lamented, "What I've been trying to be is the greatest violinist, not the greatest Negro violinist." Duke once said of his taxi trips with Cook, "I'd sing a melody in its simplest form and he'd stop me and say, 'Reverse your figures.' He was brief but a strong influence. His language had to be pretty straight for me to know what he was talking about. Some of the things he used to tell me I never got a chance to use until years later when I wrote 'Black, Brown, and Beige.'"

Within a month of Dakar, Duke was back in Japan. On his last visit, in 1964, he had won an additional army of admirers by cancelling a date in Hawaii and delaying his departure to give a special Tokyo concert, donating all the proceeds to the city of Niigata, which had just been devastated by flood and earthquake. Now he was presenting his swinging tone parallel, "Ad Lib on Nippon." Everywhere he played, the piece brought the audience out in cheers.

Despite all his travelling, and Strayhorn's absence, Ellington hadn't stopped composing. "House of Lords," a joint composition with Earl Hines, "The Twitch," "Swamp Goo," "The Second Portrait of the Lion," and "The Shepherd" (a beautiful feature for Cootie Williams) belong to this period, and earlier in the year he'd written—not altogether happily—music for the Frank Sinatra movie, *Assault on a Queen.* Conferring with Sinatra in Las Vegas about the score when the shooting of the picture had already been completed, Duke got the idea that a really swinging piece was wanted for a scene when a gang of crooks open up the safe door on the giant ocean liner they're robbing. He provided one, with a mixed band of Ellingtonians and West Coast musicians. The director didn't like it and it was dropped from the final movie. Asking Duke later what he thought of the film, the director was told it was a great Western.

The movie deal had been fixed by Norman Granz, who was still presenting all Duke's commerical tours and had first put up the idea of pairing Ellington and Ella Fitzgerald on the same bill earlier in the year. It seemed a natural development of a partnership which had begun back in 1957 when Ella had sung memorably with Duke's band on an album made for the Verve label, which Granz founded and later sold for a substantial sum to MGM in 1960. Granz, whose other artists included Ray Charles, Oscar Peterson, and Count Basie, wanted to keep the partnership alive, and in July 1966 he arranged for Duke and Ella to perform at the annual Antibes Jazz Festival at Juan-les-Pins in France, one of the loveliest festival sites in the world, on the cape which juts into the Mediterranean between Nice and Cannes. This was a one-off occasion, with no tour attached to it. Ellington and Ella were each contracted to play three nights at Antibes as separate acts, finally joining forces for a single concert.

Ellington's autobiography, so often an enigmatic document, reports the festival without comment, and he pays tribute to Granz in typically guarded words. "He did it very well," says Ellington of his first European visit under the Granz banner, "represented us beautifully as an impresario, and left me feeling very much indebted to him." Later, noting that Granz, although effectively acting as his manager, never took a percentage, Ellington rounds off with, "I was happy with him, but then Cress Courtney came back into the picture." The reference to Cress Courtney was certainly factual, for Courtney returned to Ellington's management team around this period after Duke had heard that his former associate was having a difficult time. As ever, Duke was both pragmatic and forgiving, for the two men had had stormy disagreements during their early periods of working together. It's probably significant, however, that Ellington's autobiography doesn't even mention that Duke made another European visit arranged by Granz early in 1967. It was their last collaboration until 1972, for on the Mediterranean coast of France a quarrel of some magnitude occurred between them, by no means the first altercation in their association. "There had been a big row earlier in Scandinavia," recalled Duke's nephew, Stephen James. "I think there was a kind of love-hate relationship between them. Duke had a natural power about him; and Norman was such a strong personality. They were bound to have battles."

Granz had ambitious plans for filming at Antibes. Not only did he want to capture the carefully balanced concert by Ella and Duke, but in order to broaden the appeal of his film, he shot Ellington at the Casino in Monte Carlo, at St. Tropez, watching a game of *boule*, and, most notably, in the company of the Spanish painter, Joan Miró. The site chosen for their meeting was the Fondation Maeght, a superb art museum named after a Parisian art dealer and set on a hill overlooking the bay of Cannes at St. Paul de Vence. Concerts had often been held there in a small courtyard surrounded by outstanding sculptures. Granz knew that Miró liked jazz, admired Ellington particularly, and would make a dramatic visual contrast with the musician, since he "scarcely came up to Duke's navel."

It was a good idea, but the project was threatened when Ella's sister, Frances, died in America. She cancelled her original booking for the Monday-night concert of July 25 and flew back to the States for the funeral, but returned quickly to pick up her Antibes concerts scheduled for July 27, 28, and 29, although plainly still very upset by the bereavement. Ellington, meanwhile, played his concerts, and as the day of his joint appearance with Ella arrived, went off to keep his film date with Miró. Granz was there for it, so were the Diamonds from London, and Sam Woodyard and John Lamb from the band appeared as accompanists for Duke. It was a happy day, for the admiration of the two great artists was mutual, an empathy with which the need for an interpreter—Duke spoke only English, Miró a kind of Spanish patois—did not interfere. Duke and his musicians played three tunes in various parts of the museum, with Miró as onlooker and guide. At first, there had been fears about the quality of the piano to be used, and Ellington wryly observed, "If it's out of tune at the bottom, I'll play at the top." In the event, it was perfect, and Duke lingered long enough to compose another of his instant themes, later called "Meditation." The party wound up eating a hurried meal at the renowned Colombe d'Or restaurant before hastening on their way.

Back in Juan-les-Pins, the concert finally got under way. Duke and the band were playing well. Ella was not at her best and appeared at times to be crying. Duke cut in early with the band to end the first half, apparently trying to help, and returned for the final set under the impression that Ella probably wouldn't be in a state to come back again. He was inspired. As the music built up to climax after climax, the audience lit up too, screaming for more. The more excited they got, the more Ellington played, until Granz was observed scowling up at the stage and calling out to Ellington. He was trying to get Duke to bring Ella back for her final appearance. Either Ellington didn't hear, or he chose not to hear—probably the former at first—but as Granz's voice grew louder, the message must have got through. Duke's response was to play louder and louder, longer and longer, and he said afterwards he had been affronted by what he considered to be Granz's rudeness, as well as his lack of understanding of Ella's distress. When Ellington at last ended the show, there was a confrontation between him and Granz as he left the stage. Soon, Ellington had those same dull red spots burning in his cheeks as eyewitnesses had observed during his episode in Paris with Sonny Greer (who, noticeably, had never rejoined the orchestra as had the other 1951 leavers, Hodges and Lawrence Brown), and he almost ran to his hotel, away from Granz.

Back in his room, where usually he would have a late meal, he refused to eat. Renee Diamond recalled:

I've never seen him so sad. Not angry, but sad. He spoke a little about Norman not having consideration for *anyone*—which coming from Edward was a bit hilarious—and then he asked me if I'd talk with Norman to try and smooth things over. I did. For an hour, I suppose, Norman let me know just what he thought of Duke. Terrible things. At the end, though, most of the venom had gone. He said he was concerned that Ella hadn't been brought on again. It would spoil the film he was making because Ella was billed as the star. I could understand his disappointment, but I couldn't see why he blamed Duke. Ella wasn't in any condition to perform, I thought.

Well, the next morning Duke was flying back to the States from Nice, and Norman was on the same plane. It was strange. At the airport, they waved to each other before they got on, but then they didn't exchange one word on the plane. From then on, things cooled off between them.

The quarrel with Granz wasn't the only scene involving Duke at the festival. Ben Webster and Ray Nance, two of his greatest alumni, had returned to guest with the band. When Webster first quit in 1943, his going was not entirely voluntary. Ben was occasionally allowed to play piano, and one night, carried away by the reaction of the audience, he hogged the limelight so much he wouldn't let Duke get back into action. Ellington was extremely cool after that, and when Webster tried to see him was persistently unavailable. Finally, the frustrated Webster is reputed to have cut up one of Duke's suits with a pair of scissors and soon afterwards left the band. There is only a brief reference to Webster in *Music Is My Mistress*, and it contains a sting in the tail. Recalling how he last saw Webster in Europe and was proudly shown, by Ben, a photograph of his old colleague on skis, Ellington said he observed: "How is it your skis are pointing *up* the mountain?"

At the Antibes Festival, Duke utterly refused to let Webster know what he would be asked to play during his guest appearance. Webster complained that he didn't know the current Ellington book, but Duke kept evading the issue. After the performance, which still went off without the strains being very apparent, Ray Nance, who had become a heavy drinker, demanded from Duke a fee well in excess of what he had been offered. Duke, with his usual unwillingness to be drawn into hassles over money, agreed that Nance should get $2,000 and bitterly told him that never to see Nance again would suit him very well. Then he turned to Ben Webster and smiled ruefully. "Well, if he's worth $2,000, Ben, you certainly are. That's what we'll pay you." Even for Nance, this was not the end. He was back again on an Ellington recording session in 1973 with Bob Thiele as producer. "Nance was very noisy and very nasty," said

Edmund Anderson, who was at the session, "and Thiele was so cross. But Duke just sat there and wouldn't tell Nance to be quiet. He took all this hassle because he wanted Nance to play on that date—he had that much respect for him as a musician."

After Antibes, the relationship between Ellington and Granz continued to deteriorate. Granz says that their "difference of opinion" was exaggerated, but he irritated Duke immensely with a sleeve note he wrote when an album of the Côte d'Azur concerts was issued. Granz had detected an air of familiarity about one longer number which the band played, and had been told by Billy Strayhorn that "it was just 'A Train' turned around." So in his sleeve note, Granz had named the piece "That Old Turnaround Blues." Ellington did not appreciate the quip. Granz told me, however, that the really serious rift between them occurred not at Antibes, but the next year.

> Duke didn't like his equanimity disturbed, and finally I just got tired of putting up with things which disturbed *my* equanimity. He had this terrible propensity for booking himself into dates on the spur of the moment without telling me—almost as if he was *afraid* not to be working on any day. Well, I'd been trying very hard to break the East down—I mean the European East, and not on a State Department aid basis. I mean commercially. Hungary and Yugoslavia and Poland were beginning to think of accepting American jazz, and they wanted Ella.
>
> So I'd flown to Budapest and had three days' hard talking. They *sap* you, those people, because they work in committees, but you've got only you, and they're obdurate, and they don't really care. So when I flew back to Vienna, I'd got it all fixed for Ella *and* Duke, and that wasn't easy with his twenty musicians and such. I was exhausted, but I was elated too, and the logistics of the trip were terrible. I rang Ruth Ellington to tell her, and she said something about he couldn't make it to Budapest because he was playing some American date. A high school or something. And I didn't know about that! I blew my top, and she was defending him and said he wasn't in town, but she'd let him know. I'm sorry, I guess, that we had this terrible row, but I just cancelled out the entire schedule I had arranged for Duke and I took Basie instead. You ought to know that I didn't take a penny in all the years I was manager to Duke—and I regarded that as my contribution to jazz.

So, for a variety of reasons, it seems, Duke was finally dropped from the Granz circuit after he had toured under the

ABOVE, LEFT: Ellington at work in a BBC studio, 1965. ABOVE, RIGHT: On tour, 1968. Where else but Latin America? BELOW, LEFT: Moscow, 1971. Duke tries out the traditional Russian balalaika during his successful tour of the USSR. BELOW, RIGHT: Duke received scores of honorary degrees and other awards. This was among the last—honorary Doctor of Music, Columbia University, New York, May 1973.

LEFT: Duke and Beatrice Ellis, more usually known as Evie Ellington, the woman who made a home for him in New York City for over thirty years, yet with whom he was rarely seen in public and almost never photographed. This exception to the rule was a studio party for his sixty-fifth birthday. BELOW: Mercer and Duke Ellington. "If anything we're too much alike," Mercer once said.

ABOVE, LEFT: Norman Granz, presenter of Duke's European tours for almost a decade, talks with Ellington at the Antibes Festival in 1966. They quarreled here, and their association was soon to end. ABOVE, RIGHT: Ellington and Billy Strayhorn in 1964: "an unmatched artistic relationship...a love affair." RIGHT: Dr. Arthur Logan, for so many years one of the handful of people closest to Ellington, is feted by Duke at a party in September 1969. He holds a portrait of Billy Strayhorn in his hands as his son, Chipper, looks on.

ABOVE: Duke meets Queen Elizabeth and Prince Philip for the first time, at Leeds in 1958. "When were you last in England?" she had asked. "1933, Your Majesty, years before you were born." BELOW: Duke was seventy on this day. President Richard Nixon had organized a party for him at the White House. Nixon, as well as Ellington, played the piano that evening.

On tour, 1967: Cootie Williams and the band play, Ellington conducts, the London Philharmonic Orchestra wait their turn, in a barrier-breaking concert at the Albert Hall, London.

At a Paris party, Maurice Chevalier presents Duke with one of his famous straw hats in honor of Ellington's seventieth birthday; almost forty years earlier, Duke had first conducted with a baton when his band accompanied Chevalier in New York.

RIGHT: Westminster Abbey, October 1973: Ellington, with Alice Babs and Roscoe Gill, rehearses during the last full-scale Sacred Concert of his life.

Ellington in concert with Ella Fitzgerald—one of the many memorable occasions during their Ellington tours in the mid-1960s.

Duke Ellington, 1963: "What is there to retire to? Stagnation wouldn't look good on me."

impresario's banner in early 1967, and at that time, with infla-
tion pushing up air fares and hotel accommodation, even an
Ellington tour was far from an economic certainty. Promoters in
the various European countries were hesitant about taking on
the large expense of the Ellington band, its entourage, and its
baggage, especially when they knew that Granz was not the in-
stigator. Not for two and a half years, when the young London
impresario, Robert Paterson, moved in to promote a tour by
him, did Ellington see Europe again.

However, nothing of the breach disturbed the outward appearance of Ellington's visit to Europe in February 1967. He
was seen in a bewildering mixture of contexts. Ella Fitzgerald
appeared with the band at some concerts, and the collaboration
had by now become a mature masterpiece. "Don't Be That
Way," from the days she'd enjoyed in the 1930s with Chick
Webb, summed up the way she involved herself sympathetically
with the textures of the band. First, she used her warmest,
richest voice against a quiet muted obbligato from Cat Anderson's trumpet; then there were intensely rhythmic passages during which her personal accompanists, Sam Woodyard and Jimmy
Jones, both former Ellington associates, sustained her; finally,
she rocketed into thrilling high note choruses, her voice outsoar-
ing the orchestra, from which the bass trombone of Chuck Connors could be heard stabbing out a low-down counterpoint.

At other concerts, the Ellington band had two hours or more
to itself. There was a Sacred Concert in the University Church
of St. Mary at Cambridge, and for this Ellington strikingly kept
the vow he had made at Grace Cathedral that expense was no
object on such occasions. He spent over £1,000 to bring Esther
Marrow from New York just to sing one piece—"Come
Sunday"—during the Cambridge concert. At the Albert Hall,
Duke repeated much of his Lincoln Center program, including
"The Golden Broom and the Green Apple," with the London
Philharmonic Orchestra under John Pritchard. The *Sunday
Times* review I wrote on February 26 read:

> There was at least one period during last week's barrier-breaking
> Albert Hall concert when, by his own definition of swing as "the
> ultimate in compatibility," or simply in terms of a regular rhythm
> infectious and elastic, Duke Ellington had the London Philhar-
> monic Orchestra swinging.

It came near the end of his new work, "The Golden Broom and the Green Apple." Ellington, conducting the LPO with stabbing unadorned gestures, broke off to clap his hands in time with a tumbling passage for flute, oboe and cello. The mood caught. The LPO brass began to whoop, propelled by nine basses playing pizzicato, and the orchestra's young drummer swooped into a passage of four-bar breaks—the familiar call-and-response pattern of jazz. It has probably never happened to the LPO before, and won't again until Ellington returns.

As an occasion, the concert was an overwhelming success, received with great enthusiasm, running on for close to three hours. Whenever Ellington's orchestra played with the LPO—in his tone parallel, "Harlem," in the long medley of his classic songs (from "Sophisticated Lady" to "Solitude")—there was little sense of unease or incoherence at the fusion, despite the occasional aura of under-rehearsal which was the only reservation to be made about the quality of the concert.

The whole affair, indeed, illustrated Ellington's contention that categories in music are increasingly meaningless. There is now a broad mainstream of modern music, in which swim musicians whose tastes, training and practice encompass the traditions and devices of all music, classical or jazz or whatever. Leonard Bernstein is one, and he has plainly learned from Ellington. Categories have broken down, and it is now an interesting judgment, but no longer a conclusive one, to say that one prefers "Harlem" in a version for Ellington's band only, instead of in its band-plus-symphony orchestra guise. It was, devotees sometimes forget, originally written for the NBC Symphony during Toscanini's reign.

Before Duke had arrived in London, I'd spoken with him on the telephone, when he told me that he had spent the weeks around Christmas rummaging. "Finding the old envelopes on which I've written things, the old words, the old musical jottings. Maybe I want to write a book of statements, a philosophy." That was the first inkling that he was going to put together some kind of autobiography, for he'd always refused to contemplate such "tombstones" in the past. "I can't think about it now, though. England is my desire for the moment, my favorite audience. Well, didn't they adjust my artistic perspective in 1933?"

Strayhorn had been helping with some of the music for the tour, although he was still very ill. Gruelling operations had reduced his tiny frame to a mere eighty pounds. Yet Duke still hoped and insisted: "He is the biggest man in the world. He has survived. Slowly he is going to make it." Ellington himself behaved throughout the tour in as hectic a style as ever. Before his opening concert at Portsmouth, he was onstage at the piano twenty minutes before the curtain rose, committing something new to paper. Around two in the morning later in the week, a very good Ellingtonian hour for dinner, I asked him about that. He smiled wearily, knowing he would in part—but only in part—be repeating himself. "Sure, it's still my only interest in life—writing something I'll hear tomorrow night. I'm impatient inside."

So impatient, indeed, that he had little time for anything else. The previous year, his estranged wife, Edna, had died in Washington. On the day that Edna died, Duke rang Renee Diamond in London. Death, he explained, always made him feel sad; he wanted someone to talk to about it. Afterwards, Renee telephoned Evie Ellington in New York. "I'm sad, too," said Evie. "But now I'm hoping he'll keep his promise to marry me one day. My guess, though, is that he won't."

Duke's impatience was reflected in other ways. His relationship with Fernanda de Castro Monte, his companion around Europe the previous year, was often stormy. In the car on the way to London Airport, he had a very heated row with her, accusing her of extravagance at his expense. "I've had enough—enough, enough, enough," he declared, which demonstrated his growing concern in the later years at the way his money seemed to evaporate. His rift with Fernanda was not permanent. She continued to be his companion on and off until he died, spending a great deal of time in New York, appearing especially at Christmas parties.

When Ellington left Europe as spring approached in 1967, he was rapidly approaching his sixty-eighth birthday. Billy Strayhorn, in his fifty-second year, was growing weaker all the time, but Ellington's partner was still writing. "Blood Count," a most poignant piece composed to feature Johnny Hodges, was sent by Strayhorn from the hospital for a concert by the band at Carnegie Hall. Its connotation was made even more moving when one recalled what Strayhorn had once said. "Actually, inspiration comes from the simplest kind of thing, like watching a bird fly. That's only the beginning. Then the work begins. Oh, goodness! Then you have to sit down and work, and it's *hard*."

Ellington saw a great deal of his "favorite human being" in that spring of 1967. But the work of the band had to continue. Early in the morning of May 31, Duke's sister, Ruth, called him in Reno, Nevada, to say that Strayhorn had died during the night. She was weeping. Ellington cried too and banged his head against the walls of his hotel room. Then he sat down and wrote what he was thinking—subconsciously, as he described it—before telephoning his sister to read the words and then to break the news of Strayhorn's death to all the church friends who had been praying for him.

Within three months, Ellington's orchestra recorded one of their most beautiful albums, devoted entirely to Strayhorn's compositions and entitled "And His Mother Called Him Bill." The very last track, the exquisite "Lotus Blossom," was taped at the end of the session, when the band were packing up their instruments and chattering among themselves. Slowly, you hear the noise die down as Duke plays his grieving piano solo. It is one of the most emotional three minutes ever caught on record. Afterwards, Duke observed very simply: "That is what he most liked to hear me play." Printed on the album sleeve are the words which Ellington had written in his hotel room on the morning of May 31.

Poor Little Swee' Pea, Billy Strayhorn, William Thomas Strayhorn, the biggest human being who ever lived, a man with the greatest courage, the most majestic artistic stature, a highly skilled musician whose impeccable taste commanded the respect of all musicians and the admiration of all listeners.

His audience at home and abroad marvelled at the grandeur of his talent and the mantle of tonal supremacy that he wore only with grace. He was a beautiful human being, adored by a wide range of friends—rich, poor, famous, and unknown. Great artists pay homage to Billy Strayhorn's God-given ability and mastery of his craft. Because he had a rare sensitivity and applied himself to his gifts, he successfully married melody, words, and harmony, equating the fitting with happiness.

His greatest virtue, I think, was his honesty—not only to others but to himself. His listening-hearing self was totally intolerant of his writing-playing self when, or if, any compromise was expected, or considered expedient. Condescension did not exist in the mind of Billy Strayhorn.

He spoke English perfectly and French very well. He demanded freedom of expression and lived in what we consider the most important of moral freedoms; freedom from hate, unconditionally; freedom from all self-pity (even throughout all the pain and bad news); freedom from fear of possibly doing something that might help another more than it might help himself; and freedom from the kind of pride that could make a man feel he was better than his brother or neighbor.

His patience was incomparable and unlimited. He had no aspirations to enter into any kind of competition, yet the legacy he leaves, his *oeuvre*, will never be less than the ultimate on the biggest plateau of culture (whether by comparison or not).

God bless Billy Strayhorn.

For Ellington, it was the end of an era; for music, the conclusion of one of the most fruitful partnerships in history. Ellington mourned but did not change, except to drive himself ever more furiously through composing and appearances, even more acutely aware now that time was running out. He, and most of the important members of his band, had barely seven years left.

7

1968-1972
Second Fiddle to None

"I find that I have all these other lifetimes to compete with," Duke Ellington observed during the 1960s. "And so this lifetime now is the hardest, because I have to compete with an illusion that someone has in their mental ear of what we played in 1927, or maybe 1940 after Strays had joined, or 1956 at Newport. People are full of comparisons. That's why we work so hard. How can we stop if we're to keep our reputation?"

By the time he had finished speaking, that characteristic mixture of Ellingtonian seriousness and irony was ringing in his voice. However, the fact remained that in mid-1967 he faced another kind of lifetime and a further set of comparisons. The band was growing old. Ellington was almost seventy. Strayhorn was gone.

Nothing much happened for several months. In his public performances, Duke took to rounding off the proceedings with the same solo performance of Strayhorn's "Lotus Blossom" which he had so movingly put on record, and this was to be a great feature of his concerts until the end. Yet, creatively, Ellington recovered quickly from the loss of his companion, and there can be no doubt that his religious faith—gradually deepening during the 1960s—helped him to ride the shock. The first

Sacred Concert of 1965 had signalled this development in Duke's personality. In 1966 he had composed a suite in six sections, "Murder in the Cathedral," to be used as background music for a production by Ethel Rich of T. S. Eliot's play. Ethel Rich was a drama and speech professor at Milton College, Wisconsin, and Duke had become close to her in other ways. He declared that she "sensed my role" in sacred music and often said that the Episcopal Church booklet, *Forward,* which she sent him regularly, was his daily reading. At around the same time he met Pastor John Gensel, at whose Lutheran church in New York City Ruth Ellington had been a regular worshipper for years. For over a decade, Gensel has organized a service called Jazz Vespers and acts as a counsellor and friend to jazz musicians—a fact Ellington saluted with the tone parallel that featured Cootie Williams, "The Shepherd (Who Watches over the Night Flock)." These new friends, and many others, were all part of the background to Ellington's changing existence at this time. Before 1967 was out, and following a very busy period of appearances all over the United States, Duke had laid his plans for what he considered "the most important thing I have ever done": the second Sacred Concert, which, with an entirely new series of compositions except for "99 Percent Won't Do," was premiered at the Cathedral of St. John the Divine in New York on January 19, 1968.

Musically, it is a work of great beauty and power, upon which Duke spent far more time than he had on the first Sacred Concert. In the program provided by the church, some of the introductory notes by Ellington expressed the man and his philosophy perfectly.

> I think of myself as a messenger boy, one who tries to bring messages to people, not people who have never heard of God, but those who were more or less raised with the guidance of the Church. Now and then we encounter people who say they do not believe. I hate to say that they are out-and-out liars, but I believe they think it fashionable to speak like that, having been brainwashed by someone beneath them, by someone with a complex who enjoys bringing them to their knees in the worship of the non-existence of God. They snicker in the dark as they tremble with fright.
>
> It has been said that what we do is to deliver lyrical sermons, fire-and-brimstone sermonettes, and reminders of the fact that we live in the promised land of milk and honey, where we have prime

beef and 80 percent-butterfat ice cream. I am sure we appreciate the blessings we enjoy in this country, but it wouldn't hurt if everyone expressed his appreciation more often.

We shall keep this land if we all agree on the meaning of that unconditional word: LOVE.

A week of rehearsals, lasting until an hour before the premiere, preceded the concert, a far more intense effort than had been given to the San Francisco opening in 1965. It was as though Ellington was determined to prove both the importance of the occasion and the quality of the music. Yet the prelude had, as usual, its share of apparent chaos. Only on the last afternoon did Ellington reveal (or, perhaps, decide) how the pieces of his vast musical jigsaw, rehearsed so patiently by the band, fitted together. And he did some of his thinking lying stretched out on his back on the red-carpeted stand provided by the cathedral for the band.

Several choirs, with male and female, young and adult voices had been assembled to sing with the band. They were rehearsed by a young musician friend of Duke's, Roscoe Gill, and his long-time copyist-assistant, Tom Whaley, who was immensely proud of the choirmaster role given to him in the later years of the orchestra's life. But the most crucial new factor in the mixture was the mature and glorious voice of the Swedish coloratura soprano, Alice Babs, whom Ellington had first met (and recorded an exquisite album with) in Paris in 1963. She came, at his request, from Europe to sing "Almighty God," "Heaven" (a beautiful double act with Johnny Hodges's alto sax), "T.G.T.T." ("Too Good to Title"), and to join with three other singers—Tony Watkins, Roscoe Gill, and Devonne Gardner—as well as the band soloists in "It's Freedom" and the finale, "Praise God and Dance." Duke was enthusiastic about her:

> She sings opera, she sings lieder, she sings what we call jazz and blues, she sings like an instrument, she even yodels, and she can read any or all of it! No matter how hard the intervals, when you hand her the music, she sight-reads and sings it as though she had rehearsed it a month. Every word comes out perfectly enunciated, understandable and believable. Alice Babs is a composer's dream, for with her he can forget all the limitations and just write his heart out.

That opening night in New York, she lived up to every word of his praise. The concert was not helped by the appalling acoustics or by the glare of TV lights upon the 6,000 people present, but the feeling got through even if the sound was imperfect. The following night, at a smaller church with kindlier acoustics in New Canaan, Connecticut, the glories of the work became still more apparent. The audience gave a tumultuous ovation at the end, after Geoffrey Holder had danced a stunningly exciting solo performance while the band roared through "Praise God and Dance." At St. John the Divine, two dance groups had been used, but Holder's solo seemed just as fascinating to the smaller audience, who, as in New York, remained standing silently during Tony Watkins's *a cappella* rendering of "The Lord's Prayer."

Within a week, the whole concert had been studio-recorded and given the perfection in sound which the architecture of few churches allows. The work has flaws; but sections of it are quite astonishing. Even Ellington, experimenting in unique tone colorings for years, had never before come up with anything quite like "Supreme Being." "The scoring created an impression of brooding majesty via harmonies that were unworldly in their implications of infinity," wrote Stanley Dance after hearing the first two performances. Mysterious, austere, sometimes dissonant, and sometimes naïve the sounds and chanting voices certainly are; Ellington in an extension of all his previous roles. Alice Babs was astounded that five saxophones, five trumpets, and four trombones—Harold "Money" Johnson and Benny Green having been added to the brass—could achieve such a rich effect. "When the classical people hear *that*, they will marvel," she declared. In contrast there were pin-drop sections like "Meditation," a simple duet between Duke and his bassist, Jeff Castleman; "The Shepherd," already written to pay honor to Pastor John Gensel, and performed by Cootie Williams; and the crackle of the two featured drummers, Sam Woodyard and Steve Little, on Ellington's so-called "fire-and-brimstone sermonette," "The Biggest and Busiest Intersection." Duke slipped his own explanations into the printed program from time to time, and as he explained that the wordless and difficult "Too Good to Title" was thus named "because it violates conformity in the same way, we like to think, that Jesus Christ did," so he had a long and typical note on "Intersection."

> In life, we have to make a decision every two or three minutes, whether we are going straight ahead, or left or right. This happens at every traffic intersection. In Denver, they have one with five

points, and at the Arc de Triomphe in Paris there are so many outlets that it is terribly confusing if you are not familiar with it. Down at the end where all ends end, there is an intersection with millions of outlets. If you've been a "good boy" and have made it all the way to the gate, almost, you still have to go through this last, final intersection. The pavement is slippery, and there are all kinds of pitfalls, potholes, booby traps, and snares. The commercials that the representatives of the opposition are doing are outrageous. They even have cats who come up just as you see the reflections of the golden streets and are about to put your hand on the gate. "Baby," they whisper, "I know it looks pretty in there, but you should see how those chicks are swinging down where we are!" They always whisper, you know, but you have to watch it right up to the very last second, because it is a very busy intersection.

The first Sacred Concert had been performed in more than fifty churches of many denominations; a similar exposure was given to this even more impressive second concert. Ellington delighted to point out that language barriers seemed no impediment to the concert's message. In the church of St. Sulpice, Paris, in 1969, Alice Babs was summoned to bow after bow by the applause of the packed 5,000, and the Swingle Singers were part of the concert. In Santa Maria del Mar in Barcelona, the Swingles came too, and the congregation burst into the aisles to join in the dancing finale. The choir from Barcelona came later, in the summer of 1970, to sing in the concert at the ancient Roman amphitheatre in Orange, France, one of the most striking settings for music in the world, where the seats rise almost sheer, towering above the stage below.

Reaction to Ellington's latest major work was generally good, and he pressed on through the spring and summer of 1968 in good heart, undeterred even by the major loss of his great clarinet-player, Jimmy Hamilton. Harold Ashby, primarily a tenor sax man, replaced Hamilton, so Duke was now missing an important color from his tone-palette. Hamilton's departure was for the same old reason; after twenty-six years he'd had enough of hotel rooms and buses and planes. Soon, Ellington's men were to have another round of that intensive shock treatment in an area they had never visited before, below the equator.

On September 1, Duke and his band—sixteen instrumentalists, two singers (Tony Watkins and Trish Turner), and the wives of Mercer Ellington and Johnny Hodges—left New York for his first South American tour. In the next month they played in Brazil, Argentina, Uruguay, Chile, and, finally, Mexico, the last named following a five-day break to fulfill some one-night stands in the United States. It wasn't only the obvious places they visited either. They were staggered by the sweeping bays and explosive mountain scenery of Rio de Janeiro, dominated by the lighted Christ on Corcovado. They briefly tasted the lazy high life of Acapulco, the more adventurous ones whizzing around the ocean on parachutes towed by speedboats. But the Ellington music was carried to more out-of-the-way areas as well, to a basketball arena in Tucumán in the far north of Argentina and to a country club at Mérida in the province of Yucatán, sweeping up to form the southeastern fringe of the Gulf of Mexico.

This was one of the happiest of all his tours, and was frenetic as most of the band's longer journeys. In the plane out, Ellington didn't sleep much during the night—he kept humming a few bars of a new tune he was working out. There were many early-morning departures, and at most hotels the harassed Mercer would be struggling with hotel bills and currency problems while screaming "Rollin'!" from time to time in a vain endeavor to get the musicians on the bus. Usually there was someone missing; usually they were late leaving.

Before their concert in Santiago, Ellington smilingly announced that after it there would be a 1:15 A.M. rehearsal to polish up the major "Harlem" suite, which was to be played at the farewell show in Buenos Aires. One veteran refused to attend the rehearsal and stalked out angrily, so the band put it together without him. At the concert the next night, they had to make do without Johnny Hodges, who was very sick with swollen glands and unable to play. So Willie Cook took over his place in the sax section, playing trumpet most of the time with a tin derby over the bell. At one outlandish Mexican date, a slow five-hour flight and a missing band bus made them two hours late for a concert in a ball park, where the incredibly distorted sound system led to the piano and drums drowning the horns, and no string bass line at all. Also in Mexico, Paul Gonsalves got down rather cheekily and none too steadily from the stage at another concert to serenade a girl with "In a Sentimental Mood"—a trick I also saw him pull in Las Vegas—and when he returned was immediately called on by Duke for a second solo. That was probably the Ellington disciplinary system in operation, although from time to time Duke spoke quite benignly about Gonsalves' habit of wandering off.

Everywhere, however, the performances were rapturously greeted. After the passionate approval which followed "Things Ain't What They Used to Be" in Buenos Aires, Harry Carney compared it with London's messianic fervor in 1933; he could think of nothing quite comparable since those early days. Ellington himself bore the main brunt of the tour as he always did, and the extra burden thrust upon him when he was travelling for the State Department by the endless round of functions and other official receptions, including press conferences, radio and TV interviews— all added to ceaseless performing and travelling—is often overlooked.

Duke was a sensationally good ambassador, but even he had only twenty-four hours in a day, and he invented special techniques to deal with the situation. At embassy or consular receptions after concerts he would arrive full of smiles and bonhomie, and for a few minutes would drink and chat. Then someone would announce that he had graciously consented to play. He would dedicate the piece to the wife of the most important official present. An intimate explained what happened next.

> Duke would sit at the piano and play beautifully for five minutes. Half the time he'd be looking at the audience. For the rest, he'd be sizing up the food on the buffet table. He'd make his selection, whisper what his menu would be to an aide, then wind up. Applause, everyone enchanted. Ten minutes' more chat, and he'd have to leave—he always had a plane to catch or an interview the next day—and no one would think him rude, because he'd played for them and they knew how tough his schedules were. So thirty minutes after he'd come, he'd be out of the front door carrying his supper with him in a doggy bag. What a performer!

Toward the end of his life, Ellington would become even more ruthless about socializing, despite that element of snobbism in his character which made him feel flattered to move among the high and mighty. Invited to attend a Washington party given by the Edward Kennedys for the opening of the Kennedy Center for the Performing Arts in 1972, he invented an excuse, shrugging his shoulders as he sat in a black bathrobe working on a new piece of music and observing to an aide: "It's only a lot of bowing." But in 1968, he still acted as if he had time to burn, spreading enchantment all around him. At his final public concert in Buenos Aires, crowds waited for him weeping, reaching out to touch him, thrusting gifts upon him. Yet throughout all this, he was in sparkling form, firing off answers which often weren't simply variants on what he'd said before. "Improvisation?" he declared on radio in Buenos Aires. "Anyone who plays anything worth hearing knows what he's going to play, no matter whether he prepares a day ahead or a beat ahead. It has to be with intent." In the same interview there was a delightful answer about ancient and modern styles of jazz living: "A jam session is a polite endeavor—an exchange of compliments. In the old days, they had cutting contests where you defended your honor with your instrument."

Just occasionally, as he was quite capable of doing, Duke showed his teeth—but such elegant and civilized teeth. "Do I think of Charles Mingus as a disciple of my school?" he said in Tucumán, musing over a question. "Well, that's what *he* says." To illustrate that such a remark wasn't completely out of character, Ellington had in earlier years said of Jelly Roll Morton, "He played piano like one of those high-school teachers in Washington; as a matter of fact, high-school teachers played better jazz."

Amidst all this, Ellington was still composing, promising in Buenos Aires to express his appreciation for this "inspiration of a lifetime—a virtual summit in my career" at a later date in his music. When the band reached Mexico, he had parts of what was later to become "The Latin-American Suite" nearly ready, performing them onstage under code names, in effect composing as the band played, shouting out instructions and modifications during quieter passages. On the penultimate day in Mexico, he officially premiered "Mexican Anticipacion," telling his audience: "For years and years we have wanted to come to Mexico, and we have thought of her as a beautiful woman. This is a musical reflection of our mental anticipation."

Oddly, the recording of "The Latin-American Suite" which the band later produced contained no section called "Mexican Anticipacion," nor was the suite issued for some years. The sparkling music was completely true to Ellington's methods. It's an *impression* of South America, with underlying rhythms of Latinate orientation produced by his own rhythm section without need for the congas and bongos which all other composers would surely have regarded as obligatory. Johnny Hodges has some happy moments on the album, as do Lawrence Brown, Buster Cooper, and Harry Carney, but the main soloist is Paul Gonsalves, who was a star on the tour and, because of his knowledge of Portuguese, the official interpreter in Brazil. The titles are as evocative and wittily personal as the music. "Oclupaca" (an obvious inversion) is exotic and humorous; "Chico Cuadradino," credited jointly to Duke and Mercer, reflects "a little Spanish square doing his thang," and the boisterous sound suits the conceit. "Eque" (celebrating Duke's crossing of the equator), "Tina," and "Brasilliance"—tributes to two of the countries visited—continue the jubilant word play, which fits, on this occasion, very happily with the music.

Ellington was in his seventieth year whilst he was in Latin America, and even he couldn't totally ignore this milestone. Nor, making up for many periods of neglect, could America. In the autumn of 1968, he played what was becoming a regular date at the Rainbow Grill in New York with an octet and, with Christmas past, the spring buildup to his seventieth birthday began. Between engagements, he was interviewed endlessly by reporters. He appeared in all manner of radio and TV programs. And he had been composing again too, this time the music for a new movie, *Change of Mind*.

It had a controversial subject: the transplanting of a white lawyer's brain to a black man's body, and it was not a great commercial success. It was also an Ellington curiosity. Unusually, he'd given the band a holiday, so he gathered together a skeleton crew of his own musicians to which members of the Count Basie and Earl Hines bands were added for the recordings. Some music was new, some was revised treatments of old classics from almost forty years earlier. On a theme from "Creole Rhapsody," renamed "Neo-Creole," Ellington played the electric piano he'd used in earlier Sacred Concerts. For some time he'd favored the instrument in hotel suites and at home so that he could play quietly without disturbing anyone during the night. As he once explained, "You have to write it down when it comes to you. You can remember the notes next day, but not the values and rhythm. So you go home expecting to go to bed. But then you sit down and try out a couple of chords, and when you look up it's 7 A.M." *Change of Mind* was well behind him, however, when Ellington returned to his home town on April 29, his seventieth birthday, to attend an unprecedented party given for him at the White House and to be presented with the Medal of Freedom, the highest civilian honor the U.S. government can bestow.

He was no stranger to the White House. A succession of presidents had invited him there, Lyndon Johnson on no fewer than seven occasions, either to play or as a guest. Dwight Eisenhower had bumped into him in a hotel before one such White House party and had loudly reminded him to play "Mood Indigo" during the evening; Ellington obliged—four times. On another occasion, Harry Truman had a long private chat with him in his study and Duke presented him with the original score of "Harlem." Duke had mourned the death of Franklin Delano Roosevelt in 1945 in a very special way. As the presidential funeral train brought Roosevelt's body from Warm Springs, Georgia, to his family home at Hyde Park, New York, Ellington's band played on the air for hours—all Duke's own compositions. His was perhaps the most genuinely American music (certainly played for the longest stretch) heard on radio that day, and Ellington was proud of the fact. But April 29, 1969, was in a separate category from all those other occasions.

Not that Duke was over-sentimentalizing the prospect. He had few feelings left for Washington as "home town." Maritally, its memories were soured. The remains of his parents were now buried in the wide green acres of Woodlawn Cemetery in the Bronx after a land sale a few years earlier threatened the burial site in Washington where the bodies had originally been laid to rest. Ellington had immediately chosen and bought a plot at Woodlawn with room for fourteen graves, and Ruth Ellington had supervised the removal of the remains from Washington to New York. But socially, politically, artistically the White House affair was the culmination of his life's work, both as an individual and as a representative of the black race. The White House claimed the dinner was President Nixon's idea, but the truth was more complicated. Charles McWhorter, a New York lawyer and jazz buff who worked on Nixon's campaigns, was one of those who put pressure on the President after Ellington's press agent of the period, Joe Morgen, had fed him the idea. Leonard Garment, Nixon's former law partner and an amateur clarinet player, was the other—but he, too, was a messenger, bearing to the White House the suggestion of Willis Conover, the respected jazz M.C. and director of the Voice of America's "Music U.S.A." programs. The greatest irony was that a gesture so generous and imaginative (however richly earned) should have been made by the most widely reviled president of the century and one who didn't even much like jazz, although, according to McWhorter, "he appreciated the elegance and greatness of Ellington's music."

The shape of the evening was apt and partly unexpected: first, a formal white-tie dinner for around eighty people; then the presentation of the Medal of Freedom and the arrival of around one hundred more guests; then a jazz concert compered by Willis Conover; and, finally, and unexpectedly, a long jam session with dancing.

Everyone who was there on that magical evening has particular memories. But very few have voiced one of its most poignant aspects. Most of Duke's family were there: his sister, Ruth, with whom he descended the grand staircase into the crowded Cross Hall alongside President and Mrs. Nixon, and her son, Stephen James; his son, Mercer, his daughter-in-law, Evelyn, and two of their three children, Edward K. Ellington II and Gaye. Intimates like Arthur Logan, Harry Carney, Tom Whaley (now almost seventy-seven) were present, together with his London friends, the Diamonds—the only Britons invited except for Stanley Dance, who had lived in America for many years since his marriage to his Canadian wife, Helen. There were high officials of government, like Vice-President Agnew and Attorney General John Mitchell, ministers of many religions, university presidents, lawyers, and musician-composers, who included Harold Arlen, Richard Rodgers, Benny Goodman, Count Basie, Cab Calloway (with whom Duke had had a no-poaching agreement on musicians back in the 1920s), and Dizzy Gillespie, as well as artists from other fields, like the film director, Otto Preminger, and the Stratford (Ontario) Shakespeare Theatre producer, Thomas Patterson. But the woman who had shared his life for so long, Evie, wasn't at the White House—nor, for that matter, was Fernanda de Castro Monte. Evie sat alone, at home, as so often, in the apartment on West End Avenue.

Before the evening began, Duke warmed up at a press conference. "I don't believe in the generation gap," he said. "I believe in regeneration gaps. Each day you regenerate, or else you're not living. I see something and I want to make a tone parallel. I wrote 'Mood Indigo' in fifteen minutes. I wrote 'Solitude' in twenty minutes standing up. But then I wrote 'Sophisticated Lady' and it took me thirty days. Couldn't decide which way I wanted to go on the seventeenth bar."

In the receiving line at the White House, Duke and Ruth, wearing one of her usual blond wigs and an outfit whose shade of green was close to that of Patricia Nixon's, greeted guests alongside the President and his wife. To all who passed by, Ellington administered four kisses. When Nixon inquired why, he gave the reply he had been giving for many years: "One for each cheek," which Nixon took some time to fathom. Later, at the medal presentation, he saluted the President the same way.

There were round tables of eight for the roast-beef dinner in the State Dining Room, where Duke's father had occasionally worked as a butler. Ruth Ellington sat with Nixon, Dizzy Gillespie, Benny Goodman, singer Lou Rawls, and the gospel artist, Mahalia Jackson. Duke, seated alongside Patricia Nixon, could converse with Richard Rodgers, Renee Diamond, singer Billy Eckstine, and John Johnson, owner of the magazine, *Ebony*.

When the medal presentation and the speeches began, Nixon was in a jovial mood. "Kings and queens have dined here," he said, "but never before a Duke. Now it's the greatest of all Dukes." He continued: "In the royalty of American music, no man swings more or stands higher than the Duke." He drew a warm roar of laughter when, after making the medal presentation, he glanced at the citation and remarked: "I was looking at the name on this and it said, 'Edward Kennedy . . .'" Nixon paused before he added, 'Ellington.'" In his reply, Ellington movingly recited the famous four freedoms by which Billy Strayhorn had lived; earlier he had made his often quoted remark: "There is no place I would rather be tonight except in my mother's arms."

But it was the music that night which made it an occasion like no other in history at the White House. First, a complete surprise. Nixon leapt to the Steinway grand, began to play, and led the singing of "Happy Birthday." Then there was the all-star band, playing Ellingtonia for one and a half hours: Paul Desmond and Gerry Mulligan (saxes); Clark Terry and Bill Berry (trumpets); Urbie Green and J. J. Johnson (trombones); and a rhythm section composed of Hank Jones (piano), Louis Bellson (drums), Jim Hall (guitar), and Milt Hinton (bass). Three guest pianists—the incomparable Earl Hines (whose "Perdido" brought roars of approval), Dave Brubeck, and Billy Taylor—joined in too, as well as singers Mary Mayo and Joe Williams. For the first time in history, television cameras were permitted to record this after-dinner entertainment, an indication of the importance of the event in official eyes. When, finally, Nixon called upon the Duke himself to play, he suggested impishly that he would "pick a name and see if I can improvise on it—something graceful and gentle—Pat." After which he produced a soft mood number to everyone's delight. As refreshments were served at past midnight, Duke had to listen to Vice-President Agnew playing *his* version of Ellington songs at the piano.

Then, surprisingly, Nixon announced that the East Room was being cleared for a jam session and dancing. He and his wife retired, but the music played on. Most of the all-stars joined in the jam session. So did members of the Marine Band. Ellington sat at the keyboard alongside his mentor, Willie "the Lion" Smith, who still wore his old derby hat. George Wein and Marian McPartland got to the piano too. Singers Joe Williams, Billy Eckstine, and Lou Rawls were all at the mike together at one stage, cutting each other in versions of the blues which ended with "It's a Lowdown Dirty Shame." There was dancing after chairs had been pushed back, Duke leading it off with Carmen de Lavallade, the radiantly beautiful ballerina who had been his Madam Zajj in *A Drum Is a Woman.* "Can you imagine Coolidge doing this?" observed Harold Arlen.

Ellington got back to his hotel just before three, surrounded by friends. He changed from tuxedo to travelling clothes and, stuffing congratulatory cables and birthday cards into his pocket, he departed to catch a plane. On the evening of the same day, he and the band played a gig in Oklahoma. Birthdays were all right, but business as usual remained Ellington's motto.

Business, however, hadn't been quite as usual for him during the past two years. Since the spring of 1967, in the wake of his quarrel with Granz, he had made no European tour. There were fears in London that he might not come again. During the summer of 1968, I suggested to the young London impresario, Robert Paterson, that he should try to add Ellington to his already distinguished list of artists.

During the 1960s, Paterson had become one of the most ambitious, hardheaded, and energetic entertainment figures in

Europe. Not everyone loved him, but in a business which isn't exactly dominated by charm or civilization, his cultural achievements were undeniable. He delivered the goods. In his early twenties he fearlessly approached Stravinsky when, presumably, everyone else believed that the great Russian composer was far too grand even to be asked. Stravinsky, brought to Europe for memorable concerts, was Paterson's first client. Down the years he has promoted tours by artists as different as Andy Williams, Charles Aznavour, Shirley Bassey, Neil Diamond, Benny Goodman, and Chicago. As late as 1976 he persuaded Bing Crosby to play his first-ever London theatre season at the age of seventy-two. In the middle of 1968, it seemed that if anyone could bend the reluctance of European concert promoters to present Ellington's band, it was Paterson.

The two men met for the first time in a room at the Fairmont Hotel in San Francisco. According to Paterson, Duke "was just damned awe-inspiring. I felt it with him just like I did with Stravinsky and with Bing Crosby. No one else. Just those three, and especially Duke."

Ellington and Paterson got on well enough, but there were all kinds of problems before Paterson finally brought Duke to Britain. First, Paterson reached an agreement with Duke's recently returned managerial aide, Cress Courtney, who was on the scene again after an absence of many years. Typical of their up-and-down relationship had been Ellington's explosion on observing the huge pile of green crocodile suitcases which were accompanying Courtney on a tour; the manager, Duke declared sourly, appeared to be making a better living than he was. As it turned out, Paterson almost missed getting Ellington at all when, inadvertently, a contract went off to Duke's office which Paterson himself admits was a mistake. "I missed checking it and I'm not surprised Duke's people took it as an insult to him. It had one clause which said he had to state the personnel in the band, and if anyone was ill Duke had to get *my* permission to put in a new man. I was horrified! Do you know something else? Duke was allergic to anything to do with health or accident insurance. It was his superstition again. He believed it would hasten the end to be insured like that. So I could never insure him during his tours because he wouldn't sign the forms or go through a medical examination. It was a big risk for me, but I suppose a lot of other people had to take the same chance."

The outcome of the misconceived contract was, finally, that

Paterson presented Duke in Britain, but that Duke's tours else-where in Europe were handled by the long-time promoter of the Newport Jazz Festival in America, George Wein.

So Ellington at last got back to Europe in the autumn of 1969. Earlier in the year he had been to the West Indies, playing a performance of the second Sacred Concert in Kingston, Jamaica, and on the other side of the Atlantic he made sure that many similar concerts were given; this was when he played at churches in Stockholm, Paris, and Barcelona. The tour was gruelling—a hectic series of one-night stands from Scandinavia down to Italy, and another first for Duke when he went behind the Iron Curtain for a single concert in Prague. There was, too, a joyous evening at the Alcazar music hall–restaurant in St.-Germaine-des-Prés in Paris when, at a banquet in his honor, Duke was presented by Maurice Chevalier with one of the great French artist's straw hats. "Fancy me wearing your hat," said Duke in his speech, "when no other artist in the world can ever fill your shoes."

The band which Ellington brought with him was more or less as of old, but the cracks were beginning to show, the transitions to be made. The trombones numbered only two—Brown and Connors. A new saxophonist and flautist, Norris Turney, seemed to push the reed section up to six; but he sat most of the time with the trombones, playing trombone parts. Herbie Jones had gone from the trumpets, Rolf Ericson substituting, although the irreplaceable Cat Anderson and Cootie Williams remained. The new bassist was Victor Gaskin. Most remarkable of all, there was a second keyboards man, the organist Wild Bill Davis, not appearing only as a specialty act, but adding his tone colors to several of the classic orchestrations from time to time.

Yet the performances Duke played in Britain in November, rounding off the European journey, were as scintillating as ever, seeming also to have a special significance. Rarely had anyone heard Ellington offer so much of his music at one sitting. As my review in the *Sunday Times* observed:

> It's as though he had contracted a productivity deal with his Muse. The urgency to sum up his achievement and reveal everything in his imperial storehouse has never seemed more insistent. His concerts in the past few days have contained a fresh restatement of as many Ellington classics as possible—"C Jam Blues," "Rockin' in Rhythm," "Take the A Train," "Black Butterfly," "Satin Doll,"

"Solitude," "Sophisticated Lady," "Caravan," "Mood Indigo"— with Duke mercilessly cutting through applause at the end of one number to hasten to the next.

One night in Manchester was typical. He played two concerts one after the other, each two and a half hours in duration—*and each without intervals.* He only let the audience into the non-stop secret after fifteen numbers, and at the second concert gave them thirty-two separate compositions of varying length, stayed onstage to do an encore with a quartet while Johnny Hodges led the exhausted orchestra away, and finally went off himself—but only as far as a small room at the back of the hall, where he listened to almost the whole rumbustious evening played back to him by the United Artists production team who were taping the performances. He didn't give up and seek his bed until dawn was seeping in through the cold Manchester rain.

This was the first time Duke had been recorded in England since 1933, and he wanted to make sure it was right. He must, too, have known that the orchestra couldn't continue much longer without losing some of its stars. That was probably why he laid out his riches so plentifully on these British occasions, and the performances are among the best he ever did. No one could have been surprised that when a double album of the concerts at Manchester and Bristol was issued under the title "Duke Ellington's 70th Birthday Concert," it was voted Jazz Record of the Year all over the world—a remarkable feat so late in the orchestra's career. Duke's piano playing was particularly inventive and joyous. The band swung like mad, relaxed and secure, with its soloists in sparkling form.

Paul Gonslaves was dynamically velveteen. Cootie Williams clowned gently, but still played the fattest-toned trumpet in captivity. Cat Anderson and Harry Carney, at opposite ends of the scales, seemed like men twenty years younger. For Russell Procope, Duke produced something quite unusual, "4:30 Blues," which began with a clarinet trio (Harold Ashby, Procope, and Carney on bass clarinet) before Procope took over, playing with a very "woody" tone and backed by grave, lamenting brass. This was a brilliant new piece of Ellingtonia, which drew a typically laconic remark from the leader. "He doesn't," he said in reference to Procope, "say whether it's 4:30 A.M. or P.M. It just could be he's complaining about the price."

Something else was captured on the album, too, which didn't

seem important at the time, but in the wake of Ellington's death was to prove a wonderful memento of him. This was the "finger-snapping" patter routine with which he elegantly closed so many concerts in his later years, but whose precise form is so elusive to one's memory. "Thank you very much, ladies and gentlemen," he says, while the band plays softly behind him at the end of the album. "You're very beautiful, very sweet, very gracious, very generous. This is 'Satin Doll.' We use it for the purpose of giving background to this finger-snapping bit, and you are all cordially invited to join the finger-snapping. . . . Crazy, I see I don't have to tell you—one never snaps one's fingers *on* the beat, it's considered aggressive. Don't push it, just let it fall. And if you would like to be conservatively hip and at the same time tilt the left ear lobe . . . establish a state of nonchalance . . . and if you would like to be respectably cool and tilt the left ear lobe *on* the beat and snap the fingers on the *after*-beat . . . and so, by routining one's finger-snapping and choreographing one's ear-lobe tilting, one discovers that one *can* become as cool as one wishes to be. With that we certainly want to thank you for the wonderful way you've inspired us, remind you that you're very beautiful, very sweet, very gracious, very generous and that we *do* love you madly. . . ." At which point, he sauntered into "love you madly" in around a dozen of the languages he'd picked up scraps of during his travels from Japan to Mexico.

The words weren't the greatest prose in the world, of course; but they have wit, they're apt for the occasion, yielding that distinctive Ellingtonian blend of sophistication and simplicity. To hear the calm, light huskiness of his voice speaking them now—and remembering that he delivered them after providing five hours of non-stop music, mostly his own, in the process of another hectic tour, all at the age of seventy—is a cause both of bittersweet recall and of considerable wonder that ever such an artist could have existed.

Equally and poignantly memorable was the soft sound of Johnny Hodges at these concerts. In the early-morning hours, Duke sat listening to the tapes with eyes closed, smiling like some great all-wise Buddha, and he murmured "Beautiful" more often when he heard Hodges than at any other time. "Have you ever known him play better?" he drawled later, shaking his head in wonder. On the recording you can hear a marvellous performance of "Black Butterfly," which Duke had written (with Irving Mills also credited) back in 1937. Hodges's relaxed, lush alto-sax sound is poised tantalizingly against spiky piano chords from the leader. You can also hear how Duke lets the applause start for just a second or two before he's pushing the band relentlessly into Mercer's "Things Ain't What They Used to Be," again featuring Hodges. Ellington had no time to spare now; nor, cruelly, had Hodges. Within six months, the most important single soloist Duke had ever had would be dead.

There was no warning of this, however, as the band headed back to America for Christmas and another new year of intense activity for Ellington. In 1970 he led the band off again for a Japanese visit; took in Australia, New Zealand, Thailand, and Laos for the first time; returned to Europe for a month; made memorable appearances at the New Orleans and Monterey Jazz Festivals, premiering major new compositions at each, and wrote the score for a much acclaimed ballet, *The River*, which was performed by the American Ballet Theatre. "He never thought it had done justice to his conception, though," Stanley Dance told me. "He never did think anything was as good as it should have been—except for *My People*, when he did the lot. I suppose he was unreasonable, really, because he never gave people too much of a chance. He was always working up to the very last minute, so how could you expect a dance company to have had time to fit everything together with the music?"

New Orleans, so appropriately, was to be the name associated with Johnny Hodges in 1970. For his appearance at the city's festival, Duke had written parts of what later became "The New Orleans Suite"—five sections devoted to its history and geography (including the delightfully named "Bourbon Street Jingling Jollies") and four which were portraits of its citizens who had meant much to Ellington: Louis Armstrong, Mahalia Jackson, Wellman Braud, and Sidney Bechet. Late in April, the band began recording the suite in New York with a lineup already revealing the band's slow disintegration. The reeds were intact; but the great Lawrence Brown had at last disappeared from the trombone section; Chuck Connors and Cat Anderson were missing, too, from some of the tracks. Five numbers were recorded on April 27, with Hodges and the saxophones in fine form. Then there was a hiatus; Duke was rushing to finish off his four "Portraits." On May 11, Duke was thinking how he might persuade Hodges to brush up his soprano sax playing for the "Portrait of

Sidney Bechet" when a telephone call told him that Johnny had just died at his dentist's office. Apart from the break of four years in the 1950s, Hodges had been with the band continuously since early 1928, an absolutely unique artist. Many had tried to imitate him, but none had succeeded. No wonder Ellington was moved that night to set down one of his most generous tributes, its poignancy heightened by one's realization that at times Hodges had seemed to resent Duke. He had wanted to be a bandleader himself, had believed that he should have made it when he cut loose in the 1950s, but he had ultimately failed to do so.

In his tribute, Duke wrote:

> Never the world's most highly animated showman or greatest stage personality but a tone so beautiful it sometimes brought tears to the eyes—this was Johnny Hodges. This *is* Johnny Hodges. Because of this great loss, our band will never sound the same.
>
> Johnny Hodges and his unique tonal personality have gone to join the ever so few inimitables—those whose sounds stand unimitated, to say the least—Art Tatum, Sidney Bechet, Django Reinhardt, Billy Strayhorn. . . .
>
> Johnny Hodges sometimes sounded beautiful, sometimes romantic, and sometimes people spoke of his tone as being sensuous. I've heard women say his tone was so compelling. . . . I'm glad and thankful that I had the privilege of presenting Johnny Hodges for forty years, night after night. I imagine I have been much envied, but thanks to God. May God bless this beautiful giant in his own identity.

The album of "The New Orleans Suite" itself showed how desperately Duke would miss Hodges. The saxophone genius's lazy-sounding solo on "Blues for New Orleans" was as fine as anything he ever did, whilst on "Portrait of Sidney Bechet," taped on May 13 two days after his death, the intensely emotional playing of Paul Gonsalves in the role Hodges would have filled seems to be an elegy for the man his fellow musicians knew as "Rabbit" rather than for the nominal recipient. Ellington's ability to recruit brilliant new talent still, however, shone through. Norris Turney had got better and better, especially on flute; whilst the trombonist Julian Priester, from the unlikely background of Herbie Hancock's band, sounded like one of nature's Ellingtonians. Appropriately, the album was voted 1970's Record of the Year as universally as the "70th Birthday Concert" had been for 1969.

Even without Hodges and Brown, Ellington had to make the best of it. The band's schedule was still very full, and within a month Duke had to fulfill his commission for the American Ballet Theatre, *The River*, which opened in New York on June 25 to some generous reviews. It was written in movements, with music suited to each, and each given a characteristic note of explanation by Duke. The titles were "The Spring," "The Run," "The Meander," "The Giggling Rapids," "The Lake," "The Falls," "The Whirlpool," "The River," "The Neo-Hip-Hot Cool-Kiddies Community," "The Village of the Virgins," "The Mother, Her Majesty the Sea," and, finally, "The Spring" again. Two of Ellington's notes will give the flavor of the whole. The river starts as . . .

> *THE SPRING*, which is like a newborn baby. He's in his cradle . . . spouting, spinning, wiggling, gurgling, squirming, squealing, making faces, reaching for his nipple or bottle, turning, tossing, and tinkling all over the place. When he hits the floor for the first time out of the cradle he is about to go into . . . *THE RUN*.

Later, exhausted by the rapids, the river relaxes and rolls down to . . .

> *THE LAKE:* The lake is beautiful and serene. It is all horizontal lines that offer up unrippled reflections. There it is, in all its beauty, God-made and untouched, until people come—people who are God-made and terribly touched by the beauty of the lake. They, in their admiration for it, begin to discover new faces of compatibility in each other, and as a romantic viewpoint develops, they indulge themselves. The whole situation compounds itself into an emotional violence that is even greater than that of the violence of the vortex to come. The lake supports them until, suddenly, they are over the top and down. . . .

The music written to match these moods was some of the most ambitious ever attempted by Ellington. Glockenspiel and timpani were added to the rapid machine-gun beat of Rufus Jones's drums in the section called "The Falls," which featured Paul Gonsalves on tenor sax and was distinguished by band chords of extraordinary dissonance. Whitney Balliett, the distinguished critic of *The New Yorker*, compared it with early Stravinsky. "The Mother" was swirling and ruminative, with a lovely flute solo from Norris Turney. In parts, with Ellington conducting, Wild Bill Davis was the pianist. Balliett, who had urged in the previous year (with, typically, no takers) that Duke be given a $100,000 grant by one of the foundations so that he could take time off to record or re-record his greatest works on, say, a twelve-album set, described most effectively the recording session for "The River" and its aftermath, which in its revelations of Duke's character and ambience was pure-gold Ellingtonia.

Edmund Anderson was there, recalling that in Paris the previous November, he had shot some film of the band, with particularly great footage of Johnny Hodges, "who in all the thirty-five years I knew him never said more than two words." He told Hodges about the filming. "He shouted at me, 'Not tonight! Not tonight! My eyes looked so bad!' Which was all the more amazing when you consider that on the stand Hodges kept his eyes closed most of the time."

After the session, Ellington was invited to walk a block or so to his next appointment, a meeting with Alvin Ailey. "Well, I might as well," Ellington said, "but it'll be the longest walk I've had in years," which was true. He was as opposed to exercise as he was to fresh air, and had that stiffish way of walking that suggested an old man with worn feet. Later still that evening he agreed to a TV interview at a jazz club, the Half Note. When he wandered in, he sat on a bar stool, was given a Coke, and then was drenched in blinding arc-lamp light. "You know, I'm not really dressed for this sort of thing, but let me light a cigarette, so I'll look sophisticated." Then he knocked over the Coke. "Oh, my! I'm the only nuisance who knows he's a nuisance!" During the interview he gave in one answer a variant on a statement he had made several times in the immediately preceding years. "I don't think any music should be called jazz. I don't believe in categories. Years ago, uptown, I tried to get the cats to call it American Negro music or Afro-American music, because jazz just isn't right. Louis Armstrong plays Louis Armstrong music, Art Tatum plays Art Tatum music, Dizzy Gillespie plays Dizzy Gillespie music, and if it sounds good, that's all you need." That Ellington answer never totally held water. One completely agreed with his dislike of pigeonholing and one believed (which, of course, he couldn't say) that Ellington had brought so many other elements to jazz that his music did indeed transcend categories. But the three artists he mentioned were jazzmen, popular-music men, through and through—great individualists, all touched with genius, but playing their personal way within a recognizable and distinctive game called jazz.

Once *The River* had been recorded, Duke was travelling again—a month in Europe, including his Sacred Concert at Orange in France. Edmund Anderson was again present the evening Duke departed from Kennedy Airport, having earlier in the day picked up a huge cardboard box containing Ellington's supply of vitamin pills for the trip. "I couldn't believe the order the druggist filled. All that, just for *one* month? He ate vitamins like other people eat breakfast cereal!" Duke's flight was due to leave at nine in the evening, and Anderson arrived with Ruth Ellington outside the West End Avenue apartment not long after seven. It was almost eight before Duke casually entered the car, with Anderson warning that they wouldn't make the plane. But Ellington told them not to worry. He had to make a call at Riverside Drive—to see Aunt Flossie! Anderson explained what happened then:

> I nearly folded, but I knew it was no good arguing. This was the family devotion side of him. Aunt Flossie was his mother's sister, and she lived in one of those two Ellington houses, at Riverside and 105th Street, and every time he left town it was a ritual that he had to stop and say goodbye to Flossie. By the time we got to the house it was 8:10, and Edward sauntered off inside. He came back in around ten minutes and said she was asleep and he hadn't the heart to wake her! We set off again and I've never seen him so jovial and relaxed. I'd been to an *avant garde* concert recently, and I asked him what he thought of the "new music." He laughed. "New music? Hell, there's been no new music since Stravinsky." Then he told story after story. You know, about the gangsters in Chicago and so on, and I was really sweating because there was a huge jam around the airport, and he sat there just smiling and calm, cool, collected.
>
> So finally we made it out to Kennedy at around 10 P.M. and I was wondering how we could get him on another plane, and I was carrying this damn great box of vitamins, and to my astonishment the girl at the desk smiled and said, "Ah, Mr. Ellington. We have moved the plane from the runway and we are waiting for you." God knows what the other passengers thought, though I guess the

band was used to it. So someone takes the big box, and the last we see is Edward strolling down a corridor with his needlepoint music case in his hand—it was a present from Evie and he carried his music in it everywhere around the globe—still looking as if he had all the time in the world and, would you believe, acting like holding up a plane for an hour or more was exactly what he'd expected them to do. He could be quite infuriatingly lordly and simultaneously wonderful at times.

Back from Europe, Duke had a season at the Rainbow Grill and was hotly preparing to play at the Monterey Festival in September, for which he composed music more in his usual vein than *The River* had been. This was the "Afro-Eurasian Eclipse," an idea which had been brewing since the previous year when Duke was playing a Las Vegas season at Caesar's Palace. His habit, as soon as his show ended just before four o'clock each morning, was to watch old cowboy movies on TV in his room, then write as the sun came up, then return to television for the morning chat shows. One day the Canadian sage, Marshall McLuhan, delivered himself in an interview of this observation: "The whole world is going oriental, and nobody will be able to retain his identity, not even the orientals."

Up and down the world Ellington had seen the truth of this: American and British musicians taking to the sitar, girls wearing saris, oriental food loading our tables, an obsession among the young for Eastern religions in place of Christianity, long hair, beards, and the rest. Equally, he'd watched the Westernization of the East—the skyscrapers of Tokyo, the jazz in the clubs, the girl singer who could put over an American song word-perfect without the slightest idea what she was singing about. All this, with side references to Australia and New Zealand, which he visited in 1970 during the tour that took him to Japan for the third time, he tried to put into "Afro-Eurasian Eclipse." This suite is not notably outstanding in the Ellington canon, but it provided him with one of the happiest audience introductions of his later years. "In this particular segment, ladies and gentlemen," he would mischievously tell the bemused listeners, "we have adjusted our perspective to that of the kangaroo and the dijiridoo, which automatically puts us Down Under or Out Back. From this viewpoint, it is most improbable that anyone can tell who is enjoying the shadow of whom. Harold Ashby has been inducted into the responsibility and obligation of scraping off a tiny chip of the charisma of his chinoiserie, almost immediately after the piano player completes his riki-tiki."

This was the line of talk which Ellington was giving even to the hardened hustlers of Las Vegas in that watershed year of 1970. Hodges's death was one blow. Lawrence Brown, the minister's son from Lawrence, Kansas, had also departed, tired not only with travelling, the usual leaver's complaint, but equally soured with the music business in general. "We have to recognize that being popular is nowadays more important than producing something of value," he'd said a few years before he went. Cat Anderson, the high-note trumpeter, followed him, and by 1971 the Ellington band looked to be splitting at the seams. But Duke would never say one word to suggest that he was in any way worried. Every new man who arrived was, in his mouth, a blazing new talent; and, characteristically, he chose 1971 to undertake the longest continuous overseas tour in his band's (or anyone else's) history—five weeks in Russia, five weeks in Europe, and, finally, a return to Latin America for three weeks.

As a composer, he was again tending to look backwards. Remembering the striking evening of the torches at the Goutelas Château in 1966, he premiered "The Goutelas Suite" at Lincoln Center in New York on April 16, 1971, an expression of his admiration for the people who had restored the building. It is a fine work containing one of Ellington's few fanfares, as well as a rare piece of flute playing by Norris Turney and those strange, misty tone colors from reeds which were uniquely Duke's. It became available on an album with "The Queen's Suite" in 1976, having been purchased from the Duke Ellington Foundation by Norman Granz for his Pablo label.

This was not the only debt which Duke was repaying around this time. At the Newport Jazz Festival in July 1971, he presented a new suite, "Togo Brava!" occasioned by the gesture made to him in 1967 when his head had appeared along with the heads of Bach, Debussy, and Beethoven on a set of four postage stamps issued by Togoland to mark UNESCO's twentieth anniversary. The honor paid to Ellington by the young African republic had been marked by a ceremony in New York, and Duke, wishing to be well prepared, spent hours on the telephone asking the Diamonds to research into the country for him—everything from its history to its fertility. Finally, a package of notes and other material was sent by express air freight to America. Duke gave a great deal of himself to people and often expected the same in return. Duggie Tobutt, the tour manager for Harold Davison, who used to present Duke for Norman Granz in Britain, once described how Ellington arrived while on tour at a modest Yorkshire hotel around 1 A.M. on a very wintry night and asked for tea and sandwiches. "No one else would have got them at that hour," said Tobutt, "but he did. Then, incredibly, he said he could use a piano. Half an hour later four men staggered upstairs to his bedroom carrying an old upright."

The advent of "Togo Brava!" showed that Ellington's artistic energy was far from gone even as late as this year of his life. The lists of compositions copyrighted around this time reveal much other activity as well. "The Blues Ain't," "Lovin' Lover," "Ray Charles' Place," and "Perdido Cha Cha Cha Cha," all from 1971, reflect different facets of the man who was still driving ahead as if nothing had changed, yet, equally, as if there might be no to-morrow.

The Russian tour upon which the band embarked in September was, for obvious reasons, one of the most remarkable of all modern artistic forays. Jazz certainly wasn't unknown in Russia. Louis Armstrong and Benny Goodman had made visits during the 1960s, and Duke was met when his plane landed at Leningrad by a large band marching across the airfield playing Dixieland jazz. For all that, to tour for more than a month, visiting Moscow, Leningrad, Kiev, Minsk, and Rostov, to be fêted like a genius, and to be mentioned in *Pravda*—the first time, it was believed, that the official Russian newspaper had told its readers of the presence of an American artist in the USSR—was a feat which few other than Ellington could have pulled off.

The orchestra he took with him and then on to Britain and other European countries is worth listing to note the new names and the old ones which had disappeared. The reed section, six strong, was Russell Procope, Paul Gonsalves, Harold Ashby, Harold Minerve, Norris Turney, and Harry Carney. Cootie Williams, Mercer Ellington, Harold "Money" Johnson, and John Coles were the trumpets; on trombones were Malcolm Taylor, Mitchell "Booty" Wood, and Chuck Connors. Rufus Jones (drums) and Joe Benjamin (bass), plus two singers, Nell Brookshire and Tony Watkins, completed the lineup.

Tony Watkins, who had played an important part in the second Sacred Concert three years earlier, was one of the more interesting members of Ellington's entourage during the later years, a rare example of a man who had made it from being "band boy"-cum-valet to a place on the stage, singing well when he got the right songs. Ellington's "band boys" were a crucial part of the caravan throughout his career. There were more than a dozen of them at various times, responsible not only for setting up and dismantling stands onstage, but also for baggage handling, general diplomacy, and all kinds of miscellaneous chores. Some of them became quite expert in stage lighting, able to let different theatre staffs know exactly what color effects were wanted to suit the moods of the music. Because work schedules often allowed no time for haircuts, Duke also used to carry a barber with the entourage, another reason why his money seemed to drain away as fast as he made it.

Ellington appears to have liked Russia, indulging his appetite for caviar, but missing decent steaks so much that the Embassy arranged to have them flown in especially for him. Thus fortified, he put on ten pounds and summoned up the energy to see the Bolshoi Ballet *inside* the Kremlin, to visit the great Hermitage collection in Leningrad (as well as a clandestine club), and to meet the outstanding contemporary composer, Aram Khachaturian. He conducted and played with the Radio Moscow Jazz Orchestra—an occasion which moved him as much as it did the musicians—and everywhere he went he had rapturous sell-out audiences. There were 10,000 at each of the three concerts he played in Kiev; more than 12,000 crowded into every one of his appearances in Moscow—and they'd paid heavily for the privilege. *Melody Maker* reported in London: "The black market did a roaring trade. Five-ruble ($5.55) seats sold for 40 rubles ($44). A case of free enterprise striking back." The figures were later confirmed by Ellington himself.

Pravda, of course, had nothing to say about that, nor about the Sacred Concert which Duke presented privately at the U.S. Embassy, but it was generous indeed with the band. The critic was particularly struck by their "priceless sense of ease. . . . They walk on without any special ceremony, simply, one by one, as friends usually gather for a jam session." For his concerts, Duke chose his programs carefully. He was still closing with his "Lotus Blossom" piano solo. Inevitably, there were masses of Ellington standards and pop songs—but he presented all kinds of longer works as well: the entire "Togo Brava!" suite, "La Plus Belle Africaine," and, above all, the lengthy "Harlem" from 1950. He kept on getting requests for "When the Saints Go Marching In," but he wouldn't do it. Instead, not wanting to offend his hosts, he got Money Johnson to play and sing "Hello Dolly" in the Louis Armstrong manner. When Ellington moved on to England after Russia, lots of Ellington purists didn't like "Hello Dolly," although they appreciated the other three compositions mentioned, two of which were included in a double album recorded at British concerts during October. They should, perhaps, have understood better *why* Duke had a version of "Hello Dolly" on his books. He was an entertainer as well as a musician.

Russia was successful beyond even Duke's hopes—and was, not surprisingly, the subject of warm letters to him from President Nixon and Senator Hubert Humphrey. Once he left, it was back to the one-nighter pattern all over Europe (including Poland, Yugoslavia, Hungary, and Rumania), and when he arrived in London during a springlike spell of October weather, he was looking much older and very tired. Yet he was still bubbling over with the joys of Russia, laughing as I'd rarely seen him laugh when he recalled his alarm at seeing so many police around the hall at one concert in Kiev. Don't worry, one of his interpreters told him, they're just members of the police band who wanted so much to hear you. He exulted in the lightness of his work load in Russia. "Do you know I only had to do two concerts a week there? Man, that was *easy*. So easy, I had to find something for the band to do. So I called rehearsals!"

There were incidents to remember now he was back in England, too. Robert Paterson explained:

> You always had to brace yourself when you were getting ready for an Ellington tour. Nothing would ever be tidy. You would just have got a contract organized, and the State Department would want him to go somewhere, or he'd have to fit in a special event or a Sacred Concert or something. I reckoned it was an utter miracle he never blew a date on me. Things always seemed to go wrong with his travel. One night the band bus broke down and he played three-quarters of an hour of piano solos as the first half of the show. Another time we hit the outskirts of Southport and the limousine driver took a wrong turning and we ended up on sand dunes, outside of town, with no petrol and a gale blowing. I had to

go off and look for a hitch because there was no chance of a petrol station near where we'd got stuck. All I could find after about half an hour was a man in a jeep—and that's how Duke arrived for the concert, in that jeep! And they'd put out "WELCOME DUKE" banners around the town too!

There was one particularly memorable night after he'd played a concert at the Hammersmith Odeon in London. He'd been at his most impish in the selections chosen: "Harlem," parts of "The New Orleans Suite," and "Afro-Eurasian Eclipse," together with older works like "Black and Tan Fantasy," had been mixed in with "Hello Dolly" and a penultimate rampaging piece of soul rock, "One More Once," spearheaded by his two handclapping singers, which was just about as un-Ellingtonian as you could get, in the (misguided) view of him held by many serious fans. As that re-echoed around the theatre, you could imagine the purists frowning.

Riding hotelwards later, he recalled that the previous night some of the audience had come onstage dancing to join in the fun. "If we keep playing that number," he said with quizzical irony, "then the critics can stop wondering what to pan." We were headed for the Dorchester, and he must have been very tired, but his husky voice couldn't stop talking about Russia.

> Do you know some of those concerts went on for *four* hours? Yeah, and no one complained—not the audience [managing to make himself sound surprised], not the stage hands, not even the cats in the band. The Russians came to hear our music, no other reason. Ten, eleven, twelve encores they kept on wanting. Some of them were satisfied, I guess, and some were surprised how much they were satisfied.

I asked him why Cootie Williams, who had prowled the stage at full power, whilst saving himself mainly for solos, had left the stand early. "Come, Derek," said Duke. "He is a senior citizen of our company. He has that privilege."

There was a party that night in a private suite for around twenty people attended by, among others, Robert and Sybille Paterson, Stanley Dance, Edmund and Joan Anderson, the Diamonds, and Jacques Loussier, who happened to be in town. Around four in the morning, Duke was jamming with Loussier on a single piano. It was very funny and, at the same time, ridiculously wonderful. Was the Ellington saga, despite all the evidence of age, ever going to end?

There were, already, signs that it was if one looked hard enough. Despite Duke's bonhomie, his tolerance was becoming untypically more limited whenever things went wrong. The incident at Southport was not singular. With breakdowns added, it took Duke eight hours in a limousine to arrive at Bournemouth from Blackpool for a two-concert date. Edmund Anderson found him in his dressing room looking exhausted, with no one to help him with his stage clothes.

> Why, he couldn't even shave because there was no mirror fixed to the wall. So I held one while he shaved, and he went off to do his first show, and everyone was there—Max Jones, Sinclair Traill, Stanley Dance, all the writers. And those bums who hung around Gonsalves were on the scene, too, and then Robert Paterson arrived with Sybille and she seemed upset and Duke was comforting her when Gonsalves, absolutely plastered, came into Duke's room. And, suddenly, bang, his cool evaporated. I've never seen him in such a rage. He screamed at Gonsalves to get his ticket, get on the plane, never wanted to see him again—all that kind of stuff. Another time, at the Rainbow Grill, he actually hit Gonsalves on the face. He had to, because Paul had fallen asleep on the stand and was listing dangerously. But that wasn't typical of Ellington. He was just pushed more than even he could stand sometimes. What his words meant, God knows, because the next night Gonsalves or whoever would be back on the stand. I guess they understood they *deserved* Duke's fury at times, and most of them loved him just the same.

Equally, however, Ellington could appear to be unforgiving. At a jazz festival in New York City in 1972, with Duke and the band onstage, the compere announced that Sonny Greer was in the wings. He'd returned to take his old place at the drums. Greer came on, wild applause broke out, and the drummer (then almost seventy) clambered onto a stool behind the drum kit, all ready to play. Duke wasn't, though. He waited, in embarrassed silence, until Greer stood up again, took a bow, and disappeared. Only then did the band play on.

There were also indifferent Ellington concerts on that 1971 tour. In Birmingham, Duke left the piano to announce a number to be played in tribute to Johnny Hodges. He raised his arms and conducted the band into the opening bars, but quickly brought them to a halt, crying "Stop, stop! I think we can do better than that. Kindly start again, gentlemen." Renee Diamond commented: "The rest of the concert was slipshod too, but Duke let it go. He wouldn't have it for Hodges, though." At other times toward the end, he wouldn't have it for Ellington either. He was conducting a public rehearsal of his band at the University of Wisconsin in 1972, taking the musicians through a first attempt at his latest composition.

"Letter E," Ellington proclaimed to signify where they were to start playing. But some of the musicians began elsewhere, and Duke spoke strongly. "No! E! E as in Ellington! E! E as in Edward! E! E as in Ellington! E as in Excellence! E as in Elegance, as in Edward and Ellington! E! E! E as in all good things! Edward . . . Ellington . . . Excellence . . . Elegance! E!"

However, even occasional slipshod playing was no deterrent to Duke in that autumn of 1971, and particular occasions could still inspire the musicians to efforts almost as superhuman as those of their leader. From Britain, Ellington dashed back to Europe, ended up in Spain, and in mid-November was on his way to Rio de Janeiro. This Latin-American trip went far beyond the frontiers set on the last, in 1968. In twenty-four days the band played return dates in Rio de Janeiro, São Paulo, Buenos Aires, Santiago, Mexico City, and Guadalajara, as well as adding the following cities or countries to their lists of firsts: Mendoza (Argentina), Lima (Peru), Quito (Ecuador), Bogotá (Colombia), Montevideo (Uruguay), Caracas (Venezuela), Panama City, San José (Costa Rica), and Managua (Nicaragua). In some places where feelings about the United States were, to say the least, mixed, American diplomats were apprehensive in advance about reaction to Duke's visit. He and his music dispelled fears. Enthusiasm was high everywhere in packed halls, applause deafening, tears many. Most concerts ran on for over three hours until the band could simply play no more before they had to rush and make the next travel connection. Of the many U.S. embassy reports on the tour, a paragraph from that in Nicaragua was characteristic:

The impact of Duke Ellington's performance cannot be overstated. While many in Nicaragua have only a limited exposure to jazz, and feel more comfortable with classical and popular music, all

> were impressed by the artistry of the performance and touched by
> the magnetism of "The Duke." Nicaraguans seem to understand a
> little bit better what U.S. culture is all about . . . that we're
> something "alive and now."

As usual, there was an early-morning press conference virtually every time Duke arrived in a new town. He must have
spoken thousands of words at these, many of them reiterating
what he had said similarly in earlier years. But sometimes the
phrasing or the intention of his words, in answer perhaps to a
question with a different slant, would be elegantly revealing. "I
originally began to compose because I wasn't able to play what
other composers wrote," he said, "so I had to create something
that I could play. I remain a primitive artist, extremely primitive. But paradoxically the most sophisticated music in the world
is primitive music, and no one is able to penetrate it easily." Or
again. "To ask whether jazz is music for dancing is to introduce a
category or classification I resist, but I would say that our music
is intended to inspire or sustain dancing."

The band flew from Guadalajara in Mexico on December 10
to fulfill an engagement in Chicago the next day, and the customary round of dances and concerts within the United States
was resumed. So, too, was the bestowing of honors with which
the world had for many years been acknowledging his greatness.
Five more doctoral degrees had been given to him by American
universities in 1971 to add to the near dozen (Yale's among
them) he already had. From that 1971 clutch he particularly val-
ued the degrees from the Berklee College of Music, in Boston,
Massachusetts, which had trained so many jazz musicians, and
from Howard University, which had been founded as a black
college in Washington, D.C. Some awards were uniquely American: his commission as Admiral of the Great Navy of Nebraska in
1970. In July 1972, the state of Wisconsin was to go one better
than all the cities and states which had named days in his honor
by proclaiming a Duke Ellington week. Still to come, too, were
the Legion of Honor, bestowed on him in 1973 by the French
president, Georges Pompidou, and the Emperor's Star, Ethiopia's highest honor, which he received in Addis Ababa from
Emperor Haile Selassie in the same year.

Ellington's drive as a composer was beginning to weaken as
1972 opened. One doesn't have to agree with more extreme as-

sessments of Duke's work in his last few years to recognize this. Norman Granz's view, for instance, overstates the position.

> Towards the end he did nothing musically and he was aware of that. He'd go back into the bag and recycle things. It was a combination of sheer fatigue and the age of his sidemen. They'd been so important to him. He'd wave his hands and say to Strays at the piano or to Hodges, "Do a little thing in here," and they'd do it, help him out. Now, it's one of the strengths of a great artist that he takes short cuts, but that means you get *usualness*, too. When creativity wells within you, it all comes out in the beginnings. That's how it was with Duke. The give-and-take of the early days was incredible, but later it became *usual*. So in a way, the absence of much turnover among Duke's musicians was bad as well as good. They got *too* used to each other.

Oddly enough, considering their quarrel five years earlier, Granz and Duke were back together in 1972, at least on the recording front. Granz explained how he had the chance to put some, at least, of his beliefs into practice with Ellington.

> I bumped into him at the Coconut Grove one evening, and he said it was time we got back together. So we began talking and seeing each other. I wanted him to break up and take a sabbatical, recharge his batteries. But he wouldn't—he was afraid to have a day off. He said it was a job to him and he had to keep going. But at least I managed to get him to do some albums outside the band context. There was "This One's for Blanton" with Ray Brown in 1972 and "Duke's Big Four" with Joe Pass on guitar the next year. I believe in that. A jazz musician can't get too comfortable. He needs the give-and-take of *contact*. That's why I've been a fervent believer in jam sessions, because you place musicians in strange surroundings and, okay, if it falls on its ass, it falls on its ass.
>
> When we did the "Big Four," Duke was dying. He asked me who the musicians were, and when I said Joe Pass, he asked who he was. I told him to trust me, and the chemistry worked—Duke away from the band sounded fresh and healthy. He'd broken the mold. It was better than a lot he was doing in the last seven or eight years. I heard him once in St. Tropez and I thought it was terrible and I said so to Harry Carney, and Carney said "Don't tell me—I know." Do you remember when Duke had Wild Bill Davis on organ with the band? Well, he was the *best* jazz organist, and Duke could have really incorporated him in the sound, written

something *seriously* for him. But he didn't. He just used Bill as a relief soloist most of the time.

The truth is that some of the things said about Ellington are exaggerated. Like him writing so he could hear it played the next day. That kind of propaganda was in a way a crutch for Duke. He clung to the band like a crutch, just as old people cling together in marriage because they can't think of anything else to do. Publicity spread the idea that Duke wrote specifically for each man in the band. I guess that was true at certain fixed points in his career, especially in the early days, but even then the business wasn't one-way. It wasn't only that Duke wrote for Hodges. Sometimes *Hodges* played something with *Duke* in mind. So—did he write for somebody like Norris Turney in the later days? He didn't. He played the same numbers, and he didn't make changes in the rest of the band's scores.

Such statements indicate that, as inevitably happens even with geniuses, someone somewhere will start a backlash once they are gone and (to be fair to Granz) once enthusiasm for their work has on occasions gone over the top. Granz has a point, even a useful antidote for hyperbole about Ellington, but it is exaggerated not merely in terms of taste but sometimes in terms of fact. Ellington wrote less with specific men in mind in his final year or so, of course. But his suites of the middle and later 1960s; his Sacred Concerts; his one-off short pieces, were all composed with the same faithfulness to the idiosyncrasies of his key bandsmen as had been his earlier work. To give only a few examples. He wrote for Harry Carney specifically in many Sacred Concert passages, including "In the Beginning God." He wrote for the voice of Alice Babs very particularly as late as 1968, and even in 1973. So did he for Tony Watkins's range and timbre. Wild Bill Davis *was* integrated into the orchestral sound in concerts I heard. Ellington even made room for Norris Turney's individuality in the band; Turney often played flute as well as saxophone in his time with Duke, and Ellington had scarcely (if ever) used flute before with his orchestra. Duke was continually rewriting tunes like "East St. Louis Toodle-oo" and "Mood Indigo" to use the gifts of new sidemen and to erase the parts that called for the particular talents of departed Ellingtonians. That he was less inclined to compose or to tailor material for his band by 1972 was, however, scarcely surprising.

At this stage, even Duke's superhuman frame was suffering

from his exhausting way of life. He had a major medical checkup with Dr. Arthur Logan and other specialists before he set out early in the year for yet another journey through the Far East, longer than anything he'd done in the area before. Japan and the Philippines came first, and in Manila he played a particularly important concert with the National Symphony Orchestra, which featured both "Harlem" and the long orchestral piece from 1955, "Night Creature." The NSO's conductor, Rendentor Romero, "Red" to the Ellington band, had memorized Ray Nance's violin solo from "Night Creature's" second movement and reproduced it perfectly. There were so many other highlights of the tour, which broke new ground with visits to Bangkok, Kuala Lumpur, Singapore, Djakarta, and Mandalay. The only disturbances involved a row with a TV show host in Singapore who accused Duke of "neo-pseudoism," and Duke's displeasure with a smart New Zealand promoter who, anticipating the event, had billed the band as making its "farewell concert." Mostly, though, it was sweetness all the way, especially in Bangkok, where Duke sampled the delights of the riverside barbecue at the Oriental Hotel, surely one of the most delicious experiences in the world, and appreciated the warmth and naturalness of the Thais.

The King of Thailand, who'd often come to hear the band when he was a student at Harvard, and plays the clarinet, placed a garland of flowers around Duke's neck after the concert, and he tried for weeks to preserve it in fridges and bags of ice water. When he failed, he made a drawing of it as a memento—a poignant reminder of the fact that Duke was always buying oil paints and brushes which he never found time to use. He was a fine, but completely under-exercised, painter. There were flowers in Mandalay, too. As Ellington himself recalled it, his "Road to Mandalay" led from plane to airport building and was lined with music professors and musicians, who presented him with twenty different bouquets during his progress. Duke was intrigued by the almost total silence at the concert he played in Mandalay, the local way of indicating overwhelming approval. After three hours, the audience were still quietly sitting there. Ellington had made another hit, in a new way.

From Australia, with concerts in five cities, and New Zealand he flew on via Fiji to Honolulu, Vancouver, Seattle, and Los Angeles for a series of appearances with Sarah Vaughan and Billy

Eckstine. Soon he was to be appointed official host of New York's Summer Festival, with Gloria Swanson playing opposite him as hostess. He wrote his song "New York, New York!" whose racy lyrics were as characteristic as anything he'd ever done: "New York is a glitter, New York is a glamour, New York is a sun-swept, moonshine, super grand-slammer." One day in June he was back in Honolulu to be honored by his own profession at the annual conference of the American Foundation of Musicians, who presented him with a gold card signifying honorary life membership. The irony was cruel, for he had less than two years to live.

Duke himself may have sensed this, for he had been devoting an increasing amount of time to his autobiography during the 1970s. Remembering how he had compared biographies to tombstones in his middle years, the significance is inescapable. There are two views about how Ellington viewed his last few years. Some think he believed himself virtually indestructible. That seems, in retrospect, extreme. By the very act of grappling with his autobiography—a task he disliked—he appears at last to have been taking the realistic view that he could not expect to live for many years after his seventieth birthday.

He had had a contract with Doubleday, the New York publishers, to write a book since 1963. All through the 1950s, Sam Vaughan, then a junior editor at Doubleday, and later to become its president, had pursued Ellington. He wrote annually, offering a $10,000 advance. He followed Duke into clubs and dressing rooms. "I always seemed to meet him when he had his pants off, and he'd smile and say he'd never write a book." Then one night, the chairman of the company, Nelson Doubleday, was with some friends at a club where Duke was playing. The performance was brilliant. At the end of it, Doubleday marched up to Duke, proclaimed him to be the greatest jazz genius of them all, and said he *must* write a book.

Ellington surveyed the boss of the publishing house. The vein of snobbery within him was touched. He liked to talk with the high and mighty, and this (in book publishing terms) was one of the highest and mightiest. He said only two words: "How much?"

Nelson Doubleday may himself have felt trapped at this stage. His friends watched. He could scarcely offer anything paltry.

"Fifty thousand dollars in advance, Mr. Ellington."

"Sold," said Duke, who (as always) could do with the money. Even then, however, Doubleday had to wait a long time.

In the late 1960s, Duke was beginning to scribble down things—bits of philosophy, little prose poems and verses, capsule biographies of people he'd known—whenever he had a moment, as well as looking out all the papers from earlier years. To Stanley Dance, who had chronicled Ellington's career for many years, was given the task of sorting out the pieces, rewriting, filling in the holes. He wasn't exactly a "ghost," but he was much more than an editor, receiving a typical tribute from Duke in the introductory section of the ultimate book: "Stanley Dance, I hail as Monarch Miracolissimo for extrasensory perception revealed in his amazing ability to decipher my handwriting." That was scarcely the only gift which Dance needed.

> In some ways I used to dread going to the apartment on West End Avenue, because I had to waste so much time. I'd go there and I had to sit for hours watching those terrible movies on TV before we'd get any work done. And Evie by this time could appear a pretty embittered woman. They'd shout at each other sometimes and Duke would press me to eat. I'd be starving, maybe, but I'd say no because I knew Evie didn't want to be bothered. So in the end I'd get a cup of tea, which I taught her to make. She used to drop the tea bag into the cup of hot water. I persuaded her to pour the boiling water onto the tea bag.

Lisa Drew, one of the senior editors at the book publishers, Doubleday, had the task of final editing and she determined the order of the book. It was, she recalled, not lively enough with the biographies all together, the philosophical passages together, and so on. So she broke up the sections into the looser potpourri form which was the book's final shape.

She saw Ellington over a period of two years—1972 and 1973—and says he was "a very charming guy—he charmed the socks off you." But Ellington was also quite testy at times. He disagreed with the color of the jacket chosen by the publishers and insisted it should be changed from brown to blue (his favorite lucky color) even though 25,000 jackets had already been produced. "We didn't know it at the time," said Lisa Drew, "but he must have been feeling very sick and sorry for himself." Lisa Drew also kept pressing Dance for more personal material about Duke: how, she argued, could you print an autobiography without even mentioning the name of Mercer's mother? Dance, however, said that Duke didn't want such details and would call the whole deal off if there were any suggestion of it. A conference was called one afternoon to "lean" on Duke, who had been very slow in coming up with some pages and some photographs which were urgently needed to complete the manuscript. Around four in the afternoon a meeting was arranged between Duke, Lisa Drew, and the enthusiast of old, Vaughan. The publishers went into a carefully rehearsed assault. The world was waiting for the book; it was going so well; but what about the story on Lena Horne, the picture of Benny Goodman, and so on. For five minutes they went on while Ellington, looking incredibly benign, sat silently gazing out of the window. At last, there was nothing more to say. Ellington hadn't responded. He spread his hands, still looking into the afternoon sky. "You know," he said at last, "I was just thinking what a terrible job it must be to work as a window-washer with all those skyscrapers."

Of all the beautiful, wise, and naïve words in the book, *Music Is My Mistress*, eventually published by Doubleday in the autumn of 1973, these are the most revealing of all:

> Roaming through the jungle, the jungle of "oohs" and "ahs," searching for a more agreeable noise, I live a life of primitivity with the mind of a child and an unquenchable thirst for sharps and flats. The more consonant, the more appetizing and delectable they are. Cacophony is hard to swallow. Living in a cave, I am almost a hermit, but there is a difference, for I have a mistress. Lovers have come and gone, but only my mistress stays. She is beautiful and gentle. She waits on me hand and foot. She is a swinger. She has grace. To hear her speak, you can't believe your ears. She is ten thousand years old. She is as modern as tomorrow, a brand-new woman every day, and as endless as time mathematics. Living with her is a labyrinth of ramifications. I look forward to her every gesture.
>
> Music is my mistress, and she plays second fiddle to no one.

Except, of course, to death. Nineteen seventy-two was gone. In the late spring of the new year, Duke learned what he must have suspected for some time. He had rapidly advancing cancer of the lungs. He didn't take to his bed, or even visit the hospital very much. Ellington kept on working and began to prepare for his last journey to Europe.

8

1973-1974
Can't Jive with the Almighty

"A man who's concerned is concerned about something he can do something about," Ellington once observed. "He can solve a problem. But a man who worries can do nothing, because worrying is purely negative. It eats, and it eats you. It's completely destructive."

Nothing more became him than the manner of his living in the last year of his life. Whatever he believed or did not believe about his future, he certainly gave the appearance to the world that his health did not worry him. Many who knew him have said, indeed, that he was convinced he could triumph even over cancer, at least for a time. But Ellington was concerned that he should finish one more chapter of his musical life. He wanted very much to compose a third Sacred Concert, and when he was invited to perform it at Westminster Abbey in London, the most important church of the British nation, the task gained fresh urgency. He spent a great deal of time on these sacred compositions during 1973 and wrote very little other new music. Asked why he was taking so long over it, he said: "You can jive with secular music, but you can't jive with the Almighty."

Mercer Ellington gave, in 1974, as honest a picture as is perhaps possible of his father during that final year.

He never accepted how ill he really was. And it wasn't because he was not told. His closest friend, Dr. Arthur Logan, suspected it first about a year ago and referred him to eleven of the top specialists in the country. There was no place else for him to go where he would have gotten any better care.

Just before we started our last European tour last winter, we were told that the disease was advancing rapidly, but he didn't believe it. His absolute faith in God made him believe that he could go on and on, and he did. There were times when he did become fatigued and he would lay down between shows and then he would bounce right back. I remember one point last year when we were playing at Northern Illinois University in De Kalb, we were referred to a doctor who had to send a report back to Columbia Presbyterian Hospital in New York. The X-ray didn't show any shadows where his lungs were supposed to be and this doctor was astonished at the amount of progress the disease had made and that this man still had the heart to conduct a band. If I go through life with half as much valor as he showed in the past year, I would be the strongest man in the world.

This, then, was the Duke who, in the autumn of 1973, began his last journey, whose focal point for him was unquestionably the new Sacred Concert he was to present on October 24, United Nations Day, at Westminster Abbey. "He knew it was his last shot, and he wanted it to be good," Mercer said. Incredibly, the band—now further weakened by Cootie Williams's departure and with only Chuck Connors remaining of the old trombones—flew overnight from New York and arrived in London early on the morning of October 23. The full list of musicians was this: Mercer Ellington, Harold Johnson, Johnny Coles, Barry Lee Hall (trumpets); Vince Prudente, Art Baron, Chuck Connors (trombones); Russell Procope, Paul Gonsalves, Harold Ashby, Harold Minerve, Harry Carney (reeds); Joe Benjamin (bass); and Quentin White (drums). Tony Watkins and Anita Moore were the singers, and for the Sacred Concert Alice Babs flew in from Sweden, whilst Ellington's regular partner at his church performances, Roscoe Gill, had been in London for a week rehearsing the choir.

The band had been trying out some parts of the concert at early-morning sessions the previous week following their shows at the club called Mr. Kelly's in Chicago, but as usual the early scenes in the cold surroundings of St. Margaret's, adjacent to the

Abbey, had the expected air of chaos. Duke was far from well. Only he knew the running order and all the band parts, and he acted as if he had all the time in the world. The outlook seemed even worse on the morning of the concert. Paul Gonsalves had been rushed to Westminster Hospital, very ill, after some of his evil London acquaintances had encouraged him to take too much drink and, probably, drugs as well. Duke passed Paul's solos to Harold Ashby, brought in a young saxist called Percy Marion, and went on with the rehearsals, which moved into the Abbey itself in the afternoon. He was uncomfortable with the photographers who wanted him to pose, and his shortness of temper was another indication of his ill-health. "I can sit here and do this," he told them at one stage, striking an attitude, "or do a concert." Ultimately the photographers left, with Joe Morgen, Ellington's press agent, running a nervous hand over his gray crew cut and proclaiming (according to *The Times*): "This is ridiculous—but don't put that down." Ellington was putting the band and singers through their paces until barely thirty minutes before the concert was due to begin. The musicians just had time to change and Duke had seconds to spare as he arrived at the Great West Door to greet Princess Margaret and the Prime Minister, Edward Heath.

Sir Colin Crowe, chairman of the United Nations Association, said a few words, including the observation that if the General Assembly had their debates conducted by Duke Ellington they might achieve better harmony, and Duke himself, dedicating his music, said this: "Every man prays to God in his own language, and there is no language which God does not understand." Then the music began. You will hear it better on the recording which RCA later put out than if you had been there, for the acoustics were dreadful and most of the audience couldn't see. Ellington must have known this would happen, so the concert was very different from others which had preceded it. The thrilling voice of Alice Babs, at slow tempos, was heavily used. Duke played more solo, or virtually solo, piano than ever before. Harry Carney, the most reliable musician he had, was featured a lot, too. Only rarely did Duke let the band romp at speed. Mostly the music was decorous, yet with immense bonuses. Some of the choral harmonies were as swirlingly blue as Ellington's instrumental arranging. There was one great call-and-response passage straight out of the gospel tradition. There were even

new effects from the band, like the recorder—yes, *recorder*—
passage played by trombonist Art Baron.

Musically, the sequences open with Duke and Alice Babs in
"The Lord's Prayer; My Love," continue with her voice soaring
on "Is God a Three-Letter Word for Love?" (Part I), a theme
put another way in Part II by Tony Watkins. The band and choir
swing into Ellington's conception of what the UN *ought* to be,
"The Brotherhood," which features Harold Ashby in place of
Paul Gonsalves. "Hallelujah" is a medium-paced chant for the
choir, sustained by piano and bass, and a long piece, "Every
Man Prays in His Own Language," gives space for the choir to
sing "The Lord's Prayer" and for the band and various soloists to
make musical statements at tempos both brisk and slow. The
reed section, as well as Miss Babs, *a cappella*, have rarely been
more impressive than in this eleven-minute section of the concert, during which the recorder of Art Baron, playing completely solo beneath the great arches, takes on a simple beauty.
"The Majesty of God," another long section dominated by Alice
Babs and Harry Carney, has an equally poignant serenity, and
for Tony Watkins's big voice, Duke wrote one of his most appropriate songs, "Ain't Nobody Nowhere Nothin' without God."

It wasn't the greatest Ellington concert. It couldn't be. But
the mysteriously sour air with which it was greeted by some
critics showed a superficiality which astounded me at the time,
and still does. There are no regrets from me that this is how I
wrote in the *Sunday Times* afterwards:

> After that Sacred Concert, the mind is full of mixed feelings. Oh,
> it was all a bit starchy at times, like these occasions so often are,
> because it was for a cause, with titles there and top politicians and
> diplomats and such. And who ever could believe that the Abbey
> was built for Duke's sounds? All those arches and tombs and
> echoes crucify music which is played at other than very decorous
> tempos. So the band only let its hair down on a couple of oc-
> casions. And half the audience couldn't see. And Paul Gonsalves
> wasn't playing. And the critics, a lot of them, were pretty sniffy
> about the whole thing: they said it wasn't vintage Ellington, that
> kind of remark, and there was one national newspaper reporter (if
> that's the word) who obviously couldn't tell Duke Ellington from a
> cheese sandwich, since he began his story by mis-informing his
> readers that Duke had danced into the Abbey nave to lead the au-
> dience in handclapping. It was Tony Watkins and Anita Moore

who did that, but maybe, to be charitable, the poor man was stuck behind one of those tombs.

Well I was there as a critic too, and perhaps I'm easily pleased or just get hang-ups and suspended faculties when it comes to Ellington. I'm in favour of him, at all seasons, you understand, and if he doesn't merit such warmth of attitude, who does? And as I came out of the Abbey all I could hear on every side were comments of pleasure. I noticed the smiles on the faces too. The audience, I judged, felt they had experienced something special, whatever the musical (or other) imperfections of the evening might be. And I agreed with them.

About Paul Gonsalves, who had collapsed on the day of the concert, and been replaced by a young man called Percy Marion, I cannot at this moment say more than that I'm hoping hard he has made a good recovery. He is, apart from Harry Carney, the baritone saxist, and altoist Russell Procope, the longest-serving musician in the band—an important point with Ellington's men. He was sorely missed that night, would be sorely missed in the future were anything to happen to him. Duke's ranks have been sadly thinned of his veterans in recent years. Cootie Williams, Cat Anderson, Johnny Hodges, Lawrence Brown are among the giants he has lost.

But before we look at that part of the story, let me finish about Duke's Sacred Concert. It was another of the sad aspects of the tale that although I read four or five newspapers the next day, I didn't come across a critic who thought it worth mentioning— maybe they didn't know—that Gonsalves was missing. Yet he's a crucial element both in the Ellington ensemble sound and as a soloist. There also seemed to be some uncertainty about how to deal with a Sacred Concert by Duke.

He's done only a couple such concerts in Britain in recent years. So comparatively few people have heard of them. For the Abbey audience it was, as I've said, a very *special* occasion. True. Special because it's another *aspect* of Duke and one which, in his seventies, *he* wants to emphasise. I enjoy all his music. Some of his compositions are greater than others, of course. But all of it's got a touch of genius in it somewhere. And it seems pointless to me to mark down his sacred music because it "isn't jazz," which I've read somewhere, or because it hasn't been written in "his most creative period," which I've read somewhere else.

Duke isn't writing only "jazz" when he's doing his Sacred Concerts. He's writing *music*, which happens to blend elements of his jazz style with other influences, like the European choral tradition of church music. Take it for what it is, in other words, not for what it was never intended to be. Duke has decided, with heart and brain, that what he wants to do now is to create his own personal song of praise to the Deity he knows. It's very important to him. It's another aspect of his genius, and I personally find it enjoyable and in many ways seizing. Different from "Caravan" or "Harlem Airshaft" or "Black, Brown, and Beige." But then it's meant to be. . . . So, as if it will matter to him what I think, I have to say that I gain huge pleasure from these Sacred Concerts. They have the authentic Ellington touch; they are disarmingly direct and simple—perhaps too much so for some sophisticated tastes, but then that's true of some other of his lyrics too; and in the context of his huge output down the years, they have an important place.

With hindsight, the concert was even more poignant than such writing made it appear. Duke was really ill at this time, so much so that he disappeared from the platform for ten minutes in a state of near collapse, leaving Alice Babs and the band unexpectedly to carry on without him. They responded magnificently. "Whatever their relationships with him were at that time," said a friend afterwards, "and the band was disintegrating then, they knew he was paying for that concert himself—playing his own way towards heaven, if you like. So although they were old and tired, they did their best for him. It was touching in a way I thought I'd never experience." After the concert, a party was being given for him by Edward Heath of 10 Downing Street. Duke dragged himself there, didn't even take his coat off, and left after fifteen minutes. Next day, he heard that Nips, the wife of Sinclair Traill, the editor of *Jazz Journal*, had fallen and broken her hip. His own ill-health did not prevent him acting as naturally and generously as was his wont. An enormous basket of fruit and flowers arrived at her hospital bed with a card that read: "Merrie Mending."

Despite the way he felt, Duke had a massive program to fulfill before he was due back in England a month later to appear before Queen Elizabeth at the Royal Command Performance held at the London Palladium. He swung, as usual, through Europe on a concert schedule. He went to Ethiopia for the State Department, receiving in Addis Ababa the Emperor's Star from the aged Lion of Judah, Haile Selassie, who, more than forty years earlier, had chosen W. C. Handy's "St. Louis Blues" as the imperial battle song. Zambia was also on his State Department itinerary, and from there he telephoned his sister, Ruth, who, with the Diamonds, was awaiting his return to Paris.

"He was so puzzled that Arthur Logan wasn't coming to see him," Ruth recalled. "He'd been looking forward to it so much, joking about how his doctor would tell him how great he was feeling. I was puzzled, too, because Arthur had flown halfway round the world to be with him at other times. So I called Arthur and his voice, well, it was just terrible. He said to me: 'I've got this bug—and a lot of things are bugging me.' That was his style, you know, but he sounded *so* strange."

On Sunday, November 25, Logan fell to his death in New York. Ruth Ellington heard the news on the transatlantic telephone from Cress Courtney. "I'd had a dream after I'd been to communion at Notre Dame. I can't remember what I dreamed, but it was enough to have me ringing Arthur in New York all day. They kept saying he'd be back in half an hour. But he was always still not in whenever I rang back. Then finally Cress came on. I couldn't believe it. At the time, Edward was making this twenty-three-hour flight from Zambia to London, not arriving till around six in the morning of the twenty-sixth, when he was due to play before Queen Elizabeth. We were desperate what Duke's reaction would be to Arthur's death."

Fearing he would cancel his Palladium show, Ruth and Mercer decided they would not tell him. Normally, a full-scale rehearsal for the Command Performance takes place the day before. Ellington missed that. He flew into London on the morning of the show exhausted, "acting like a zombie," as one observer put it, to face a further crisis. The band's instruments had gone astray—to Rome.

The show began at 7:30 P.M. Not until 8:45 did the instruments finally arrive at the theatre. Probably for the first time in the history of these shows, the top-of-the-bill act, Duke Ellington and His Famous Orchestra, took the stage without a rehearsal. They didn't really need one, of course. Ellington graciously got through the show, was presented to the Queen and Prince Philip, went back to the Audley Suite at the Dorchester—which his sister and Fernanda de Castro Monte were sharing—and prepared to travel to Edinburgh the next day for a public concert in the evening.

Edinburgh was played; then Glasgow on November 28. On the way to Dublin on November 29, the day Arthur Logan was being buried in New York, Ruth and Mercer could keep the news from Duke no longer. Many of his musicians had known as they played before the Queen. Ellington kept asking questions, wondering when Logan was going to appear. Mercer broke the news to him.

"That night he cried himself to sleep and it was the first and only time I had ever seen him cry," Mercer said later. "If ever he lost a friend, it was Arthur. I saw him affected by Billy, but nothing like with Arthur."

Logan's widow, Marion, remembered the day in this way. "Edward called me and said, 'The worst thing has happened to me. I just don't believe that it's so. I don't know what I'm going to do. I'll never ever get over this, I won't last six months.' "

Logan's death has remained something of a mystery. His involvement in social causes, especially on behalf of the city's blacks, had been outspoken and consistent. He was chairman of New York's Council against Poverty during the turbulent days of the mid-1960s, and when the Poor People's March on Washington took place in 1967, he mobilized a medical team to treat the demonstrators who were camping out under canvas in the so-called "Resurrection City." At his funeral, the outstanding black artist, Roberta Flack, sang, and the NAACP executive director, Roy Wilkins, characterized him as "one of the most successful local men who did not forget his less fortunate fellow citizens."

Logan fell to his death from a viaduct of the Henry Hudson Parkway at 134th Street in upper Manhattan, where he had apparently gone to look at the site of a bus terminal whose removal was going to allow an extension to the Knickerbocker Hospital—later renamed as a memorial to Logan—for which he had campaigned for several years. The manner of his death was not classified as accident, suicide, or homicide because of incomplete information, but any assumption of suicide was hotly contested by many of his friends. "Doctors don't walk off bridges, even if they want to die," said one of them. "They know a hundred ways to die with more dignity than that." There were rumors of Logan's having made underworld enemies, some of whom were involved in the property business. It was suggested that the site was wanted by these men for different purposes. Some of Logan's acquaintances believe he was murdered, but others completely dismiss the idea. Edmund Anderson simply said: "I haven't the slightest notion of the true cause of his death, but I have to think

Logan knew during 1973 that Edward wouldn't live to see his seventy-fifth birthday. And something died inside Arthur's soul."

"Who will ever know," Ruth Ellington commented. "Marion said some time afterwards that there had been reports of some-one in Florida confessing in jail to killing Arthur—that this man had said if he'd realized Arthur was black, he would never have done it. But to me it's still completely a mystery. The personal blow to Edward was staggering, however. Apart from Billy— they were on the same chord in every way—Arthur was *the* one. He loved Edward and his music, and Arthur was so gentle, beautiful, and brilliant, both as a doctor and a human being, that Edward loved him in return."

Logan's death certainly struck hard at Ellington as that November of 1973 came to an end. But he had to finish the tour. He played Dublin, Preston, and Eastbourne, where a doctor had to be called to him by Sinclair Traill, and on December 2 he was back in London. In his day he'd played the Palladium, the Festival Hall, the Albert Hall, the Hammersmith Odeon. He'd never, however, appeared in so scruffy and unsympathetic an auditorium as the rock emporium at Finsbury Park, the Rainbow Theatre, whose high-camp 1930s-Gothic architecture was now overlaid by dust, dirt, and a general air of hopelessness. Maybe Duke was too depressed; maybe the place got him down. Whatever the reason, his performance lacked lustre and—not knowing the full truth—I had to write this in the *Sunday Times:*

> Of course it was marvellous to hear the band and Ellington's music—music of genius—again. And although the old solo strength is sadly depleted, it is remarkable that Duke continues to discover such brilliant new musicians as Art Baron and others.
>
> But it really is now true that the band is showing signs of strain. The singers used were ordinary and unnecessary. There was too much clowning and not enough substance in the items chosen. Perhaps even Duke's countless thousands of admirers, of whom I am one, may feel that in his seventies he might allow himself to ease up on his endless hurtling progress around the world.

The words, like those of others at the time, were sadly prophetic. He flew back to America for Christmas, was ill on the plane, but still went ahead with his by now regular engagement at the Rainbow Grill in New York City. On December 23 he performed the Third Sacred Concert, which had been premiered at Westminster Abbey, for the second and final time, at St. Augustine Presbyterian Church in Harlem. Some of Ellington's friends were puzzled to see the name of Roscoe Gill, Jr., given equal weight with Duke's in the printed program, which was surely fanciful on someone's part. The next day, Christmas Eve, Edmund and Joan Anderson dropped in to see him just before the last show at the Rainbow Grill. Anderson placed a small Christmas tree on the piano, and when Duke saw it he picked it up, waved it delightedly around, and went into a sort of dance. Later, in the dressing room, Anderson said they'd skipped church to come. "You're in church when you're here," Ellington replied. "Don't forget, wherever you are, *Somebody Cares*" (one of his Sacred Concert titles). Anderson mentioned the spiritual quality of the Westminster Abbey concert, and Duke said simply: "I have so much more to do, so much more I have to do." For a few days, Ellington was missing from the stand at the Rainbow Grill. He was undergoing tests in a hospital.

With the opening of 1974, Ellington had his band back on the road again. At a January concert in Washington, D.C., he collapsed. Back in New York he went into hospital—the Columbia Presbyterian Medical Center—and the band's engagements were cancelled, never to be resumed again with Duke as the leader. Evie Ellington visited him daily, bringing him food, staying until the evening. By February, he was out of the hospital. He returned to the apartment on West End Avenue to stay with Evie. His precise condition was still uncertain. "It was nothing but tests, tests, tests," said Ruth Ellington. "It just wasn't clear how ill he was." To her friends, she insisted that Duke would be all right.

But many who knew him noticed ominous changes in him. "He kept saying he felt terrible," said one. "He may have been a hypochondriac, but he was always an optimist. Not now. He didn't want steak, which he adored. He didn't even say yes to grapes. I think he was just homesick, otherwise he would have stayed in the hospital." His friends were further depressed when a report reached them that a specialist who had recommended the hospitalization of Ellington a year earlier had examined the latest findings, shaken his head, and pronounced: "It's a catastrophe."

A further blow was to come. Evie Ellington began to feel ill herself. She was often in severe pain. During February, an Arthur Logan memorial dinner dance was held. Ruth and Mercer Ellington, Stephen James, the Andersons, and other friends attended. Duke and Evie could not go, but a place was kept for them at a table. Ellington produced a large card on which he'd drawn a heart around the names DUKE and EVIE, and the card stood on the table at the dance.

In March, Evie went into the hospital. Lung cancer was diagnosed. When he heard that she had had an operation, he wept. They were never to see each other again. Ellington's health steadily declined. By early April, he was back in the Harkness Pavilion of the Presbyterian Hospital.

Officially, he was allowed only family visitors. But there were more than that. Ruth and Mercer were, of course, with him regularly, and friends like the Andersons and Pastor John Gensel came frequently. There were associates and admirers—from Robert Paterson and Cress Courtney to Frank Sinatra. His on-off companion of many years, Fernanda de Castro Monte, was also a caller. Another woman, white and married, who had pursued him for years, infatuated, had at one stage to be removed from the hospital. Each day, Norman Granz sent him a jar of caviar, which he scarcely touched. Evie by this stage was back at West End Avenue, being cared for by a nurse. She could not come to the hospital. Duke telephoned her continually, pledging his devotion, insisting that she was the only woman who had really meant anything to him. "At the end," a friend observed, "I believe he really regretted not marrying Evie, but I guess he wasn't too crazy about the institution of marriage." At times in the hospital, Duke would act like his old exuberant self. The doctors tried to cure this tendency by placing a notice on his door: NO FOUR KISSES PLEASE.

What they couldn't cure, however, was the rage to work, which was still upon him. Ellington wanted to alter and improve some of the music from the Third Sacred Concert, so Ruth and Mercer had his electric piano moved into the hospital. He worked, too, almost until the end on the comic-opera venture, *Queenie Pie*, which he had begun over a decade earlier and had been commissioned to complete two years earlier by Channel 13, the public service TV station in New York. *Three Black Kings* (named for a monarch of the Nativity, for King Solomon, and for Martin Luther King) was another venture he attended to. Ultimately it was jointly credited to Duke and Mercer Ellington and used for a ballet by Alvin Ailey. Talking about his father at this time, Mercer said:

> Over the years we had our fights in the recording studios about tonal qualities—bounce and things like that. But during his hospital stay, for the first time, he entrusted the judgment to me of what I should do to improve this or that—and I think that was the only time he came close to alluding or admitting that he wouldn't be coming out of the hospital.
>
> But apart from that, he carried himself with decorum. He walked every day, and when he got to the point where he couldn't walk in the corridors, he made sure he walked somewhere, even if it was just across the room. Just so he could say he walked somewhere that day.

Ellington's seventy-fifth birthday on April 29 was approaching. Its highlight for his New York circle was to be a concert of selections from his Sacred Concerts at St. Peter's Church, then in a temporary location at Sixty-fourth Street and Park Avenue. The band, which hadn't been working while he was ill, was to be reconvened. Without Duke, who was to conduct and who was to play the piano? When he heard that Roscoe Gill was to lead, and a young follower and Ellington expert called Brooks Kerr was to sit at the piano, Duke urged that a different conductor and pianist be used in each section of the program. He believed the band might resent the implication of a take-over by these younger men; Ellington also didn't like the way that Kerr's press agent was pushing the pianist as Duke's "protégé," and he'd observed the equal billing given to Gill on the Sacred Concert at Christmas. Such emotions in Duke had been foreshadowed two years or so earlier during an evening party at Ruth's Central Park South apartment. Duke had been sitting at the white piano, framed against the setting sun blazing through the window, playing as he was moved to. Someone challenged Kerr, who was present, to play the second song Ellington had ever written—"What You Gonna Do When the Bed Breaks Down?" "Duke jumped in and said no, he'd do it instead," recalled Edmund Anderson. "He *wouldn't* let Brooks take over that piano. And he sang it too, and he remembered every word."

But Ellington's desires for the St. Peter's concert were not practical. Kerr and Gill were probably the only two men available who knew enough about Ellington's plans, music, and habits to act as a two-person substitute for him at short notice and with little rehearsal. So they performed their roles all the way through what was a marvellous evening of music despite the last-minute summoning of the band. Only three musicians had turned up for the rehearsal the day before the concert, although the turnout was better the following morning, when even Paul Gonsalves, who was frequently in an alcoholic and narcotic haze by this stage, rolled up at 11 A.M.

Ellington never heard the tape of the concert. He was visited on his birthday by Ruth, Stephen James, the Andersons, and Fernanda de Castro Monte (wearing white slacks and a blue top—in deference, doubtless, to Duke's color preference), who carried to him a cake and some caviar.

Duke was now sinking fast. He stopped walking, he stopped playing; pneumonia threatened. In the week which ended on May 18, 1974, Paul Gonsalves and Tyree Glenn both died, two musicians who meant much to him, especially Gonsalves. In January, the bass player Joe Benjamin had also died following an automobile accident. Gonsalves had been in Holland, playing by invitation, having left New York with only a few borrowed dollars. From Holland he flew to Britain, seeking friends or drink or heroin, no one quite knows. He died in London. Although his erratic habits in the last few years had at time infuriated Duke, there was the closest of bonds between the men. "We call him 'the strolling violins,' " Duke said of him, "because he will take his horn and walk over to a group, or do his whole solo to one child in the audience. . . . He has respect for respect, but never makes demands for himself. There is never an evil thought in his mind."

No one told Duke of the latest deaths among his alumni, believing that the news would do him no good. He had already outlasted virtually all of those who had started out with him or joined him along the way. Tricky Sam Nanton, Bubber Miley, Arthur Whetsol, Shorty Baker, Freddie Guy, Toby Hardwick, Johnny Hodges, Ben Webster, Rex Stewart, Jimmy Blanton, Billy Strayhorn, and singer Ivie Anderson were among those who were dead. The notable survivors who were not now playing in the band included at this stage Sonny Greer, Cootie Williams, Cat Anderson, Ray Nance, Barney Bigard, and Lawrence Brown.

Early in the morning of Friday, May 24, during the hours

when he had always been so vibrantly and creatively alive, Ellington himself died. Pastor John Gensel was with him until a few hours before his death; he was continually calling for Evie Ellington to be with him. It was seven months to the day since his Westminster Abbey concert, just one day earlier than the date on which his mother had died in 1935, and little less than the six months he had given himself to live after Arthur Logan's death.

Duke's body was taken to the funeral parlor of Walter B. Cooke at 1504 Third Avenue, and that night the bodies of Ellington, Gonsalves, and Glenn all lay there. The next day, and throughout the weekend, thousands came and stood in line on Third Avenue to pay their respects as Ellington lay in an open coffin, the Emperor's Star of Ethiopia about his neck, his Legion of Honor and the presidential Medal of Freedom also upon him.

Two Masonic services were held for Duke in the funeral parlor—an interesting sidelight on the man, for few had realized his fascination with freemasonry. Friends, colleagues, and admirers from all over the world came to pay their respects. Norman Granz, later to begin issuing several hitherto unheard Ellington record sessions, was there. Robert Paterson, his successor as Duke's presenter in Britain, stood, at Mercer Ellington's request, for an hour by the bier. On the first night, Edmund Anderson and Harry Carney mourned Duke's death together. "This is the worst day of my life," Carney told him. Within six months, Carney too would be dead, on October 8, aged sixty-four, the best friend among his musicians that Ellington ever had.

Many words were written and spoken about Duke at this time by hundreds of statesmen, musicians, ministers, and writers. Even a book can encompass only a few of them. Joe Williams, the blues singer, spoke for the musicians. "You don't have to say much about Edward because he said it all. To me he was a Messiah. And everybody whose life was touched by his, that even came close to him . . . we're a better people for it, for having known Duke Ellington. I thank God he happened in my lifetime."

Richard Nixon, still in the presidency, spoke for the rest of the world. "The wit, taste, intelligence, and elegance that Duke Ellington brought to his music have made him in the eyes of millions of people both here and abroad, America's foremost composer. His memory will live for generations to come in the music with which he enriched his nation." Enriched, indeed, and gloriously so, for Ellington had always been a patriot. He'd burned himself out, partially, carrying the torch for the State Department abroad, and for the simple reason that he felt America had treated him well. He was immensely proud of his country, whatever its shortcomings on the civil rights front for many years.

Hundreds of newspapers and magazines around the world attempted in more detail to sum up the achievement of the man whom his alumnus, Rex Stewart, had once called the first, and perhaps the last, of the genuine creative founding fathers of "Music Americana." The *New York Times* gave approval to Ralph Gleason's assessment of him as "the greatest composer this American society has produced." An innovating founder he indubitably was, a trait which he once had characteristically shrugged off during an interview with these words: "I'm so damned fickle. I never could stick with what I was doing. Always wanted to try something new."

So novel were his approaches that every important big jazz or dance band after him had betrayed his influence, directly or indirectly. His innovations within modern music were unmatched. He revolutionized the role of the tenor and baritone saxophones through Ben Webster and Harry Carney; his "jungle" sound had done something similar for the brass section; the double bass was never the same after he'd amplified it for Wellman Braud on "Hot and Bothered" (his variation on "Tiger Rag") in 1928, and Jimmy Blanton had expanded its range still further—a history which many rock bass players probably don't realize. He'd begun the use of the human voice as an instrument when he blended Adelaide Hall with the band on "Creole Love Call," and continued the fashion later with the coloratura sopranos, Kay Davis and Alice Babs. With Johnny Hodges in 1938, he'd invented the echo chamber. He'd given a start to "Latin-American jazz" with his colleague Juan Tizol and their "Caravan."

There was much more, too. He had written more different kinds of composition in the popular idiom of his century than any other man, and had uplifted his work into a class where the word "popular" seemed no longer applicable, giving scores of jazz and "pop" composers who came after him a standard and a dignity to aspire to. He'd also been a great pianist: oblique,

surprising, and dominating, often despite the spareness of his
sound. "One chord from him can set the machinery of his entire
band running perfectly," as another piano virtuoso, Earl "Fatha"
Hines observed. The horizons he had shown for every artist
working from the starting point of the Afro-American musical
tradition were virtually illimitable. One comparison put it this
way: the two most original American contributions to world culture are Duke's music and Disney's cartoons.

On the day of the funeral, Monday May 27, Ellington's body
was moved to the Cathedral of St. John the Divine, and Alistair
Cooke made his own—and I think the best—summary of Duke's
life. He cast his eye upon the 10,000 people packed within the
cathedral, and the thousands outside, and mused how it would
have probably shocked the founders to know that they were
there to honor the life and mourn the death of a genius in an art
that "began in the brothels of New Orleans"—an understandable
oversimplification on Cooke's part. Ellington once murmured
before the California Arts Commission, on hearing someone observe that jazz came from brothels: "They didn't learn it there."
Cooke had other things to say, however. He recalled Ellington
being "put to the piano," keeping at it every day; Ellington
"sleek as a seal" in white tie and tails; Ellington naked except for
undershorts and towel on his head going at his apartment breakfast (at two or so in the afternoon, of course) "like a marooned
mountaineer"; Ellington as a man with whom all problems of
color disappeared. Cooke was one of those 4,000-odd people
who received Duke's last Christmas card, sent out, as it always
was, long after Christmas so that it would arrive in April or May.
This card had, Cooke recalled, the words GOD and LOVE set in
the form of a cross, with the letter "O" as the link. Its color was
blue, Ellington's favorite, and inside were these words, casual
and almost naïve: "Merry Christmas is Merrie Happy New Year
is Happie, Compounded with LUV and Blessings, and May Your
Total Future Be the Greatest!" Duke was, said Cooke, as used
to be said of Joe Louis, "a credit to his race." He paused. "The
human race, that is."

Then came the final *coup*, as Cooke, substituting names,
rewrote the words with which the novelist John O'Hara had
mourned George Gershwin. "Duke Ellington died last week. I
don't have to believe it if I don't want to."

Nothing, one suspects, could more truly have said what millions in the world must have felt that day in May. The weather was rainy as, before the service, some of the cars among the several dozen in the cortége drove a route around the city which passed many of the places dear to Ellington: his old apartment on St. Nicholas Avenue, the former site of the Cotton Club, the Roxy Theatre, the Apollo. Robert Paterson was riding with Mr. and Mrs. Count Basie, Benny Goodman, Judy Collins, Edmund Anderson. "In Harlem, many of the shops were shuttered," Paterson said. "There were thousands standing in the streets, both men and women, many of them weeping.

The service at the cathedral, at Amsterdam Avenue and 110th Street, on the very edge of Harlem, was as ecumenical and stately as Duke's own life had been. Every religion in the world, or so it seemed, was represented at the cathedral. The suffragan bishop of the New York diocese, the Right Reverend Harold Wright, himself a black man, took the service. Among his assistants, inevitably, were Duke's friends and jazz experts Pastor John Gensel and the Reverend Norman O'Connor. Ella Fitzgerald sang the most moving performance of "Solitude." There was music, too, from Joe Williams, Ray Nance, Jo Jones, Billy Taylor, Earl Hines, Mary Lou Williams, and Hank Jones. Pearl Bailey (the White House's representative) and her husband, Louis Bellson, attended together with Alice Babs, Sonny Greer, Aaron Bell, Sy Oliver, Buddy Rich, Jack Dempsey, Dick Gregory, and hundreds of other notables who joined Ellington's family in mourning. "Duke once gave me his definition of music," Bellson recalled. "Mass unity sounding in concert— M-U-S-I-C."

With dignified emotion, Stanley Dance gave the address. "He was loved," said Dance, "throughout the whole world, at all levels of society, by Frenchmen and Germans, by English and Irish, by Arabs and Jews, by Indians and Pakistanis, by atheists and devout Catholics, and by Communists and Fascists alike."

And who was he? He was "at once sophisticated, primitive, humorous, tolerant, positive, ironic, childlike (not childish), lionlike shepherdlike, Christian. He was a natural aristocrat who never lost the common touch. He was the greatest innovator in his field and yet paradoxically a conservative, one who built new things on the best of the old and disdained ephemeral fashion."

Dance spoke, too, of the reverence which Duke had for freedom of expression. Ellington never wanted to be restricted or confined to the idiom of jazz within which he was the unchallenged and acknowledged master.

"His scope constantly widened, and right up to the very end his creative force was still at work. He worked hard, he did not spare himself, and he virtually died in harness. Music was indeed his mistress."

Two hours after it had entered the cathedral, the white copper coffin was carried away by pallbearers who included Edmund Anderson, Harry Carney, the son of Irving Mills, and George Wein, the jazz impresario who was Ellington's major promoter in the final decade. As they moved down the aisle, the sounds of Alice Babs's voice and Johnny Hodges's saxophone were poignantly heard, offering music from the Second Sacred Concert which had first been presented at St. John's in 1968. He was buried beside his father and mother at Woodlawn Cemetery, in the Bronx. A linden oak tree, flanked by rosebushes, shaded his grave in the section of the cemetery called Wildrose, at the junction of Heather, Fir, and Knollwood Avenues. For a few minutes during the burial service, the cool, drizzly day was illuminated as the sun broke through.

On the next day, May 28, Mercer Ellington led the band to Bermuda to fulfill a two-week engagement at the IBM convention which Duke had accepted some time before his death. He was convinced that his father would have wanted the band to continue honoring engagements: the customary Ellington philosophy of the show must go on. Not everyone agreed with him. Some of the musicians were hesitant about the journey, believing that the engagement should be cancelled as a mark of respect. Mercer, however, was equally determined to try to keep the band together. Harry Carney, who was ill, and Russell Procope did not go.

Epilogue

On June 12, there was a London tribute to Duke in the form of a memorial service at St. Martin-in-the-Fields, the historic church looking out over Trafalgar Square. Because I was involved in its organization, with the aid of a group of ushers drawn from the staffs of *The Times* of London and its associated newspapers, my comments are bound to be prejudiced, but it was indeed a joyous occasion. The church, inevitably, was packed, and among those who came to honor Duke were the American ambassador, Walter Annenberg, and his wife, Mr. and Mrs. Yehudi Menuhin, the Honorable Gerald Lascelles, who had been instrumental in getting Ellington to play before the Queen back in 1958 and who now read the Lesson, and most important of all a superb band of British musicians and soloists.

Britain even rediscovered its own "Ellingtonian," for Adelaide Hall, who as long ago as 1927 recorded "Creole Love Call" with Duke, sang that song again. "Time had dealt leniently with her sweet voice and lovely face," wrote Sinclair Traill, the doyen of British jazz journalists, in *Jazz Journal*, "and one had a feeling that it was only their surroundings which kept the beautifully behaved congregation from bursting into spontaneous applause."

235

This was not the only musical and emotional highlight. A choir led by the exuberant Ian Hall wonderfully caught the spirit of Duke's Sacred Concerts. In pin-drop silence after the address, Larry Adler walked down the aisle playing "Mood Indigo" on his harmonica before joining Cleo Laine and the band in a version whose finale had, in Sinclair Traill's report, "outright beauty of blues perfection."

The band for the occasion was led by John Dankworth, and within it were Humphrey Lyttelton, Chris Barber, Mike Gibbs, Danny Moss, Tommy Whittle, Mike Page, Stan Tracey, Lennie Bush, and Tony Crombie—as glittering a representation of native jazz talent as could possibly have been assembled by the leader—and they played better, most critics thought, than they had ever played in their lives. No one who was there will ever forget the ten minutes after the official service had finished. The band was playing "A Train" as their recessional. No one left. They stayed, and after a time they were urging on the musicians with stomping and handclapping, reinforced by hundreds who hadn't been able to get into the church, now flooding in from Trafalgar Square outside. St. Martin's had never before seen anything like this and perhaps will never see it again.

In February 1975, Mercer Ellington led what had become known as "The Duke Ellington Orchestra" to London for a concert at Hammersmith. He was warm and charming, and he had a good band within whose ranks were Cootie Williams and Chuck Connors from the great years, and Harold Minerve, Harold Johnson, and Art Baron of Duke's recruits in the later days. Mercer and the musicians were anxious, fearing that they wouldn't be liked and would be unfavorably compared with Duke's former caravan. In fact, the band played with considerable flair, had some good new soloists, including an explosive modern tenor saxist of around twenty, Ricky Ford. The tunes were partly Ellington's, sounding something like they did in the old days, but with obvious differences. There was much non-Ellington material—"Basin Street Blues," "Blueberry Hill," "The Way We Were." Mercer also did one extremely courageous thing: he closed the three-hour, good-value show with his own classic, "Things Ain't What They Used to Be." It was a title which invited the obvious comment. Things ain't and weren't, but no one could wish Mercer other than success in his desire to carry on the tradition, in his own way.

He did precisely that. Two years later, after mixed early fortunes, the band was still performing in America, and was featured at the Newport Jazz Festival in New York in the summer of 1976. Cootie Williams and Harold Ashby had by this time departed—Ashby after a quarrel with Mercer—and only Chuck Connors from Duke's 1960s band remained, together with Harold Minerve, Percy Marion, and Barry Lee Hall, who had played with the seniors in the 1970s. Some new arrangements—"Sophisticated Lady" and "Caravan"—hovered between the style of Stan Kenton and Ellington, which called to mind what the symphony orchestra conductor and jazz pianist, André Previn, had once said of the mysteries within the creation of Duke's sounds. "Stan Kenton can stand in front of a thousand fiddles and a thousand brass and make a dramatic gesture, and every studio arranger can nod his head and say, 'Oh yes, that's done like this.' But Duke merely lifts his finger, three horns make a sound, and I don't know what it is."

There was, however, one fascinating aspect to Mercer's leadership of his reconstituted Ellington band. Longer compositions by Duke which the great bands had rarely played in full more than a few times were being avidly sought out and rehearsed for special occasions, as when Mercer and the orchestra played a fortnight's season with Alvin Ailey's City Center Dance Theater in August 1976. "Ailey Celebrates Ellington" was the title of this impressive contribution to America's bicentennial year, and it gave almost a panoramic view of Duke's many kinds of music. In his program note, Ailey emphasized how Ellington loved to have his music danced. "He thought that dance was a major means of communicating what he was trying to get through to people, which was a love of life and a caring about mankind." The choreographer also paid a striking tribute to Duke as "a man who spoke to all mankind, a poet, a voice crying out against darkness and negativism . . . a man whom the black community revered; a man who was to us a God. . . . He wrote the heartbeat and the rhythms of this century and, more than that, he celebrated the beauty and the uniqueness of man." The music to which Ailey's company were dancing included "Harlem," "The Liberian Suite," "Night Creature," "Reflections in D," parts of "Such Sweet Thunder," "A Drum Is a Woman," and "Anatomy of a Murder," as well as shorter pieces like "Black Beauty," "The Shepherd," and "Creole Love Call." The restoration of so many important sections of the Ellington repertoire was justifiably applauded, and by the end of 1976 it had been enlarged by a ballet to the music of *Three Black Kings*. The invitation to Mercer Ellington's orchestra to play at the Inaugural celebrations for President Jimmy Carter in Washington in January 1977 was an apt and deserved accolade.

On April 7, 1976, Evie Ellington died of cancer, aged sixty-four, in the New York Hospital after a long and painful illness which, in her uncertain circumstances, was particularly frightening for her. A sense of insecurity had haunted her during her last years, especially since Duke left no will when he died. This was partly a reflection of his superstition, in line with his reaction to insurance and biographies; he believed the act of preparing for death and disaster would help them to happen. It was also, however, a facet of his whole life style. He had no time to make wills; his incredibly tangled financial affairs, still being sorted out in 1976, would have made the preparation of a sensible will a nightmare; and, at all events, he gave away money and goods so lavishly while he lived—to his family, his girl friends, his companions and colleagues—that by the time he died he may not have been as wealthy as many people imagined.

Evie often complained about her uncertain material and emotional status down the years. She was particularly bitter that Duke had never married her, although that bitterness decreased as she moved toward the end. Why Ellington did not marry again will remain a mystery. Many of his friends thought it incredibly unfair to Evie; others believed that, knowing his own nature so well and the long periods of absence which his musical life imposed, he was in a strange way following the kindliest course he could. Evie knew, of course, that Fernanda de Castro Monte was frequently in Duke's company during the 1960s and 1970s and was supported by Ellington whilst living in New York until the day he died, later returning to Europe. Under stress, she often challenged assessments of Ellington's doings. "*That's* what the public thinks," she would say tartly. Yet a friend of hers could still assert: "She had a tremendous tolerance—for people, for the way things had panned out. That tolerance was based on cynicism, which life had taught her. About Duke, though, she was never cynical." It was certainly a bizarre, unpredictable, and only partially explicable set of arrangements.

In the last year or so of her life, Evie was closer to Mercer

Ellington and Edmund Anderson (he and his wife, Joan, telephoned and talked with her daily and made frequent visits) than to anyone else. Mercer was particularly devoted. He helped her move from the West End Avenue apartment to a smaller, more practical one in the same building, for she was out of the hospital for part of 1974 and most of 1975. He paid her hospital bills, which were heavy when she returned to the New York Hospital for the last time in 1976. He tried to calm her fears about money and ensured that she was well looked after. In fact, Evie left a considerable sum on her death. "I adored her," Mercer told Anderson during the final days. "She was wonderful to me all though my life. When I was in the hospital, she came every day to see me and brought me food and things. She was a marvellous lady." He was at her bedside, comforting her, during her last hours, as was Anderson.

Evie was widely described as Duke Ellington's widow when she died—in, among many other newspapers, *The Times* of London and the *New York Times*. *Jet*, the American magazine, knew better. In a phrase of understanding and beautiful tact it called her "his First Lady, Beatrice (Evie) Ellis Ellington." There was no question in Mercer's mind what should happen upon her death, nor, apparently, in that of Ruth, who had tried very hard in the last years to heal the breach with Evie. And so she was buried beside Duke in Woodlawn Cemetery. The Ellington plot is simplicity itself. Two white crosses carry the inscription, "The Lord Is My Shepherd." One small tablet in gray stone states: "James Edward Ellington 1879–1937 and his wife Daisy Kennedy 1878–1935." Another, identical, has only these words: "Duke: Edward Kennedy Ellington 1899–1974."

By the autumn of 1976, Ruth Ellington had left her old apartment on Central Park South and was established in 750 Park Avenue, at the junction with Seventy-third Street. The sitting room was dominated by a large cross, an open Bible, a religious mosaic, a colored peacock, and a white piano which Duke had often played. Among her treasures was a minute New Testament covered in gold filigree, which Duke had sent her from Jerusalem in 1963 with a marker in the page beginning "Let not your heart be troubled. . . ." She said simply, "He showed me how to live, and he showed me how to die. I understood what he said and meant. 'We love you madly' was his way of saying the love of Christ and the Christian heritage." Ruth was still running the

Tempo publishing business with Michael and Stephen, her sons from her earlier marriage to Dan James, a journalist and writer, who had helped her to get Tempo moving in the 1940s, but said she would like to sell it if a buyer with the right attiude of love and respect, as well as the right money, came along.

Norman Granz was, as ever, moving between Europe, Britain, and California, making records for love as much as money, declaring that he could, if he wanted, say terrible things about Duke. "That myth of graciousness. It's been built by idolaters. Gracious sometimes, sure, but he could be monstrous. I saw him behave so badly to his son."

Pastor John Gensel was hard at work in his ministry at St. Peter's Lutheran Church, at whose new site, the junction of Fifty-fourth Street and Lexington Avenue, the foundation stone was consecrated on October 31, 1976. The new St. Peter's is a remarkable conception for a place of worship, built with graceful modernity on three levels as a vault set into the base of the fifth tallest skyscraper in New York. The new, still-building St. Peter's was also to become the site of the Duke Ellington Center, part of an arts complex within the church. Intended as a jazz rehearsal and workshop room, the Center would remain open twenty-four hours a day: "to realize a dream," in John Gensel's words, "for a permanent home of the Jazz Community in New York City." Billy Strayhorn's piano would be part of the furniture.

Gensel had continued even more firmly with his care for the jazzmen and women of Manhattan following Ellington's death. In that same month of October, he had celebrated eleven years of his weekly 5 P.M. Jazz Vespers services at St. Peter's—for which Duke was only one among 300 artists who had played or sung—with a twelve-hour service until 5 A.M. featuring coffee, cake, and a hundred musicians. "All Nite Soul," it was called; the venue was a synagogue close to the new church. The previous year, on April 29, New York had honored what would have been Duke's seventy-sixth birthday by proclaiming a "Duke Ellington Day," during which Gensel had organized a twenty-four-hour service with music by several Ellingtonians (Greer, Procope, Tony Watkins, Matthew Gee, Francis Williams) and many musicians who could not claim that honor.

"Duke," said Gensel a week before the foundation stone of St. Peter's was consecrated, "had the ability to make the eternal contemporary."

That perspective was widely shared by all kinds of people, those who had known him and those who had not. Even in death, Ellington could be many things to many souls: Artful Dodger, enigma, god, genius unfathomable. Who could know best? A musician, perhaps, one of the handful of survivors?

On June 4, 1976, Russell Procope and Wild Bill Davis came to the 100 Club in London to play in a concert called "Echoes of Ellington" along with the British jazzman, Chris Barber. They were substituting for Sonny Greer and Brooks Kerr, who had fallen ill at the last moment. Procope sat in a tiny dressing room, playing Duke's phrases during his warm-up before taking the stand. He was edgy at first. "Well, I'm a sitting duck. Everybody asks me about Duke. I'm an introvert. I don't like the spotlight."

But after a time, he relaxed. "Why did I stay twenty-eight years? Well, hell, I joined him because I loved his music. It was the greatest. Besides which, it was a chance to go round the world. Besides which, it was security. Sure, security. What else are we here for? In a profession, to do what you like doing *and* getting paid for it—isn't that what everyone wants?"

To the question of why he wasn't playing in an old-Ellingtonians band, and particularly Mercer's band, he replied, "There aren't many Ellingtonians left. A lot of guys who played with Ellington are *not* Ellingtonians. He achieved what he did *despite* them rather than because of them. People say he didn't fire many people. Yeah, and he didn't hire many either. It was special, very special. So that's why I don't want to play in no 'Ellington' band now. There's nobody really left. Mercer isn't even playing the old book. If only he would."

It was getting on to be time for the show. He hitched his sax up over his shirtfront, picked up his clarinet, and walked to the door. He turned.

"Don't let nobody tell you any different. While it was happening it was the greatest thing that ever took hold of your soul. When it ended, it ended."

Chronology of
Duke Ellington's Life

1899   Born in Washington, D.C., on April 29; named Edward Kennedy Ellington.

1914   Writes first composition, "Soda Fountain Rag," soon followed by "What You Gonna Do When the Bed Breaks Down?"

1915–18   Informal tuition with Oliver "Doc" Perry, Henry Grant, and other Washington musicians.

1918   Running local bands in Washington. Marries Edna Thompson on July 2.

1919   Mercer Ellington born on March 11. Duke meets Sonny Greer who, with Duke's neighbor, Otto "Toby" Hardwick, forms the nucleus of first Ellington band.

1922   Brief engagement in New York with Wilbur Sweatman for Duke, Greer, and Hardwick. Informal study with James P. Johnson and Willie "the Lion" Smith.

1923   Thomas "Fats" Waller persuades the trio to return to New York. With Arthur Whetsol and Elmer Snowden they get their first club job at Barron's in Harlem, then on Broadway at the Hollywood (later Kentucky) Club. Band called The Washingtonians.

1923–24	Composing songs for Tin Pan Alley ("Blind Man's Buff," "Pretty Soft for You") and a revue, *Chocolate Kiddies*, with lyricist Jo Trent.
1925	James "Bubber" Miley joins band. Sidney Bechet also a member for a time.
1926	Joe "Tricky Sam" Nanton and Wellman Braud join band. Meets Irving Mills, who becomes manager of Duke's affairs. "East St. Louis Toodle-oo" (written with Miley) becomes band's signature tune.
1927	Harry Carney and Barney Bigard join band for opening at the Cotton Club in Harlem on December 4. Compositions include "Creole Love Call" (recorded with Adelaide Hall) and "Black and Tan Fantasy."
1928	Johnny Hodges joins band. Compositions include "The Mooch" and "Black Beauty."
1929	Band appears in Florenz Ziegfeld's review, *Show Girl*, as well as at the Cotton Club and in short movie, *Black and Tan Fantasy*. Cootie Williams and Juan Tizol join band; Hardwick and Miley (who dies three years later) leave. "Saturday Night Function" among compositions. Duke's father and mother, sister Ruth, and Mercer in New York City.
1930	First Hollywood movie for band—*Check and Double Check*. New York concert with Maurice Chevalier. Richest year yet for compositions: "Mood Indigo," "Ring Dem Bells," "Rockin' in Rhythm," "Old Man Blues," "Wall Street Wail."
1931	Ivie Anderson joins band, stays till 1942. First longer composition, "Creole Rhapsody."
1932	Another great year for compositions: "Sophisticated Lady," "It Don't Mean a Thing (If It Ain't Got That Swing)," "Lazy Rhapsody," "Ducky Wucky." Lawrence Brown joins band. Concert at Columbia University.
1933	Band's first European tour. Plays Palladium, London; Duke meets Prince of Wales, Duke of Kent. Hardwick rejoins band. "Drop Me Off in Harlem," "Harlem Speaks," "Daybreak Express," and "Merry-Go-Round" among compositions.
1934	Begins all-American tours, including southern states. Relationship with Mildred Dixon under way. Rex

Stewart joins band, which is featured in movies, *Belle of the Nineties* and *Murder at the Vanities*. Compositions include "Solitude," "Rude Interlude," "Jungle Nights in Harlem," "Stompy Jones."

1935   Duke's mother dies. "Reminiscing in Tempo" composed for her. Other music includes "In a Sentimental Mood," "Delta Serenade." Wellman Braud leaves band; replaced by Billy Taylor (and Hayes Alvis).

1936   Ivie Anderson appears in film, *A Day at the Races*, with Marx Brothers, for which Ellington provides some music. Duke meets Edmund Anderson. Compositions include "Echoes of Harlem," "Clarinet Lament," "Caravan" (with Juan Tizol).

1937   Duke's father dies. Relationship with Beatrice ("Evie") Ellis begins. "Harmony in Harlem," "Azure," "Diminuendo and Crescendo in Blue," "Black Butterfly," "I've Got to Be a Rug Cutter" among compositions. Season at new Cotton Club (on Broadway) and Apollo Theatre (in Harlem). Whetsol leaves band through illness. Duke meets Dr. Arthur Logan.

1938   "Prelude to a Kiss," "Boy Meets Horn," "I Let a Song Go out of My Heart," "Pyramid," "I'm Slappin' Seventh Avenue with the Sole of My Shoe," "Jeep's Blues," "Wanderlust" among compositions. Harold "Shorty" Baker joins band briefly. Returns 1943–51 and again later. Concert at St. Regis Hotel, New York, with Philharmonic musicians also on bill.

1939   Second European tour (excluding Britain). Billy Strayhorn, Ben Webster, and Jimmy Blanton join band; Billy Taylor leaves. "Something to Live For," his first joint composition with Strayhorn, "Ko-Ko," "Subtle Lament," "Portrait of the Lion," "Serenade to Sweden," among compositions.

1940   Cootie Williams leaves band; replaced by Ray Nance. Duke switches from Mills to William Morris Agency. Compositions include "Never No Lament" (later "Don't Get Around Much Any More"), "Jack the Bear," "Cotton Tail," "All Too Soon," "In a Mellotone," "Day Dream" (with Strayhorn), "Morning Glory," "Harlem Airshaft," "Bojangles," "Warm Valley."

1941   Strayhorn's "Take the A Train" written, and later becomes band's signature tune. Mercer Ellington writes "Things Ain't What They Used to Be." Duke's first full-length show, *Jump for Joy*, opens in Los Angeles; compositions include "Just Squeeze Me," "I Got It Bad and That Ain't Good," "Rocks in My Bed." Tom Whaley joins Ellington organization.

1942   Bigard leaves band; Jimmy Hamilton joins. Death of Jimmy Blanton. "What Am I Here For?" and "C-Jam Blues" among compositions. Juan Tizol writes "Perdido." Band appears in movie, *Cabin in the Sky*, with Lena Horne.

1943   First major suite, "Black, Brown, and Beige," premiered on January 23, marking the start of annual Carnegie Hall concerts for band. "Concerto for Cootie" has lyrics added to become another big hit, "Do Nothin' till You Hear from Me." Band appears in movie, *Reveille with Beverly*. "New World a-Comin'" premiered at Carnegie Hall in December. Ben Webster leaves band, but rejoins for few months in 1948. Al Sears joins.

1944   Cat Anderson joins band; Rex Stewart and Juan Tizol leave. Long seasons at the Hurricane Club and Capitol Theatre in New York. Paul Whiteman premieres Ellington's "Blutopia." Other compositions include "I'm Beginning to See the Light," "I Didn't Know about You" (version with lyrics of "Home"), "Main Stem."

1945   "The Perfume Suite" premiered at Carnegie Hall. "I'm Just a Lucky So-and-So," "Blue Cellophane," "Air-Conditioned Jungle," "Everything but You," "Transblucency" (with Lawrence Brown) among other compositions. Russell Procope and Oscar Pettiford join band, the former staying until Duke's death. Otto Hardwick leaves.

1946   "The Deep South Suite" (including "Happy-Go-Lucky Local") premiered at Carnegie Hall. "Pretty Woman" and "Magenta Haze" among other compositions. Death of "Tricky Sam" Nanton.

1947   Tyree Glenn joins band. "The Liberian Suite," commissioned for centenary of the black republic, premiered at Carnegie Hall.

1948   Wendell Marshall replaces Oscar Pettiford. "The Tat-
       tooed Bride" this year's Carnegie Hall premiere.
       Duke (minus the band, but with Ray Nance and
       singer Kay Davis) plays the Palladium, London, plus
       other British cities, and tours in Europe.

1950   Paul Gonsalves joins band. Third European tour for
       band. Compositions include "Love You Madly."

1951   Johnny Hodges, Lawrence Brown, Sonny Greer all
       quit band; Willie Smith, Juan Tizol (again), Louis
       Bellson join, followed by Clark Terry, Willie Cook,
       and Britt Woodman. "Harlem" premiered at Car-
       negie Hall.

1952   Willie Smith leaves band; replaced by Hilton Jeffer-
       son.

1953   Louis Bellson leaves band; replaced by Butch Ballard.
       "Satin Doll" (with Strayhorn–Johnny Mercer lyrics)
       among compositions.

1955   Duke plays summer show, *Aquacades*, at Flushing
       Meadows, Long Island. Writes play, *Man with Four
       Sides*; composes "Night Creature," premiered at Car-
       negie Hall by Symphony of the Air and his band.
       Johnny Hodges rejoins band and Sam Woodyard also
       joins. Other compositions: "She," "Orson," "Kinda
       Dukish," "Twilight Time," etc.

1956   Comeback at Newport Jazz Festival is à triumph. El-
       lington appears on cover of *Time* magazine. Composi-
       tions include "Newport Jazz Festival Suite," "Rock 'n'
       Roll Rhapsody," "Lonesome Lullaby," "Suburban
       Beauty."

1957   Major return to composing with presentations of "A
       Drum Is a Woman," "Royal Ancestry (Portrait of Ella
       Fitzgerald)," his Shakespearian suite, "Such Sweet
       Thunder," "Shades of Harlem," "Café au Lait," etc.

1958   Band tours Europe. Duke presented to Queen Eliza-
       beth, Princess Margaret, etc., at Leeds Festival.
       "Toot Suite" written for Newport Festival. Other
       compositions include "Blues in Orbit," "Princess
       Blue," "Pauline's Jump," "Mr. Gentle and Mr. Cool,"
       "Happy Reunion."

1959   "Booty" Wood joins band, which tours Europe again.
       "Idiom 59" written for Newport. Dukes first movie
       score: *Anatomy of a Murder*. Duke's "The Queen's

Suite" composed, recorded, and unique pressing sent
to Buckingham Palace.

1960   Lawrence Brown returns to band. "Suite Thursday"
(tone parallel for John Steinbeck's *Sweet Thursday*)
composed for Monterey Jazz Festival. Versions of
Tchaikovsky's "Nutcracker Suite" and of Grieg's "Peer
Gynt Suite" produced. Music written for movie, *Paris
Blues*, and for play, *Turcaret*, performed at Palais
Chaillot, Paris. *Asphalt Jungle* theme for TV. "Come
Sunday" (from "Black, Brown, and Beige") played by
Duke at Midnight Mass in Paris. Relationship with
Fernanda de Castro Monte under way.

1961   Recordings with Louis Armstrong, Count Basie, Coleman Hawkins, etc.

1962   Cootie Williams rejoins band; Buster Cooper joins.
European tour. "Money Jungle" (recorded with
Charles Mingus and Max Roach), "Lazy Rhapsody,"
"Blue Mood," "The Feeling of Jazz" among composi-
tions.

1963   Ellington writes and produces *My People*, major show
for the Century of Negro Progress exposition in Chi-
cago. Also composes *Timon of Athens* suite (for
Shakespeare Theatre at Stratford, Ontario) and "Afro-
Bossa" suite. European tour and then tour of Middle
East and Far East for U.S. State Department.
Records with Alice Babs in Paris.

1964   Mercer Ellington joins band as road manager and
member of trumpet section. European tour plus first
visit to Japan. "The Far East Suite" written, but not
yet recorded.

1965   Band performs at White House, in Virgin Islands, and
again in Europe. First Sacred Concert at Grace Cathedral, San Francisco. Duke plays with Boston Pops
Orchestra. Compositions include "The Virgin Islands
Suite" and "The Golden Broom and the Green
Apple." Pulitzer Prize committee rejects recommendation for special citation for Ellington.

1966   Duke receives President's Gold Medal by order of
Lyndon Johnson. Visits to Europe with Ella
Fitzgerald (plus Sacred Concert at Coventry Cathe-
dral, England), to Dakar, Senegal (for World Festival

of Negro Arts), to Japan. Compositions include movie score, *Assault on a Queen*; stage-play music, *Murder in the Cathedral*; plus "La Plus Belle Africaine," "The Shepherd," "Swamp Goo," "Drag," "House of Lords" (with Earl Hines), "The Twitch," "The Second Portrait of the Lion." Death of Edna Ellington.

1967   Bill Strayhorn dies. Album, "And His Mother Called Him Bill," recorded. Jeff Castleman joins band. Last European tour with Granz follows rift in 1966–67. More concerts with Ella Fitzgerald. Sacred Concert performed at Cambridge, England. Honorary degree for Duke from Yale University.

1968   Second Sacred Concert—all but one of the compositions brand-new—premiered in New York, featuring Alice Babs. Jimmy Hamilton leaves band, replaced by Harold Ashby. Tour of South America and Mexico. Compositions include "The Latin American Suite," movie score *Change of Mind*, "You Make That Hat Look Pretty," "My Lonely Love."

1969   Duke honored at White House seventieth birthday party; presented with Medal of Freedom by President Nixon. European tour (now presented by George Wein and, in Britain, Robert Paterson), including first visit to Eastern Europe (Prague) and Sacred Concerts in Paris, Barcelona, and Stockholm. Duke honored at banquet by Maurice Chevalier. Tour of West Indies. Norris Turney, Wild Bill Davis, and Victor Gaskin join band.

1970   Johnny Hodges dies. Lawrence Brown leaves band. Compositions include *The River* (for American Ballet Company), "The New Orleans Suite," "Afro-Eurasian Eclipse" (for Monterey Jazz Festival). Visits to Europe and Australasia and Far East.

1971   Cat Anderson leaves band. Newer recruits include Harold Minerve, Harold "Money" Johnson, John Coles, Joe Benjamin, Rufus Jones. Tour of Russia and Europe; second tour of South America and Mexico. Compositions include "The Goutelas Suite" (premiered at Lincoln Center, New York) and "Togo Brava!" (premiered at Newport Jazz Festival).

1972   Longest tour of Far East: Japan, Philippines, Thailand, Singapore, Indonesia, Australasia, Fiji, etc. Compositions include "New York, New York."

1973 Third Sacred Concert premiered at Westminster Abbey, London. Duke plays Royal Command Performance at Palladium, London. European tour plus visits to Zambia and Ethiopia. Presented with the Emperor's Star (Ethiopia) and Legion of Honor (France). *Music Is My Mistress* (his "autobiography") published. Dr. Arthur Logan dies.

1974 Ellington collapses, January. Enters hospital for final time in March. Further work on "opera," *Queenie Pie*, and "Three Black Kings." Ellington dies, May 24, within days of Paul Gonsalves and Tyree Glenn. Funeral service at Cathedral of St. John the Divine, New York. Harry Carney dies, October 8.

1975 Mercer Ellington leads "The Duke Ellington Orchestra" to England. This band continues to perform, including series of ballets with Alvin Ailey's City Center Dance Theater in New York (1976).

1976 Beatrice Ellis (Evie Ellington) dies on April 7; buried beside Duke Ellington and his parents in Woodlawn Cemetery, New York. Duke Ellington Center being built in St. Peter's Lutheran Church, New York.

Select Discography
and Bibliography

Inevitably, this is a limited choice from the hundreds of Ellington recordings. With regular deletions from catalogues, import albums, and reissues some records may not be available or have different serial numbers, although specialist shops often have odd copies of deleted items. Such shops also carry imported recordings, which are marked with an asterisk in the discography.

COLLECTIONS

*The Age of Ellington (3 LPs) British RCA PL 420 86(3) 1/3 (recordings 1926–67 from RCA archives, chosen by Derek Jewell).
The Ellington Era, Vol. 1 (3 LPs) Columbia C3L–27 (1927–40 recordings).
This Is Duke Ellington (2 LPs) RCA VPM–6042 (1927–45 recordings).
The Golden Duke (2 LPs) Prestige 24029 (1946 recordings).
The Best of Duke Ellington Capitol SM–1602 (1953–54 recordings).
Hi-Fi Ellington Uptown Columbia CPS CCL–830 (1951–52 recordings).

Ellington at Newport   Columbia CS–3684 (1956 recording).

Ellington Jazz Party   Columbia CSP JCS–8015 (1959 recordings, with guests Dizzy Gillespie and Jimmy Rushing).

The Great Paris Concert (2 LPs)   Atlantic 2–304 (1963 recordings).

70th Birthday Concert (2 LPs)   Solid State 19000 (1969 recordings).

Togo Brava Suite (2 LPs)   United Artists UXS–92 (1971 recordings, including *La Plus Belle Africaine*).

Eastbourne Performance   RCA APL1–1023 (last officially issued album of band under Ellington's leadership; recorded December 1, 1973).

NOTE: French RCA and French Columbia have undertaken complete editions of all Ellington recordings in their respective catalogues. The RCA series, *The Works of Duke, Complete Edition*, consists of single LPs and has reached sixteen volumes at this writing; the Columbia, *The Complete Duke Ellington*, is issued in 2–LP sets, of which eight have been released to date.

SUITES AND LONGER WORKS

Such Sweet Thunder   Columbia CSP JCL–1003 (1957 recording).

The Ellington Suites   Pablo 2335–743 (*The Queen's Suite*, 1959; *The Goutelas Suite*, 1971; *The Uwis Suite*, 1972).

The Nutcracker Suite /Peer Gynt   Columbia Odyssey 321–60252 (1960 recording).

My People   Flying Dutchman 10112 (1963 recording).

Second Sacred Concert (2 LPs)   Fantasy 8407/08 (1964 recording).

The Latin-American Suite   Fantasy 8419 (1969 recording).

The New Orleans Suite   Atlantic SD–1508 (1970 recording).

Afro-Eurasian Eclipse   Fantasy 9498 (1971 recording).

Third Sacred Concert   RCA APL1–0785 (1973 recording).

SOLOS AND SMALL GROUPS

The Duke's Men   Columbia CPS JEE–22005 (1936–39 small group recordings).

Piano Reflections   Capitol M–11058 (piano solos by Ellington, including *Reflections in D*, recorded 1953).

Blues Summit (2 LPs)   Verve 6S–8822 (small groups led by El-
   lington and Hodges, recorded 1958–59, originally issued as
   Back to Back and *Side by Side*).
The Violin Session   Atlantic 1688 (Ellington, Strayhorn, Gon-
   salves, and violinists Nance, Svend Asmussen, Stephane
   Grappelli; recorded 1963).
This One's for Blanton   Pablo 2335–728 (Duke on piano, plus
   Ray Brown, bass; recorded 1972).
Duke's Big Four   Pablo 2310–703 (Duke on piano, plus Joe
   Pass, guitar; Ray Brown and Louis Bellson, drums; recorded
   1973).
NOTE: At this writing, Fantasy Records is preparing the first au-
   thorized issue of Ellington's famous 1943 Carnegie Hall con-
   cert, including the only complete performance of *Black,
   Brown, and Beige*.

There are chapters or essays on Duke in scores of books and
magazines too numerous to list here (from Constant Lambert's
Music Ho! in 1934 onwards), but books devoted to him alone
are, oddly enough, few. This list is virtually comprehensive.

Dance, Stanley, *The World of Duke Ellington* (Scribner, New
   York, 1972).
Ellington, Duke, *Music Is My Mistress* (Doubleday, New York,
   1973).
Gammond, Peter, ed., *Duke Ellington: His Life and Music*
   (Dent, London, 1958).
Lambert, G. E., *Duke Ellington* (Barnes, New York, 1962).
Montgomery, Elizabeth Rider, *Duke Ellington, King of Jazz*
   (Garrard, Champaign, Ill., 1972—for younger readers).
Ulanov, Barry, *Duke Ellington* (Da Capo, New York, 1976; re-
   print of 1946 edition).

Index